Mastering
Wirework Jewelry

Mastering
Wirework Jewelry

15 intricate designs to create

Rachel Norris

First published 2017
by Guild of Master Craftsman Publications Ltd
Castle Place, 166 High Street, Lewes,
East Sussex BN7 1XU

ISBN 978 1 78494 331 8

Publisher Jonathan Bailey
Production Manager Jim Bulley
Senior Project Editor Dominique Page
Editor Nicola Hodgson
Managing Art Editor Gilda Pacitti
Designer Gary Thompson
Photographers Rachel Norris & Andrew Perris

Color origination by GMC Reprographics
Printed and bound in Malaysia

Note: The Resting Moth Brooch (page 48) design
was originally published in Beads & Beyond
Magazine in 2015 and is reproduced here with
the kind permission of Traplet Publications.

This book is dedicated to my dear
husband, Peter, and my children
Gemma, Joseph, and Jack, who
have been such a support, and to
the wonderful jewelry-making
friends I have met during my
wireworking journey.

Contents

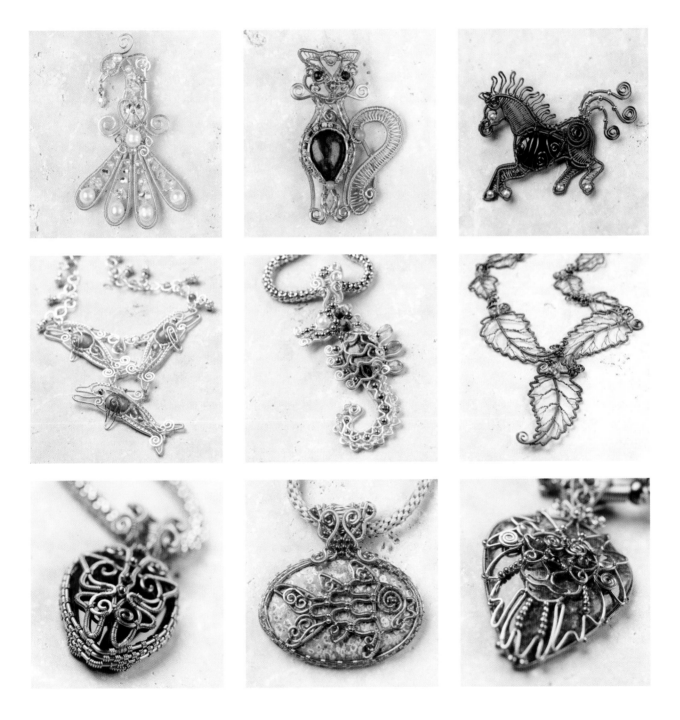

Introduction

WIREWORKING IS A MEANS OF CREATING BEAUTIFUL JEWELRY without soldering, using handmade wrapped and bound wire connections to produce artisan, bespoke, pieces. It has been around for more than 2,000 years, with artefacts made by many cultures including the ancient Sumerians, Romans, and Vikings.

I have written this book for wirework artists of all levels, to help inspire them to create beautiful pieces of jewelry, and to help them achieve the amazing design potential for this wonderful craft.

My designs are inspired by natural forms in the animal and plant kingdoms, and include some popular pieces I have made in the past along with many new designs. Each project carefully guides you through the stages, step-by-step, breaking down the design into achievable sections. The projects are of an intermediate to advanced level but I hope that by making them you will develop your wireworking skills further and gain more confidence with this medium.

There are also templates for you to use at the back of the book to help you form the outline frames for each design. You can photocopy and print these out in various sizes to tailormake your designs. There are methods explained within the projects to help you make your own templates if you don't wish to use the ones provided. I detail how to make some of the findings, links, and clasps used to make the pieces and have used other findings, materials, and components that are easily available from most jewelry suppliers. A list of suppliers can be found on page 299.

I hope you enjoy creating the designs in this book and that you progress to create your own using the techniques taught here.

Basic tools

Four tools are essential for making wirework jewelry: flush cutter pliers, round-nosed pliers, flat-nosed pliers, and chain-nosed or bent chain-nosed pliers. Other useful tools include nylon-jawed pliers, a chasing hammer and steel block, a wire coiling Gizmo, a ruler, rubber bead mat, pen and paper.

General tools

In the projects I refer to the general tools you will need: these are listed below. Any additional item specific to a project is given in the tools section for that piece.

- flush cutter pliers
- jeweler's hammer
- round-nosed pliers
- steel block
- chain-nosed pliers
- pen, paper, ruler
- flat-nosed pliers
- rubber bead mat
- nylon-jawed pliers

Pliers

The main thing to remember is to choose pliers with a comfortable grip and spring-loaded handles for ease of use and to avoid hand fatigue.

FLUSH CUTTER PLIERS
A flush cutter (**A**) cuts the wire to leave one end flush or flat and the opposite end sharp or pointed. Place the flat side of the cutters toward the wire you are working on to gain a flat-plane cut edge. This is perfect for making jumprings with good closure and a professional finish to your wirework. The other face of the cutter will produce a squashed, more triangular, wire end.

NOTE: There are many wire cutters on the market, but you need to buy those described as "flush" cutters. These cutters are only suitable for cutting silver or copper wire and can be ruined by steel or memory wire. A specialist memory wire cutter is required for the latter.

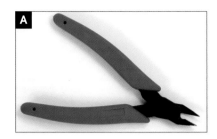

ROUND-NOSED PLIERS

Round-nosed pliers (**B**) have perfectly round and smooth tapering conical jaws. They are used to make loops, coils, and curved bends in wire. You can grasp the wire and curl it with the pliers, or use your fingers to wrap the wire around the pliers. The plier ends taper from a wide base to the tip, so you can make different size loops depending upon where on the pliers you place the wire. You can mark a level on the cones with a marker pen if you want to make many loops of the same size. For the best wire-shaping results, make sure your pliers have a narrow end tip width of 1–1.5mm with a gradually increasing diameter to the base.

NOTE: Do not use round-nosed pliers to grip flat sections of wire, as the curved plier surface may mark the wire.

CHAIN-NOSED OR BENT CHAIN-NOSED PLIERS

Chain-nosed or bent chain-nosed pliers (**C**) have flat, tapering, smooth jaws with rounded outsides and flat inner surfaces. They are versatile and can be used for gripping and holding wire and for shaping and bending wire. They can be used to manipulate jumprings and crimp beads and for grabbing and pulling tiny ends of wire through small spaces. They are perfectly designed for grasping wire and for fine shaping movements of wire (better than your fingers). I tend to work near the tips of my chain-nosed pliers, and I choose fine-tipped pliers with a $^{1}/_{32}$in (1mm) tip. Look for "fine-nosed" pliers and check with the supplier for the width of the tip.

FLAT-NOSED PLIERS

Flat-nosed pliers (**D**) are flat on both inside surfaces, with squared ends. They are used to keep surface or wire shapes flat in the same plane or to make angular bends in wire. They have a large surface for grasping wire. They are useful for making flat spirals, as the large plier surface keeps a large portion of the coil flat as you are shaping it. I use these less often than chain-nosed pliers, but they are useful as the second set of pliers used when opening and closing jumprings.

NYLON-JAWED PLIERS

Nylon-jawed pliers (**E**) are flat on both inside surfaces, with squared ends. The jaw surfaces are made from nylon rather than steel. They are used in a similar way to flat-nosed pliers, but are less likely to mark or mar the wire surface. I find them slightly clumsier to use than flat- or chain-nosed pliers, but sometimes it is worth the extra effort to use them to achieve an unmarked surface finish.

Hammers and blocks

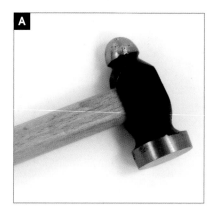

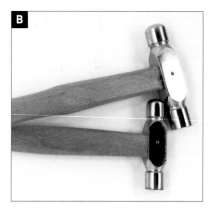

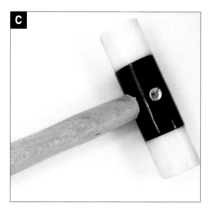

Tip
Make sure your hammer has a smooth, flat surface that won't mark your wire and an easy-to-hold handle.

There are many types of hammers available, but for the projects in this book you will need either a chasing hammer or a ball peen hammer ("peen" is another word for surface).

HAMMERS
The ball peen hammer (**A**) is a good all-round hammer. It has one flat-sided surface for flattening and work-hardening wire and a domed surface to create curves and domes in flat metal.

The larger, flatter surfaces are characteristic of a chasing hammer. The one shown in image A is a perfect size hammer with a chasing head and ball peen faced head. Also useful are small-faced hammers (**B**) for hammering onto smaller workable areas without hitting surrounding work.

NOTE: Make sure you don't use this hammer to hit tools or chisels into metal or you will damage the smooth surface of your hammer; you need specialist steel hammers for this.

Also available are rawhide or nylon-faced hammers (**C**). These offer a softer blow and are less likely to mark your wire, but will only work-harden and not flatten the wire greatly.

Some hammers have patterned surfaces for creating surface texture (**D**). Jewelers' hammers have sharp ends to create lines on metal.

BLOCKS FOR USE WITH HAMMERS

A hammer should be used with a steel or rubber block. A steel bench block **(E)** offers a perfectly flat surface for working and flattening wire or sheet against with a hammer. It can be used to support work being riveted or textured.

These blocks are usually made from extra-hard carbon steel with a polished smooth surface so as not to mark your metal surface. Often they are delivered oiled to prevent rusting; wipe away this excess before first use. To help prevent rust, which eventually forms undesirable dimples in the surface of your block, wipe over every so often with light-duty oil. Fine emery cloth can be used to gently smooth rust off the surface.

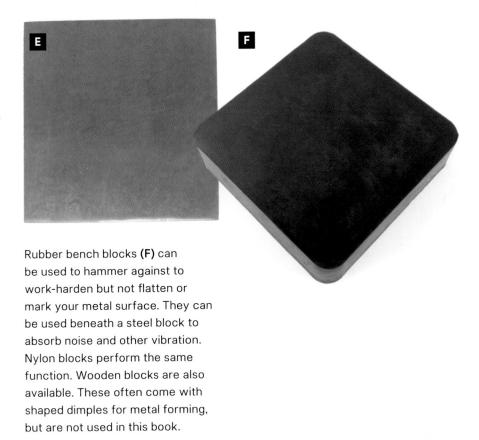

Rubber bench blocks **(F)** can be used to hammer against to work-harden but not flatten or mark your metal surface. They can be used beneath a steel block to absorb noise and other vibration. Nylon blocks perform the same function. Wooden blocks are also available. These often come with shaped dimples for metal forming, but are not used in this book.

Mandrels and Gizmos

Mandrels are rods of various shapes and diameters used to form metal and wire around the mandrel. Most mandrels are circular, as shown below right. I use them for making jumprings, round frame shapes, bales, and earring findings. Larger mandrels are used for making ring shanks and even larger ones for forming bracelets or bangles. I generally use metal mandrels, but wooden ones are also used, especially for silver clay.

You can hammer against the larger mandrels to shape metal and wire. Other shapes of mandrel are available: small ovals for making oval jumprings; larger ovals for oval bangles; triangles for triangular jumprings; and square and rectangular shapes. Some mandrels also fit into the various forms of coiling Gizmo (see image overleaf).

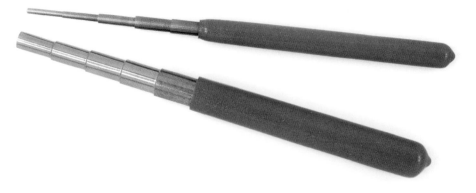

WIRE COILING GIZMO

Different types of wire coiling Gizmo **(A)** are available: basic, deluxe, and professional. All were invented by LeRoy Goertz, a sculptor and wire artist in Oregon, USA, as a tool to create uniformly neat coils of wire that are useful in many jewelry designs.

The basic Gizmo comes with a U-shaped bracket, which can be handheld or clamped to a work surface with a C-clamp, and two mandrels, 1.6mm and 3.2mm in diameter. The mandrels are $5^{1}/_{2}$–6in (14–15cm) in length.

The deluxe Gizmo is a better buying option and is used for the projects in this book. It comes with a U-shaped bracket with its own built-in clamp and five mandrel rods with turning handles, 1.2mm, 1.6mm, 3.2mm, 4.2mm, and 5.2mm in diameter and the same length as the basic Gizmo.

The professional coiling Gizmo comes with five much longer mandrels ($15^{1}/_{2}$in/38cm) than the basic and deluxe versions. These are long enough to make necklace-length sized coils. The two clamp brackets, one with a drill chuck for rod insertion, are used to stabilize the mandrels during turning as they are clamped to the workbench at either end of the mandrels. Multiple wires can be inserted into the drill chuck to be twisted together. The Beadsmith Conetastic tool™ has mandrels that also fit into the drill chuck. See page 29 for details on how to use a Gizmo tool.

WAGS WICONE

The Wags Wicone **(B)** is another useful tool, invented by Gary Wagstaff. It comes in three sizes and is used to make cone-shaped wire spirals to cover cord ends, Viking knit, and act as bead caps.

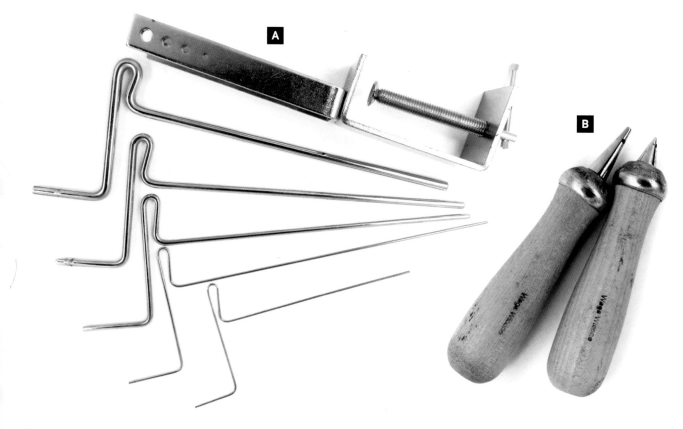

Other useful items

There are several other items you may find useful to keep to hand.

PEN, PAPER, AND RULER

Always have a pen and paper for jotting down design ideas, tracing template shapes, and noting wire lengths and bead sizes required for a design. A ruler is also useful.

RUBBER BEAD MAT

There are many types of bead mats available, but the Beadsmith is excellent. It has a sticky surface to stop beads rolling about, and has useful measurement guides in inches and centimeters and in both straight and curved lines for measuring wire, necklace, and bracelet lengths.

I use the bead mat for template making: I place a piece of paper over the mat, press a wire shape into it, and trace over the impression with a pen to create a template that can be used repeatedly to create almost identical reproducible shapes. The bead mat also offers a useful work surface for setting cabochons: When you press onto the setting and cabochon on one of these mats, it absorbs excess pressure and prevents cabochon breakage. You can place it under your steel block to absorb vibration. It can also be rolled up easily for storage and transport.

Wire & gemstones

Wire and gemstones have been used in jewelry making for thousands of years. Today, in addition to the stunning natural gems that are available, beautiful manmade beads and modern wire production methods provide the wirework artist with an extensive and diverse range to work with.

Materials for wire

Wire is available in a variety of materials and prices. All will handle slightly differently and offer different levels of flexibility, malleability, and ability to hold their shape.

PRECIOUS METAL WIRE

Precious metal wire, such as sterling silver, fine silver, and gold, is traditionally used for wirework design.

Sterling silver is a mixture of 92.5% silver and 7.5% copper and zinc. It has wonderful malleability and good shape-holding ability. On the other hand, 100% pure silver is very soft and can sometimes distort out of shape even under its own weight.

Gold wire is a high-end material; it is very soft and prohibitively expensive.

COPPER WIRE

Copper wire is commonly used in wirework jewelry and is a cost-effective way to create larger and more experimental designs. It is a beautiful metal in its own right with its lovely pinkish hue. It is easy to shape and form as it is very malleable.

Some copper wire is coated with silver plate and/or colored enamels to create colored coatings. These offer an increased palette to the designer and also act as a tarnish-resistant surface. I have mainly used copper and enamel-coated wire in the projects in this book, but all the designs could be made with sterling silver or other wire materials.

OTHER WIRE MATERIALS

Other wire includes brass, which is stiffer than copper. Gold-filled wire is also available; this is a thick layer of gold over a base metal or silver core.

Memory wire is made from steel with a "shape memory." It can be useful as it is thin and strong, but cannot be used for weaving and cannot be cut with flush cutters; it requires specialist memory wire cutters.

Lastly, you may come across beading wire: this is a stranded stainless-steel wire with a nylon coating and is used to strand beads.

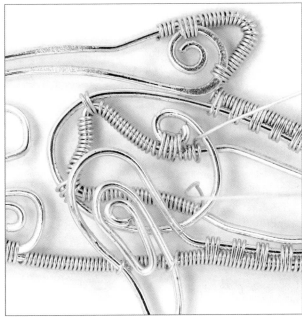

Wire shape

Wire can be formed in many cross-sectional shapes including round, square, half-round (like a semicircle), and flat, twisted, and patterned. I use round wire in all the projects in this book, as it is the most commonly used and easily available wire. Using square wire, with its geometric reflective surfaces, will change the look of the piece you are creating, while the flat side of half-round wire will fit against a stone surface better, so it can be easier to set a stone into a frame.

Wire hardness and work-hardening

Wire hardness is altered by a process called annealing. This involves heating the wire until it glows but does not melt and then quickly "quenching" the wire by plunging it into cool water. The heating moves the metal molecules into a higher-energy state with fewer chemical bonds between the atoms, and the rapid quenching "freezes" those connections in the higher-energy state so the metal is soft and flexible. Conversely, if you hammer, bend, or even tap wire, you allow more chemical bonds between the metal atoms to form; these bonds are more resistant to movement so the wire becomes stiffer. Therefore the metal is termed "work-hardened."

You can buy wire already work-hardened, or you can do it yourself by working with the wire or by tapping with a hammer.

Wire can be supplied in three main grades of stiffness or "hardness," which affects its ease of bending and manipulation. These grades are soft, half-hard, and hard. I usually work with soft to half-hard.

Soft wire is pliable, easy to shape, form spirals, and wrap gemstones. However, unless work-hardening takes place, the design can still be bent out of place. I try to work-harden as I go along and tap loops and frame wires, especially to create a stronger structure. This is especially important when making clasps, as you don't want them to bend out of shape during use.

Half-hard wire is a medium stiffness and is good to work with for tight angular bends, loops, and coils. It also makes an excellent frame wire. It can work-harden to hard quite quickly so you can find you are working with hard wire!

Hard wire is very stiff, a bit springy, and may not stay in place without a lot of hard pulling. It is hard on the hands to work with. It is an excellent frame wire but not good for making small and complex shapes and spirals. Hard wire is also likely to break if you try to work it into complex shapes and tight bends, or repeatedly bend the wire in the same place.

Over-worked wire can become work-hardened. This is because so many bonds between the atoms have been created that there is less flexibility for metal movement.

Try this with a piece of wire: Repeated bending in one point will harden the wire and eventually cause it to break at the join. For this reason, avoid repeated reshaping or bending at the same point.

Wire diameter or gauge

AWG No.	Diameter (mm)
1	7.35
2	6.54
3	5.83
4	5.19
5	4.62
6	4.11
7	3.67
8	3.26
9	2.91
10	2.59
11	2.30
12	2.05
13	1.83
14	1.63
15	1.45
16	1.29
17	1.15
18	1.02
19	0.91
20	0.81
21	0.72
22	0.64
23	0.57
24	0.51
25	0.45
26	0.40
27	0.36
28	0.32
29	0.29
30	0.25

There are various thicknesses of wire available and each has a different potential use. There are a few different gauge number systems around the world. In this book we give both the American wire gauge (AWG) and the diameter in millimeters.

There is a UK based standard wire gauge (SWG) system but this is used less frequently now and will not be quoted in this book.

Thicker wire of 18–12AWG (1–2mm) is useful for frames, chokers, bangles, and jumprings. Medium-diameter wire of 22–20AWG (0.6–0.8mm) wire is useful for making ear wires and wire coils.

20AWG (0.8mm) wire can be used if work hardened as a frame wire for small, delicate pieces such as brooches and earrings.

22AWG (0.6mm) wire can be used as a heavy-weave wrapping wire.

Thinner-diameter wire of 30–26AWG (0.25–0.4mm) wire is used for weaving, wrapping, and coiling wire.

Some beads have a hole drilled into them, which will accept a certain diameter of wire. So, after checking the wire will fit through the stone, choose the wire diameter best suited for what you want to do.

Gemstones

There are many books dealing with the wonderful variety of natural gemstones available (see page 299). I use easily available standard gemstone sizes in this book, some with drill holes through which you can thread wire or thread, and some undrilled in the form of cabochons. A cabochon is a flat-backed stone with a slightly domed smooth and polished front surface.

Stones come in all shapes, colors, and sizes. Each one offers many possibilities for your designs.

Basic techniques

This chapter will lead you through some basic techniques that are referred to in many of the projects. You will find instructions on how to make necklace links and clasps, shape, coil and weave wire, and make a simple brooch pin.

Making rosary links for a necklace

Rosary links are made with wrapped loops either side of the bead. The beads shown in images A and B are 8–10mm diameter rounds set on 18AWG (1mm) wire. 24–20AWG (0.6–0.8mm) wire can be used for smaller, more delicate, beads. There is also the option of making swirly curls at the end of each wrapped loop either side of the bead, as in image B. Make the swirly curls using ³/₈in (1cm) lengths of the wire tails at the end of the wrapped loops.

NOTE: The wire you use may depend on the size of the drill hole through the bead.

Tip

I prefer to work with longer lengths of wrapping wire so I don't run out along weave lengths. If you want to work with shorter lengths, try to spot a point where you can add in new wire, tucking in the old end and adding in new where there is the least disruption to what you are trying to do.

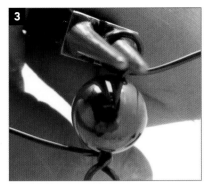

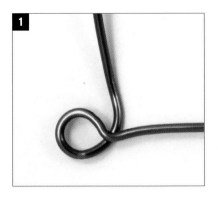

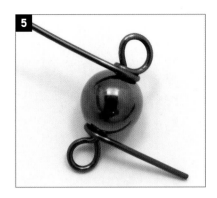

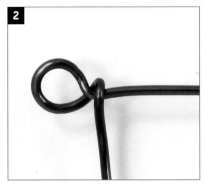

TO MAKE A WRAPPED
LOOP NECKLACE LINK

1 Take a 4–4³/₄in (10–12cm) length of 18AWG (1mm) wire and loop it as shown about 1³/₈in (3.5cm) from one end of the wire, into a round shape using your round-nose pliers.

2 Grip nearer the base of the loop with chain-nosed pliers (if possible with the pliers placed flat across the whole loop). Bend the shorter wire tail to the side where it crosses under the longer length of wire. Straighten the longer length of wire, bending it slightly at the crossing point. Pull the shorter wire tail to wrap it around the longer wire length at the crossing point so that it points in the opposite direction.

3 Thread a bead onto the longer length of wire so that it lies tight against the first loop you made. Make a loop at the other side of the bead using chain-nosed pliers, adjusting the loop so that there is no "play" or gap between the loops and the bead.

Tip

Try to make sure the loops are all the same size by making them at the same point on your chain-nosed pliers.

4 Grip each loop with chain-nosed pliers and wrap the wire tails around the base of the loop with your fingers or another set of pliers. You have a few options now:

• You can cut the wire tail with flush cutters and press the ends down around the wrap to press the cut ends in so they don't catch on skin or clothing.

• You can wrap the wire tails over to the other side of the bead (see the hook end of the clasp, page 23).

• You can make a swirl curl detail over the bead, as follows:

5 Cut the wire tails to ³/₈–⁵/₈in (10–15mm) depending on the size of curl you want to make over the bead or the size of bead you are working with.

6 Spiral the wire tails (see page 27). Press the wire tails down over the bead using your fingers or the rubber ends of your pliers. Your little link is finished. Make more in the same way, but make sure you add on one link to the next before you close that loop.

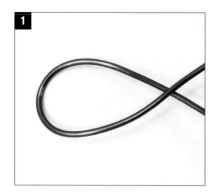
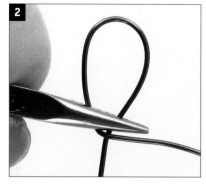
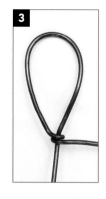

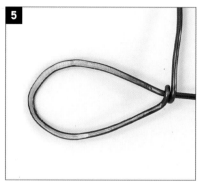

Making the loop end of the clasp

The loop end of the clasp is made in the same way as the links except with a much larger loop on the loop side.

1 Take a 6in (15cm) length of 20–18AWG (0.8–1mm) wire and loop it near one end of the wire into a teardrop shape. Use your fingers or a pencil-sized mandrel to make a more circular loop.

2 Bend the shorter wire tail to the side where it crosses over the longer length of wire. Straighten the longer length of wire, bending it slightly at the crossing point.

3 Grip the base of the loop with chain-nosed pliers and pull the wire tail to wrap it once around the longer wire length at the crossing point in a 180-degree loop.

4 At this stage you can alter the shape of your loops using the chain-nosed pliers. You can make the loop teardrop shaped, angular, or completely circular by placing the loop around a ring mandrel to shape the wire.

5 Hammer the large loop on a steel block to create a flat, reflective surface.

6 Thread a bead onto the long length of wire so it sits tight against the large loop. Make a smaller loop on the other side of the bead as in Step 4. Grip the smaller loop with your chain-nosed pliers and pull the wire tail around the top of the bead to make a spiral over the end of the bead around the closed loop.

7 Cut the wire tail at this end to $^{3}/_{8}$–$^{5}/_{8}$in (10–15mm). Grip the larger teardrop-shaped loop with your chain-nosed pliers near the base of the loop and across both sides of the loop, spiraling the wire end around and along the loop for a few wraps (you can also wind down over the bead; it is your choice).

8 Cut the wire tail at the large loop end to $^{5}/_{8}$–$^{13}/_{16}$in (15–20mm).

9 Spiral the wire tails: Press the spiral at the small loop end over the bead and the spiral at the larger loop end over the base of the loop.

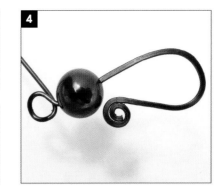

Making the hook end of the clasp

1 Take a 6in (15cm) length of 18AWG (1mm) wire and make a small spiral at one end as shown on page 27.

2 Shape this end of the wire into a shepherd's crook shape. You can wrap the wire around a mandrel, bale-making pliers, or a round pen. Make a slight bend at the base of the hook leaving a straight wire tail (see arrow in image above).

3 Hammer only the "crook" end, leaving the straight wire tail unhammered.

4 Thread a bead onto the straight wire up to the base of the crook and the edge of the hammered wire section. Make a loop at the other side of the bead using round-nosed pliers.

5 Make a closed wrap loop (see page 21). Pass the wire tail over and around the bead to wrap the wire tail at the base of the hook end a few times, leaving a $^5/_8$–$^{13}/_{16}$in (15–20mm) wire tail.

NOTE: The wrap around the bead may cause the bead to travel up the hook end a little. Hold the bead in place as you make this wrap; once you have a few coils around the base of the hook the bead will be held in place.

6 Curl the wire tail as on page 27 and press into place over the base of the hook end.

7 Your clasp is now finished. You can join it to the rest of your necklace with a few jumprings or by slipping it onto a necklace link before you wrap and close the loop.

Tip

If the wire is difficult to thread through spaces, use your pliers to help grab the wire. Trim the tip if it looks ragged to make it thread through more easily.

Making a bend sharper

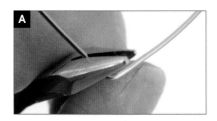

I often use diagrams as templates over which to shape my wire forms. This allows me to make many uniform and symmetrical pieces of wire frame. The rounded wire bends you make will need to be made more angular and defined with a sharper bend. To achieve this, make your bend using chain-nosed pliers. Then clamp either side of the little bend with your pliers, as close as you

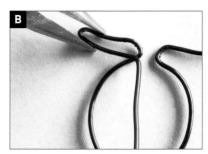

can to the bend (see **A**). Repeat this clamping process with your pliers several times alternating either side of the bend. This will make the bend much sharper.

Another technique to make a bend really sharp and bring the wires either side of the bend close together is to clamp either side of the bend on the outside edge of the bend (see **B**).

Standard two-by-two basket weave

I use some very basic weave techniques and these are required for almost every project in this book. The frame space you are weaving across may be a different shape in each design, and the weave ratio of wraps around the frame before making each weave traverse may be different, but the essential technique remains the same. See the books listed in the bibliography (page 298) if you want to learn more weave patterns. Weaving wires can be 30AWG (0.25mm) for a fine weave, 26AWG (0.4mm) for a medium-grade weave and a bit more strength, and 24AWG (0.6mm) wire for a strong but very coarse weave. The steps below apply if you are weaving a bale.

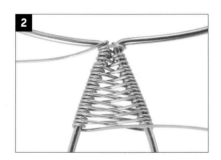

1 Take a 40–120in (1–3m) length of 26AWG (0.4mm) wire, depending upon whether you are weaving a smaller or large bale. Attach 8in (20cm) from one end of the 26AWG (0.4mm) wire to the base of the

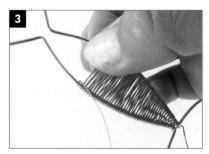

bale and start a two-by-two cross weave up the bale with the longer end of wire.

2 Use a standard figure-of-eight weave with two wraps of the wire around each leaf side before each traverse to the opposite side bale wire (passing from front to back and back to front in a figure-of-eight pattern).

NOTE: A figure-of-eight weave is a lovely basic weave. If your wrap around the main frame comes out at the front edge of the frame wire, pass the wire across the gap you are weaving across within the frame to the back edge of the frame wire you are wrapping toward. Then wrap around this part of the frame for the correct number of times. Pass the wire from the front edge of the frame wire you have just wrapped, across to the back edge of the frame wire you started from, and so on until you finish the weave. Keep your weave as tight as possible.

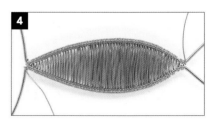

3 Hold the weave as you progress with thumb and forefinger to keep adjacent weaves close together. This is especially important as you move along the bale: it is easy to wrap into an expanding shape, as the weave traverse is too short to move upward into a larger traverse space.

4 Stop at the top of the leaf section of the bale. Do not cut the wire ends unless requested in the project: you might need to use them to bind the base of the bale together or bind on beads, for example.

The basket weave can progress into a weave across multiple wires as in the Seahorse Pendant bale

(page 172), or in the setting for the cabachons in the Butterfly Cabachon Pendant (page 242) or the Little Fish Pendant (page 259).

Tip

Keep checking for kinks in the wire and stop them from forming. This gets easier with practice.

Finishing the tip of a weave frame

If you are weaving a petal with a tip, or a feather shape, you will need to finish the end off differently.

1 Weave until 3/16in (5mm) from the end of the tip.

2 Wrap around the tip until you reach the weave on the other side of the frame.

3 Make a traverse or two up to the tip, wrapping tightly to "click" the weaving wire into the wraps around the tip already in place.

4 Cut and tuck in the wire neatly, smoothing the wire end around the frame wire with your chain-nosed pliers to finish off that petal.

Tip

It is easy to weave along a frame with wires that are parallel, but in this example I am weaving a petal shape. As you weave in a shape that changes from a large traverse to a smaller traverse, the weave can tend to slip upward, so holding the weave in place is really important. A tight bind around the frame can also help, as the wire will grip into the frame better.

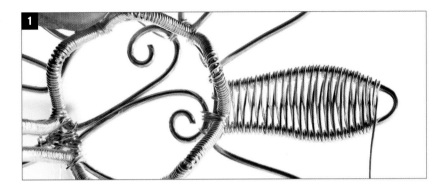

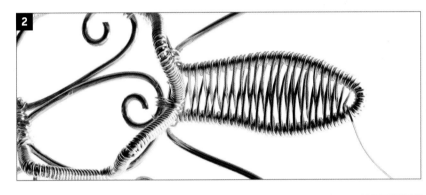

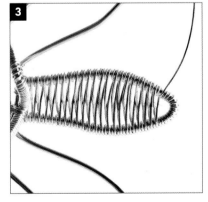

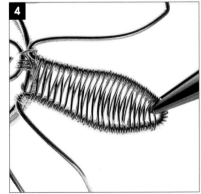

Making a three-by-three weave

With this weave, you have two frame wires, usually placed parallel to each other. If they are not already bound together at one end, bind them with some scrap wire near the end you are starting from. Wrap around just one frame wire first for three wraps if you are using 26AWG (0.4mm) wire, and four to five if using 30AWG (0.25mm) wire, to help keep the definition of the pattern with the finer-gauge weave wire. Wrap across both wires. Hold the frame wires close to where you are weaving to help keep the wires slightly separated.

Wrap around just the frame wire you started with. Make sure wraps are neatly placed, as an overlapping wire will stand out. Push wraps together as you go with your fingers, or with side-to-side gentle pushes with the edges of chain-nosed pliers (be careful not to damage the wire). Be consistent: if you swap the frame wire that you are wrapping only once around in an alternating pattern up the weave, you build up a whole new pattern. If this is not what you intended, you may need to re-weave the section, especially if you have done this in only one or two places. But if done intentionally, this can be quite an attractive effect in its own right. For example, if you add in more wires and wrap across different numbers of frame wires, you build up different patterns, as in the Golden-Eyed Owl Necklace bale weave (see pages 148–149).

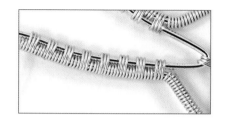

Tips

Make sure you place wires carefully during wire weaving; run your hand over the wirework to ensure there are no wire ends that could catch, and always tuck the wire ends in neatly.

Do not bind the frame wires too tightly or you won't be able to insert the next wrap around just one frame wire properly and the frame will distort.

Criss-cross bead attachments

This attachment is helpful when using smaller wire gauges to give strength to the binding on of a bead to a frame. This ensures the gemstones are wired in place with two strands of the wire and is a much stronger attachment. It also helps prevent the bead rotating around the frame, as it is held on more securely.

If wrapping onto a frame wire and not into a frame space, wrap above and below the bead to help secure it. There is an option to "bezel wrap" the wire around the base of the bead to add detail and further security to the attachment. This technique is used in several projects, including the Egyptian Cat Brooch, Lion's Mane Pendant, Running Horse Brooch, and Seahorse Pendant. In the example here I am using the attachment to add a bead into a small frame space for the eye in the Resting Moth Brooch (see page 52).

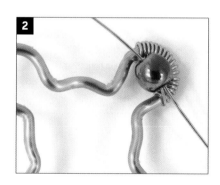

1 Thread a bead onto one wrapping wire end and pass the other wrapping wire end through the opposite side of the gemstone (see arrows in image).

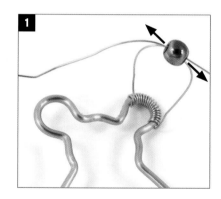

2 Pull the wire ends firmly to pull the little gemstone into place within the eye socket frame.

Making a spiral coil: inner to outer

This is a method for making a spiral coil, working from the center of the spiral outward. This technique is used throughout the book to finish off frame wire ends and add embellishment and details.

1 Once you have cut your wires to the desired length and perhaps wrapped along some of the wires with wrapping wire, you can curl the bare wire ends. Shape the bale wire ends using round-nosed pliers to start the curl and use fingers and pliers to finish the curl.

2 When you start the curl, it will look like a "P" with a straight end. This won't curl into a nice circle easily and might even curl into an oval shape.

3 Cut the end off with flush cutters so the curl is rounder.

4 Curl the ends using round-nosed pliers initially for the first spirals.

5 Use flat-nosed pliers for the outer spirals. Use your other hand to help guide the wire into the curl as you use the pliers on the end of the wire. Stop when you have reached the desired spiral size.

NOTE: Do not use pliers on wrapped wire or you might damage the wire.

Spirals can be made tightly coiled, as shown here, or loosely coiled to suit your design. Press the curled ends into place with your fingers and adjust them so they are balanced and symmetrical. You can arrange them in any pattern you wish over the design in later stages. You can also hammer the spiral to obtain a flat reflective surface.

Tip
Practice making the shapes and the wraps with scrap wire so you are happy that you can get the shape right with the real thing.

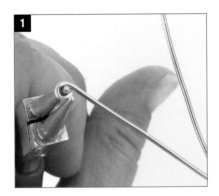

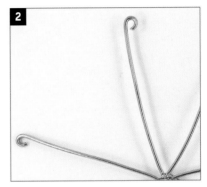

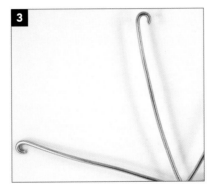

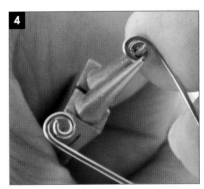

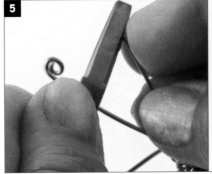

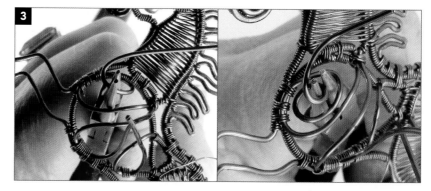

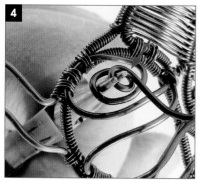
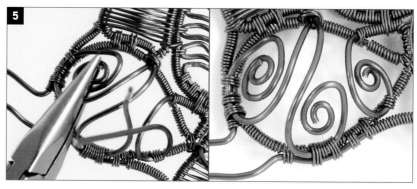

Making a spiral coil: outer to inner

In this spiral coil technique we are working from the outside of the spiral inward rather than from the inside of the spiral outward. This technique is useful when you don't know how much wire you need to make a certain spiral shape, when you need to fill a specific sized space and you can't make the spiral on a flat surface or template. In this example I am spiraling the wire inside the body frame of the Running Horse Brooch (see page 100).

1 You can start to form the outside edge of the spiral curl with your fingers to start to fill the space.

2 Place your round-nosed pliers inside the curl made with your fingers and grip the wire near the base of the pliers where the pliers are the widest diameter. Pull the wire with the other hand around in a counterclockwise direction to form a spiral curl to fit inside the curl made in Step 1.

3 As you pull the wire around the pliers, gradually move the wire curl up the pliers to smaller and smaller-diameter plier sections.

4 While you pull the wire around the smaller-diameter section of the round-nosed pliers, the curl will get smaller until you reach a point where the final curl is made at the very tips of the pliers. Cut the wire where it crosses the inside curl (see red arrow in image).

5 Press the curl to flatten and shape it with pliers or fingers.

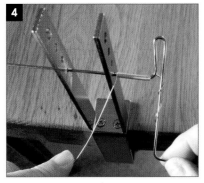

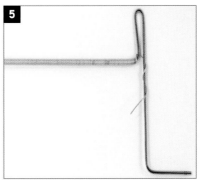

2 Wrap your chosen wire around the loop of the mandrel rod a few times to anchor it. Here I used the 1.6mm-diameter rod with 26AWG (0.4mm) wire. Make sure the little wire end is as short as possible so it does not catch on your hand as you wind the handle.

3 Wire of varying diameter can be attached to the mandrel handle. It is advisable to work from the wire reel, as it is hard to judge the exact length of wire that you will need. Insert the mandrel rod into the Gizmo bracket.

4 Hold the winding wire firmly with your left hand, keeping it taut. Start to coil the wire by turning the handle on the mandrel with your other hand, letting the wire slide through your fingers. Keep the coils neat as you wind. If there are gaps in the coils, push them together with your fingers or by pressing the coil end on the mandrel against the side of the bracket.

5 If your wire starts to overlap, reverse wind the mandrel to undo the overlapping wires and start that coiled section again. Keep winding until you have made the desired length of coil for your project. Here I made a 5¹⁄₂in (14cm) long coil. Take the coil off the mandrel and snip off the excess uncoiled wire ends. Trim carefully so there are no sharp edges.

Making coils with a Gizmo tool

This tool enables you to generate long, very neat, wire coils. Larger-diameter wire, such as 20–18AWG (0.8–1mm), creates coils with greater strength but less flexibility. Smaller-diameter wire such as 26–22AWG (0.4–0.6mm) is used to make coils that are more flexible but less strong.

Coils can be cut up to be used as spacers, or longer lengths can be wrapped around and woven through wire weaves. Coils can be threaded onto wire and curved to create shapes such as closed loop links, clasps, hearts, and flower petals. Coils made on a larger mandrel can be cut or sawn to create your own jumprings.

Wire coils can be coiled again to make coiled coils using "core" wires threaded through the coils. The core wire gives strength and stops the coil separating and collapsing. 20–18AWG (0.8–1mm) diameter is recommended for this.

MAKING A SIMPLE COIL

You can use these coils as spacers and coverings for bare wire in many situations.

1 Clamp your U-bracket to a work surface using a G-clamp or the integral clamp for the bracket.

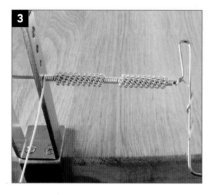

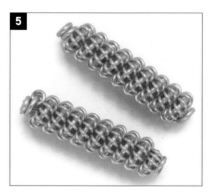

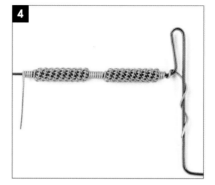

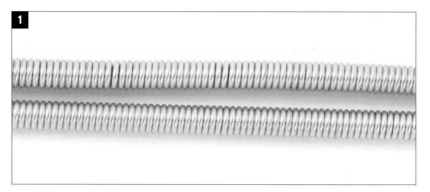

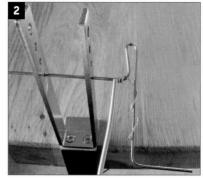

MAKING A COILED COIL

Different coil lengths can be used as spacers or as integral to different wrapping designs.

1 To make a spacer bead of a regular size, cut the coil into two equal lengths, such as 2$\frac{1}{2}$–2$\frac{3}{4}$in (6–7cm). By using the same length of coil, you can ensure your coiled coils will be the same length as each other.

2 Take a core wire (working from the reel, uncut). You can use 22–18AWG (0.6–1mm) core wire for different levels of strength or flexibility. I used 18AWG (1mm) wire with the 2$\frac{3}{4}$in (7cm) length coils made in Step 1 threaded onto it. Attach the core wire to the mandrel handle. I used the same mandrel as before, but you can choose a wider or narrower one depending upon the effect and length of coil you want to make. Reinsert the mandrel into the bracket, and wind the core wire a few times to create one or two bare wire coils about $\frac{1}{8}$in (3mm) in length. Slide the outer coil tightly up to the top of the mandrel rod. Hold the bottom of the first coiled length.

3 Wind the Gizmo handle, winding the core wire and its coil "sheath" around the mandrel to produce spirals of coiled coils.

4 Make sure you have a few turns of core wire at either side of the coiled coil. Repeat for the second 2$\frac{3}{4}$in (7cm) coil length.

5 Take off the mandrel and snip into two sections.

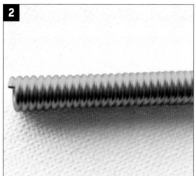

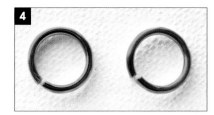

Making jumprings from Gizmo coils

Take a Gizmo coil made with 18AWG (1mm) wire on a mandrel. The internal diameter of the rings will be about the same as the mandrel; the outer diameter is the width of the mandrel plus twice the diameter of the wire. Thus, a 3.2mm mandrel and 18AWG (1mm) wire will make jumprings of about 5mm outer diameter and 3.2mm inner diameter.

Make sure that both ends are properly flush cut so they fit well together when the rings are closed. The aim is to gain an almost seamless closure, which is less likely to catch on skin and clothing, and have a more aesthetic look.

FLUSH CUTTING THE RINGS USING PLIERS

1 Take a pair of flush cutters and cut the coil at one end with the flat-edged flush-cutting side facing the coil end.

Tip

Look at your cutters and make sure you know which is the flat edge and which the angled edge.

2 This will result in a nice flat edge to this end of the wire. If you use ordinary cutters or use the flush cutters the other way around, the end will be squashed and conical rather than nice and flat and won't form a jumpring that will close neatly.

3 Rotate the flush cutters and cut the next coil along from the end at the same level as the cut end you made in Step 1. Don't cut too much above the first cut edge or the jumpring ends will overlap, or too much beneath the first cut edge or the wire ends won't meet and there will be a gap in the ring. The rotation of the pliers ensures the other cut edge faces the first cut edge you made.

4 Repeat Steps 1–3 along the coil until enough jumprings have been made.

5 The image above shows a flush-cut jumpring on the left and a jumpring cut with ordinary cutters on the right. The neat flat edges on the left will close neatly, whereas the crushed triangular ends of the non-flush-cut jumpring on the right will have poor closure.

Tip

I flush cut these jumprings using pliers, but if you have the equipment to saw cut them, you will gain an excellent flush-cut edge and lovely clean closure of the rings.

Making a brooch pin

A brooch pin is a simple fixing for a brooch. It can be made to fit the piece you are making in the same color wire. You can use wires from the design to bind to the pin, or you can wrap 30–26AWG (0.25–0.4mm) wire along the back wire of the pin and use that to bind the pin onto the design.

Here I used 18AWG (1mm) round wire; 20AWG (0.8mm) wire is also ideal. This one fits the Resting Moth Brooch (see page 48).

NOTE: You should make the brooch pin to fit your design: the total length may need to be smaller or larger than the one made here.

1 Take a 5^1/$_2$in (14cm) length of 18AWG (1mm) wire (less wire will be used for a small brooch pin and a little more for a longer pin). Start to make a 180-degree loop 2^3/$_4$in (7cm) along the wire using round-nosed pliers just under halfway along the cone tip of the round-nosed pliers (see image top right). Moving the loop around and perhaps onto the other cone tip of the round-nosed pliers, and making sure you stay at the same width/level on the pliers so your loop stays even, pull one wire end around the round-nosed pliers so it makes a 360-degree loop. Both wires should now be in the same direction lying parallel on opposite sides of the cone of the pliers.

Stroke the wire firmly away from the loop along both parallel wires with your thumb and forefinger to start to straighten it out. Measure it against your design to ascertain the length of the brooch pin you require. Make sure the fixing wires you have left in the design can attach near either end of the pin you are making.

2 Bend the end of longer wire, 1^3/$_{16}$in (3cm) away from the edge of the loop end sharply at 90 degrees to the plane of the wire you are bending.

3 Using chain-nosed pliers, make a sharp turn in the lower pin's projecting wire about ^{3}/$_4$in (18mm) along from the 90-degree turn that you made in Step 2 to make a 180-degree sharp reverse turn in the wire.

4 Squash this 180-degree turn (side to side) with your chain-nosed pliers, repeating this little squash moving from the tip of the turn down to the base. This action will make the 180-degree bent wires lie as close together as possible.

5 Make a 90-degree bend in the bottom wire just beyond the 180-degree turn, so that it lies in line with the main pin.

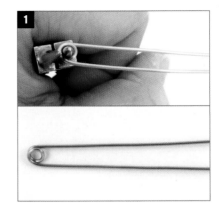

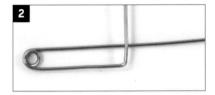

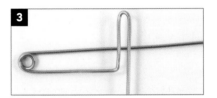

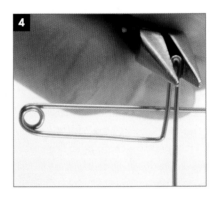

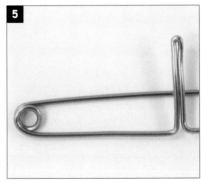

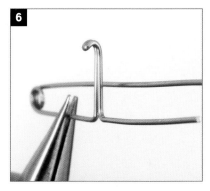

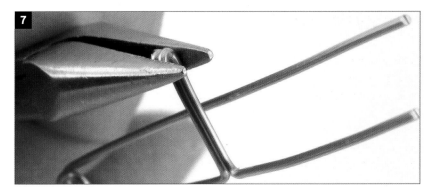

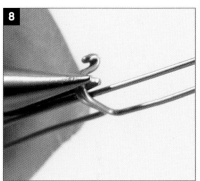

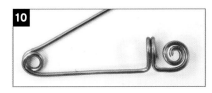

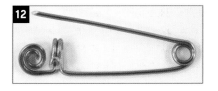

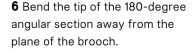

6 Bend the tip of the 180-degree angular section away from the plane of the brooch.

NOTE: You may need to hold the wire/brooch firmly at the base of the 180-degree section with flat-nosed pliers or fingers to stop the bottom line of the pin frame distorting out of its plane.

7 Squash this little curved tip front to back using chain-nosed pliers to neaten the curve.

8 Place the chain-nosed pliers back on the 180-degree section 3/16in (5mm) below the first curve you made. Start to curve this section in the other direction so it curves gently around the upper pin of the brooch.

9 Move the pliers further down the 180-degree section and make the bend more curved. Gradually move the pliers down this section, making little curves in the same direction until the loop bends around the upper pin. This curved loop will form the secure catch for the brooch. Cut the end of the lower wire of the brooch pin to a 1in (25mm) length.

10 Make a loose spiral using round- and chain-nosed pliers to act as a pin guard for the brooch.

11 On a steel block, hammer the spiral section only, not the rest of the pin. Use flush cutter pliers to cut the upper brooch pin at a sharp angle to create a pin end.

Tip

You can cut the other side of the pin to make the point even sharper. You can use a nail file or jewelry needle file to file the end at an angle all around to create a beautiful sharp point.

NOTE: Move the brooch pin inside the curved loop securement/catch to check that the sharp point is not longer than the guard (it may cause injury) or shorter than the catch (it won't secure properly).

12 The total length of this brooch pin is 1 9/16in (4cm).

THE PROJECTS

Spring daisy necklace

This daisy flower necklace combines the natural beauty of turquoise and quartz. The design can be easily adapted to use smaller or larger cabochons and can be converted with loops or clasps to make necklace components and brooches.

Templates
See page 291 for the template for this design.

Materials

FOR THE PENDANT
18AWG (1mm-diameter) silver or silver-plated copper round wire
26AWG (0.4mm-diameter) silver or silver-plated copper round wire
33 x 3mm-diameter round silver or silver-plated copper balls (through hole); use 2mm or 4mm for a smaller or larger pendant
1 x 20mm-diameter round flat-backed turquoise cabochon. Use a smaller or larger cabochon depending upon the size of pendant you want to make.

FOR THE NECKLACE SIDES
20 x 8mm-diameter rounded faceted clear quartz
18 x crackled quartz through-drilled leaf- or teardrop-shaped beads
18 x ball headpins
56 x 4mm-diameter round silver or silver-plated copper balls (through hole)

Tools
General tools (see page 10) plus:
Large marker pen or ring mandrel
Deluxe Gizmo coiling tool

Dimensions of finished piece
The pendant is 2⁹/₁₆ x 2¹/₂in (6.5 x 6cm) (bale adds to length)

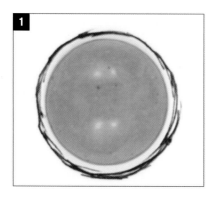

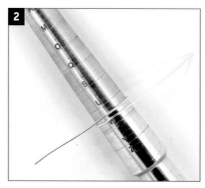

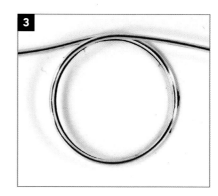

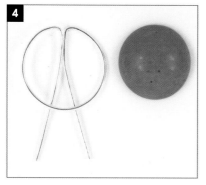

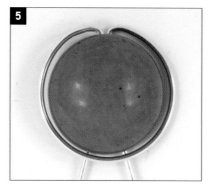

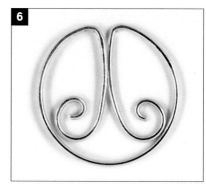

1 Place the cabochon on a piece of paper. Draw a circle around the cabochon with a pen, leaving a $1/32$in (1mm) gap. This gap will allow for weaving and the attachment of the petals around the cabochon later on in the assembly.

2 Take a $4^3/4$in (12cm) length of 18AWG (1mm) round wire and form a circle around a ring mandrel. The circle size needed to fit around the 20mm cabochon was US ring size $9^3/4$ (UK T).

3 Check the wire circle made in Step 2 against the drawing made in Step 1.

4 Using chain-nosed pliers, sharply bend the wires where they cross so that they bisect the circular shape. Trim the wire ends to project $5/8$in (15mm) outside the edge of the circle.

5 Check that the cabochon fits inside this shape with a $1/32$in (1mm) gap around it.

6 Using round-nosed pliers, curl the ends of the 18AWG (1mm) wire so that they loosely curl to fit inside the circular shape with the curl just touching the inner edge of the circle. This will form a backing plate for the cabochon to sit on. Using a flat jewelry hammer, gently hammer the shape against a steel block to work harden but not flatten it. Make sure the backing plate is nice and flat. Set the backing shape aside.

7 Cut a 12in (30cm) length of 18AWG (1mm) wire to form the triangular prong setting for the cabochon. This involves making little zigzag shapes that will fold over the stone. These extend from the base of the cabochon and will eventually be attached to the backing shape to about half to two-thirds the way up the stone. They must not extend any further or the stone will be covered by the prongs and they may meet, which is undesirable. The central portion of the stone will still be uncovered when you come to set the stone and, as the prongs are quite open, much of the stone under the prongs will still be visible.

This stone is $13/16$in (20mm) in diameter, but the curve of the frontal dome of the cabochon is nearer $1^3/16$in (3cm) in length; thus the zigzag needs to be $1/2$in (13mm) in length and $5/16$in (8mm) in depth

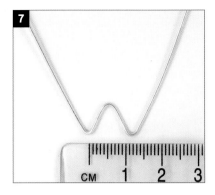

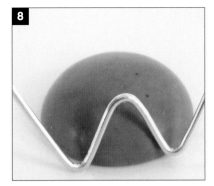

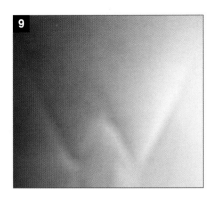

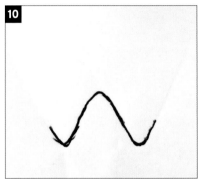

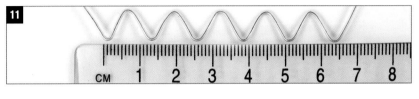

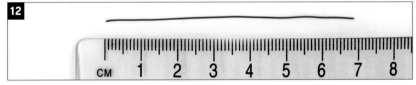

to fit this size stone. To start making the first triangular prong shape, use chain-nosed pliers to make a sharp bend in the wire about 1³/₈in (3.5cm) from one end.

8 Check the fit against the stone before making more prongs.

9 You may be able to judge the next four prongs by eye; however, if you are not confident or want to ensure accuracy, make a template from your first prong and use this to make the next four as identical as possible.

Place a sheet of paper over a rubber bead mat. Press the wire into the paper, running your fingers over it so that the impression is as true to the wire shape as possible.

10 Remove the wire and trace over the shape with a pen. Place the original wire shape over it to check it is the same size.

11 Make four more prongs until you have a shape as shown. Use the template from Step 9 to check the prongs are exactly the same size and shape.

Do not trim the long wire end yet; you need to check that the prong setting fits the stone and you may need to make more prongs! I made five prongs, but six or more may be required if your cabochon is very large.

The prong setting for this stone is 2⁹/₁₆in (6.5cm) in length along the base of the prongs.

12 If you have an awkwardly shaped or sized stone, you can judge the length of your setting roughly by using a scrap piece of wire to make a circle the same size as the shape you made in Step 1. Mark where the wires cross, then open out the scrap wire so it lies along a ruler. Now measure the circumference of the circle to make it easier for you to gauge the length of the prong setting you need to make. In this case, the circumference of the setting was about 2⁵/₈in (6.75cm) in length, so the prong setting I made could fit around the stone with a little gap.

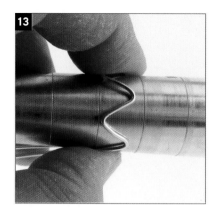

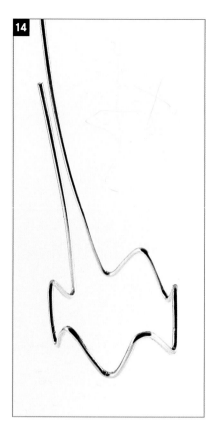

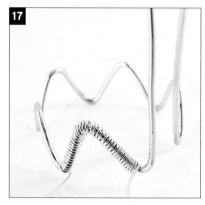

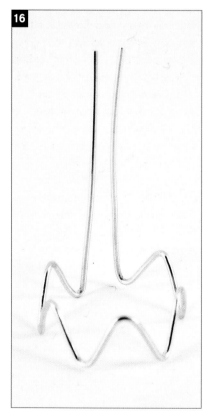

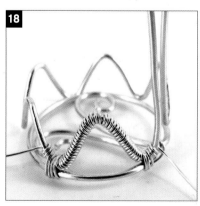

13 Gently bend the prong setting into a circle at the base of the prongs; either use your fingers or bend it around a marker pen or ring mandrel.

14 As a ring mandrel is tapered, make sure you are shaping around US ring size 9³/₄ (UK T) (for this stone). Only press at this level, or your prongs will either splay or point inward. Bend the wire ends so that they point straight upward like a little crown and they don't cross over each other.

15 Check the fit of the prong setting around the stone. Stretch or compress the prongs slightly to get a good fit or make more prongs if required. Make sure these adjustments are even all around the setting to keep the prongs looking identical.

   The setting can be smaller than the backing plate by about ¹/₈in (2–3mm). Don't worry if the setting looks as if it is not long enough—you will still be able to attach the setting securely. It makes it easier if there is a little gap between one end of the setting where it meets the other end when it makes the circular form.

16 If the setting looks right and you have made all the adjustments required, trim the other end wire to 1³/₈in (3.5cm), the same as the first end.

17 Cut a 60in (1.5m) length of 26AWG (0.4mm) wire. About 12–16in (30–40cm) from the end of the wire, start to wrap along one of the prongs nearest to one end of the setting. Wrap neatly, making sure the wires lie next to each other. Try to avoid gaps in the wrap, although this is difficult to avoid at the tips of the prongs. Use your fingers and pliers to help push the wire wraps together. Use a sideways push of the 26AWG (0.4mm) when using pliers and be careful not to damage the 26AWG (0.4mm) wire by crushing across the wire too roughly. This will take a bit of practice and you will get lovely results if you compress the wraps like this. Wrap along the prong until you get to the base of the prong on either side.

18 Now attach the prong setting to the backing. Place it over the backing section so that the gap in the prong setting lies over the gap in the backing plate.

Wrap the 26AWG (0.4mm) wire ends around both the base of the prong setting and the backing section three times. Lock this wrap into place by starting to wrap along the next prong on one side.

The other side will need to be locked into place by wrapping a couple of times around the gap in the backing plate with a figure-of-eight weave within this little space. Then pass the 26AWG (0.4mm) wire up to the base of the 18AWG (1mm) wire end of the prong setting (which is sticking straight upward) and start to wrap along up this 18AWG (1mm) wire end.

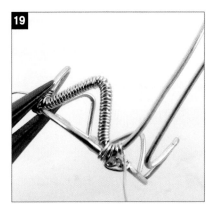

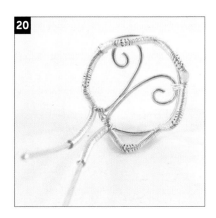

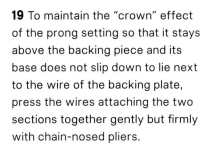

19 To maintain the "crown" effect of the prong setting so that it stays above the backing piece and its base does not slip down to lie next to the wire of the backing plate, press the wires attaching the two sections together gently but firmly with chain-nosed pliers.

20 Continue to wrap along the prong setting, attaching it to the backing plate at each base of the prong until you reach the other end of the prong setting. At any stage where the curled wires in the backing piece also touch the points on the backing circle and the base of a prong setting, wrap across all three wires. This strengthens the backing section and saves you doing it at a later stage when attaching the petals.

21 Wrap up the end wires on either side of the prong setting for $^{13}/_{16}$in (20mm), leaving $^5/_8$in (15mm) of bare 18AWG (1mm) wire. Cut the 26AWG (0.4mm) wire with flush-cutter pliers. Press in the ends around the 18AWG (1mm) wire with chain-nosed pliers so there are no sharp ends to catch on the skin.

22 Check that the cabochon fits nicely inside the prong setting. Then put this flower center component aside.

23

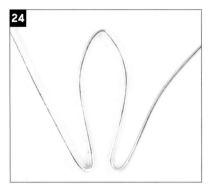

24

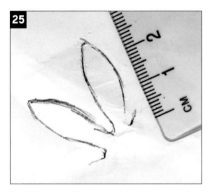

25

26

23 To make the petal section, first decide on the length and number of petals for the flower design. I drew up a rough diagram to help me, and decided to make ten petals to fit around the flower center component. Changing the petal number and length will completely alter the look of the flower.

The petals need to be in proportion to the stone and also to the pendant size you wish to make. When placed on either side of the stone, the petal length will make the pendant much larger than the stone itself, although this will be moderated by the bending and shaping of the petals in the later stages.

The template (shown at actual size on page 291) will help you plan the flower design. It is 2¹/₂in (6cm) across. You will make equal shaped and sized petals from templates in later stages.

24 Take a 40in (1m) length of 18AWG (1mm) wire. Make a petal shape 1in (25mm) long and ³/₈in (9mm) at its widest point about 4in (10cm) along the wire (leave this 4in/10cm length to help make the bale later). Use your fingers and chain-nosed pliers to shape the wire.

Tip

To make the bend in the wire at the petal tip sharper, clamp either side of the bend repeatedly with the chain-nosed pliers as close to the bend as possible.

25 You can use the template on page 291 but if you are making different sized or shaped petals, you can use the impression technique (as in Step 9) to make your own template. To make my first template, I made impressions of the first petal I made, placed next to each other to help me gauge the spacing between petals and the little curve at the base of the petal.

26 Use this template to make a run of ten petals, leaving at least a 4in (10cm) length of wire at the end that will make the other side of the bale.

NOTE: Don't trim the wire ends to 4in (10cm) just yet. You may need to make more petals to fill the space around the flower center.

27 Check the fit of the flower frame around the stone and make more petals if required. However, ten is usually enough. You can then cut a 4in (10cm) length of wire at the end to form the other side of the bale in the later stages. Gently hammer the petals against a steel block to slightly work-harden them, but not to flatten the wire.

NOTE: The 4in (10cm) wire ends for the petal section will cross over to lie on opposite sides of the bale from the side of the flower they originated from. This arrangement will help the flower petals at the top sit better and not be spaced out too far by the bale, which will sit in a space between petals.

28 Now attach the flower petals to the flower center component. Using 60in (1.5m) of 26AWG (0.4mm) wire, start to attach the top of the central flower component to the center of the petal shape about 12in (30cm) from one end of the 26AWG (0.4mm) wire.

It is important to place the petal shape so that the end bale wires cross over each other to lie on opposite sides (see arrow in image). When you bind the 26AWG (0.4mm) wire with this first fixing, you bind across the base of both

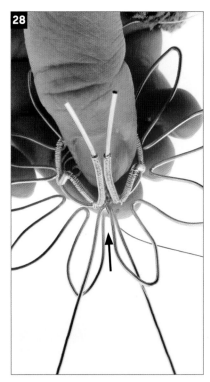

bale wires and in between the wires projecting at the top of the central petal complex. This ensures the tops of both components line up nicely and you are already starting to give some strength to the piece.

One end of the 26AWG (0.4mm) wire will be used to weave the bale; the other will be used to help attach some petal beads in later stages.

29 Make a couple of traversing weaves at the base of the bale with the long wire end, but don't progress any further as you will weave the bale in later stages. Tuck this wire out of the way for the moment by wrapping gently and loosely around the bale.

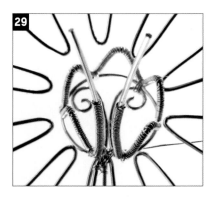

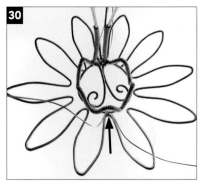

30 Take an 80in (2m) length of 26AWG (0.4mm) wire and start to attach using the midsection of the wire at the space between the bottom two petals, opposite the first attachment made in Step 28, at the center of the space under the bottom prong (see arrow in image). This ensures the petals are centered and evenly spaced around the flower as they have been attached at two opposite points around the central flower component. Bind three times and pull the wire tight to secure the petal.

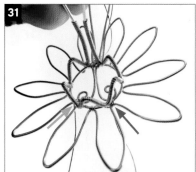

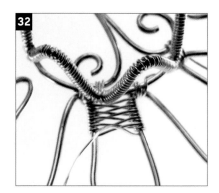

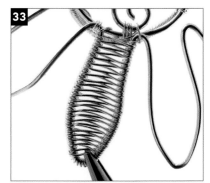

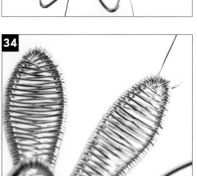

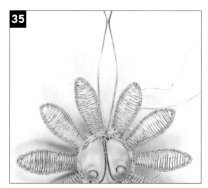

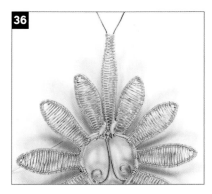

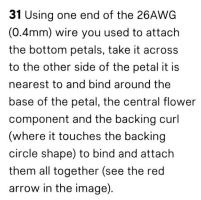

31 Using one end of the 26AWG (0.4mm) wire you used to attach the bottom petals, take it across to the other side of the petal it is nearest to and bind around the base of the petal, the central flower component and the backing curl (where it touches the backing circle shape) to bind and attach them all together (see the red arrow in the image).

Do the same with the other end of the wire at the base of the flower and attach the other side of the petal on the other side of the bottom midline as shown (see the blue arrow in the image).

This not only attaches the petals and the central flower component together, but also attaches the backing curls of wire into place so the stone won't drop out of the back of the setting.

32 Start to weave along one of the petals with the 26AWG (0.4mm) wire ends. Use a standard figure-of-eight basket weave with two wraps of the 26AWG (0.4mm) wire around each petal side before each traverse to the opposite side petal wire (passing from front to back and back to front in a figure-of-eight pattern) (see page 24).

33 As you approach the tip of the petal, stop the traversing weaves about $^3/_{16}$in (5mm) from the tip and finish the petal end as shown on page 25.

34 Use the other 26AWG (0.4mm) wire end at the base of the flower to weave up the adjacent bottom petal.

NOTE: The image shows where the final traverse is positioned before pulling the 26AWG (0.4mm) wire tightly and firmly into position.

35 Attach more 26AWG (0.4mm) wire in between unwoven pairs of petals around the flower. Weave them in the same way as in Steps 32–34 until all the petals are woven. In the image I have also shaped the bale wires into a narrow diamond shape $1^9/_{16}$in (4cm) long with splayed wire ends $1^3/_8$in (3.5cm) long.

36 Weave up the bale with the long length of 26AWG (0.4mm) wire you attached in Step 28 using the same weave used for the petals. Stop the weave at the top of the long diamond-shaped section. Cut and tuck in the 26AWG (0.4mm) wire. The weave is in a small space between the top two petals; you might need to press the weaves together with pliers as you go.

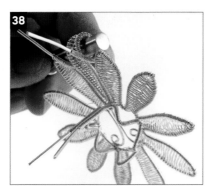

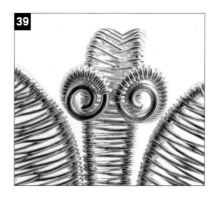

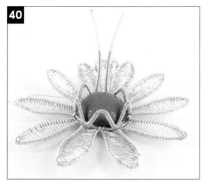

37 Add a 12in (30cm) length of 26AWG (0.4mm) wire at its mid-section at the end of the diamond section of the bale using a figure-of-eight weave around both bale wires. Use each 26AWG (0.4mm) wire end to wrap up the sides of the bale end wires for ¹³/₁₆in (20mm). Cut and tuck in the 26AWG (0.4mm) wire ends on either side, leaving ⁵/₈in (15mm) of bare wire.

38 Take a 6mm-diameter mandrel (or use a pen, Gizmo rod or knitting needle) and use your fingers to bend and curl the bale around the mandrel.

39 Use round-nosed pliers to start curling and shaping the bale wire ends, and fingers and pliers to finish the curl, as on page 29.

NOTE: This bale is adjustable; it is not wired into place at the base as in other designs. The work-hardened bale wire is very rigid. This is a nice variant for those who prefer interchangeable necklaces. To make a more secure bale, wire the end wires in place by not trimming the bale wrap wires from Step 37 and using them to bind the bale wires to the front of the bale where they cross it. Press the bale's curled ends into place with your fingers and adjust them so they are balanced and symmetrical.

40 Now place the cabochon into the setting. I set cabochons on a soft surface like a rubber mat; this means I am less likely to break a cabochon either due to pressure from the prongs or from dropping the cabochon if it falls out during setting.

41 Use your fingers to gently press the prongs down against the stone. Pressing opposite prongs simultaneously with thumb and forefinger, or even four fingers (using both hands), can help as evenly applied opposing pressure helps to set the stone balanced in place. It will be difficult to press the prongs completely flat against the stone with your fingers alone. The prongs will look like the image—the stone will not fall out but it is not properly set yet.

42 Use the soft rubber handle of your pliers to press the upper part of each prong into place.

43 Work from opposite prong to opposite prong until they lie flat against the stone.

44 Curl the prong setting ends using the same methods to curl the bale wires in Step 33 and press them into place with your fingers. Adjust them so they are balanced and symmetrical.

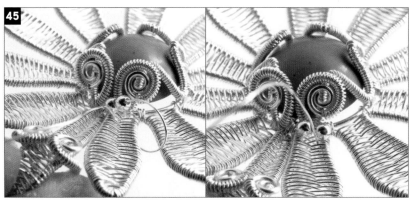

45 Now add the silver ball details to the base of the petals. Take the 26AWG (0.4mm) wire end left over from weaving the bale and use this to start adding the balls. You may need to add in more wire, but this can be done at any stage.

Thread the 26AWG (0.4mm) wire up along the outside edge of the base of the nearest petal. Thread on two 3mm-diameter round silver balls. Attach with a firm wrap around the opposite edge of the base of the same petal, bringing the wire up in the midline of the petal ready to attach a third bead.

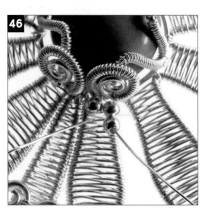

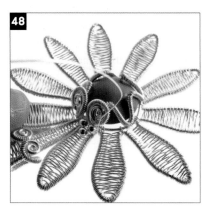

46 Attach a third bead. Thread the 26AWG (0.4mm) wire back through the middle of the petal through a different set of weave wires so that the third bead is caught on top of the petal and sits in between the first two silver balls added in Step 45.

47 Pull the 26AWG (0.4mm) wire tight and thread it up inside the cabochon setting next to the next petal.

48 Pass the wire over the edge of the circular backing plate through the midline of the bottom of the petal. Pass the wire up to the side of the base of the petal, ready to add on more beads. Pull the wire tight.

MASTERING WIREWORK JEWELRY

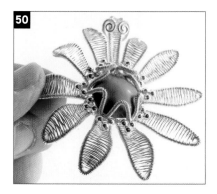

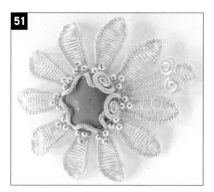

49 Add on beads to the base of each of the rest of the petals. Add more 26AWG (0.4mm) wire if you run out, and cut and tuck in at the base of the bale. You can choose to add beads to the base of the bale. I have done this in one flower, but I omitted them in the other as the bale was too narrow.

50 This next step is up to you! You can either have the daisy petals sticking straight outward, as in Step 43, or you can make a little curve in the petal with your fingers to shape it slightly.

51 Do this for each petal. Experiment to see what looks right for you.

52 Make a necklace bale component section to support the bale. Use a $^{5}/_{16}$–$^{3}/_{8}$in (8–10mm) length of Gizmo coil made with 18AWG (1mm) wire on a 1.6mm-diameter Gizmo mandrel.

Place an 8mm-diameter faceted clear quartz gemstone either side finished with a wrapped loop either side.

53 Make up the necklace either side of the bale component using wrapped loop links made with two 4mm-diameter silver beads either side of an 8mm-diameter faceted clear quartz. Attach dangle drops of teardrop crackle quartz and a 4mm silver bead on a wrapped loop headpin attached to the bottom wrapped loop of each necklace link.

54 The loop end of the clasp is made in the same way as the links, but with a much larger loop on the loop side. Hammer the large loop to create a reflective surface.

55 For the hook end of the clasp, make a spiral at one end of a $4^{3}/_{4}$in (12cm) length of 18AWG (1mm) wire and then a shepherd's hook shape.

Hammer this section and then thread on a 4mm silver bead, an 8mm quartz and another 4mm silver bead. Then make a wrapped loop at the other end to attach to the rest of the necklace.

Add embellishment to the clasp by wrapping the wrapped loop wire end across the beads and quartz. Wrap around the edge of the bead toward the hook end and make a little curl to secure the beads in place and stop them moving up along the hook.

56 Your beautiful necklace is now finished and ready to wear!

Resting moth brooch

This brooch is set with turquoise and lapis lazuli gemstones embellished with metallic beads. The design offers the option of different wing finishes.

Templates

See page 290 for the templates for this design.

Materials

18AWG (1mm-diameter) round copper wire
26AWG (0.4mm-diameter) round copper wire
30AWG (0.25mm-diameter) round copper wire
(Antique bronze, bare copper, silver or gold-plated wire can be used instead)
79 x 3mm (8/0) round gold-plated copper beads with 1mm-diameter hole
2 x 4–5mm round antique bronze-plated copper beads with 1mm-diameter hole
2 x 3mm round rainbow coated hematite gemstone beads, through-drilled
1 x 20 x 15mm turquoise pear cabochon, no drill hole required
1 x 15mm smooth puffy coin-shaped lapis lazuli gemstone (the one I used had a drill hole but is not used in the design. A 15mm round lapis lazuli cabochon could also be used)
1 x 4–5mm diameter round turquoise gemstone
1 x 6mm-diameter round turquoise gemstone

Tools

General tools (see page 10)

Dimensions of finished piece

Beaded wing brooch: 2¹/₂in (6cm) in length x 3¹/₄in (8cm) maximum width
Hammered spiral wirework wing brooch: 3¹/₄in (8cm) in length x 2³/₄in (7cm) maximum width

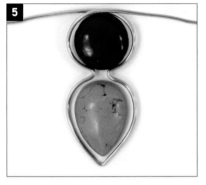
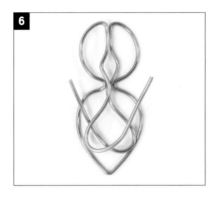

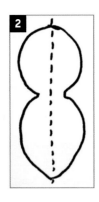

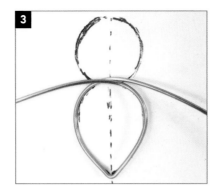

1 Place the 20 x 15mm turquoise cabochon and the 15mm coin lapis lazuli on a sheet of plain paper in the position of abdomen and thorax respectively. Draw around them with $^1/_{32}$in (1mm) clearance around each gemstone (to allow for wire wrapping space in later stages). (There is a template on page 290 that you can use if you prefer.)

2 Draw a midline vertical dotted line to make sure you place the gemstones correctly.

3 Cut a 12in (30cm) length of 18AWG (1mm) wire using flush cutter pliers and make an angle in the midline of the wire. Placing the wire over the abdomen part of the drawing from Step 1, shape the wire over the diagram using your fingers.

Tip

Clamp either side of the angle at the tip of the abdomen with your chain-nosed pliers near the angle; this will help you achieve a sharp angular bend in the wire.

4 Make a little bend at the top of the abdomen section to create a waist for the moth using pliers and fingers shaping over the diagram.

Tip

Gently squashing either side of each bend of the waist with your chain-nosed pliers will help you create a more acute angle.

5 Continue to shape the wire ends in a circular form either side of the lapis gemstone until they meet at the top.

6 Shape the wire ends to form a backing plate for the gemstone cabochons and attachment sites for wires in later stages. Bend the wire ends sharply downward into the thorax circle for about $^1/_4$in (6mm), taking care not to distort the circular shape. Check that it still fits around the lapis gemstone every so often. Make an angle in each wire $^1/_4$in (6mm) into the thorax space, splaying the wires outward slightly. You will have made a diamond-shaped space in the thorax backing shape. Angle back inward, toward the midline, another $^1/_8$in (3mm) further along the wires. Bend then straight downward to pass through the middle of the waist section. Curve each wire within the abdomen wire frame space so they touch the outer frame one-third of the way up from the abdominal tip on each side. Then curve the wire ends upward so they point

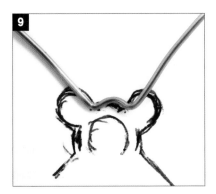

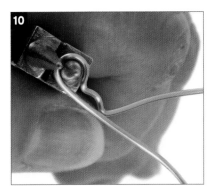

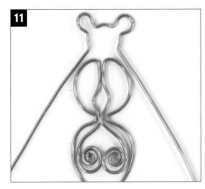

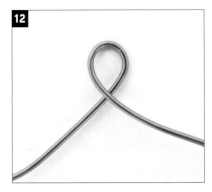

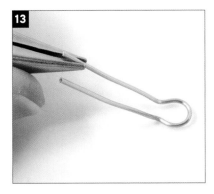

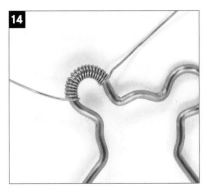

out over the opposite edge of the abdominal frame, about two-thirds up from the tip. Cut the 18AWG (1mm) wire ends so they project about ¹/₂in (12mm) from the side of the lower abdomen shape.

7 Curl the 18AWG (1mm) wire ends from Step 6, with round-nosed and chain-nosed pliers, into a loose spiral (see page 27) so they form an upside-down heart shape fitting inside the abdomen frame space.

8 Place the frame made in Steps 1–7 onto plain paper and draw a head section with the head bead you are using as a guide.

NOTE: The bead in the image is slightly smaller than the one I eventually used.

9 Take a 32in (80cm) length of 18AWG (1mm) wire and make a shallow W-shape at the midpoint of the wire using your pliers. Make sure it fits over the top of the head drawing in between the eye frame shapes.

10 Using round-nosed pliers, make the eye frame shapes on either side of the W-shape. The base of the pliers will have the girth required to make the right sized space.

11 Place the shape next to the thorax and abdomen shape with the wire ends projecting downward and outward ready to make the wings.

12 Take a new 4in (10cm) length of 18AWG (1mm) round wire and make a circle at its midsection using a wrap around the base of your round-nosed pliers. This should fit inside the head section with a little gap to allow for wire weaving. This is termed the "inner head frame section" in later stages.

13 Make bends in the ends of the wire shape so you have straight wire ends projecting about 1in (2.5cm) from the circular shape. Bend the wire ends upward from the plane of the circular shape so that the shape you have made does not lie flat.

14 Take an 8in (20cm) length of 30AWG (0.25mm) wire and wrap it around the midsection of one eye frame (made in Steps 9–11). Stop when halfway around each side of the eye socket.

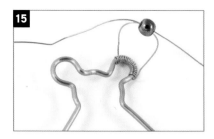

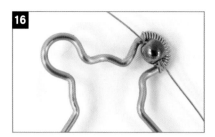

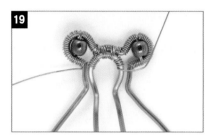

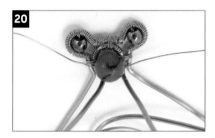

15 Thread a 3mm-diameter coated hematite onto one 30AWG (0.25mm) wire end and pass the other wire end through the opposite side of the gemstone. This ensures the gemstones are wired in place with two strands of the wire and makes a much stronger attachment. I call this a "criss-cross bead attachment" in later steps.

16 Pull the wire ends firmly to pull the gemstone into place within the eye socket frame.

17 Continue wrapping the 30AWG (0.25mm) wire ends to the base of the eye socket. Cut the wire ends and tuck them in neatly around the frame wire.

18 Take a 40in (1m) length of 30AWG (0.25mm) wire and wrap it around the middle of the head frame three times.

19 Take the inner head frame section made in Steps 12–13 and bind it to the outer head frame using three wraps of the 30AWG (0.25mm) wire across and around both frames on either side of the three wraps made in Step 18. Wrap only around the top of the outer head frame for two to three wraps (depending on space). Pass the 30AWG (0.25mm) wire ends back to the inner head frame and wrap around that until you reach a level at the base of the eye socket on either side of the head section.

Tip

Gently squeeze the wraps front to back to neaten them. Use pressure from your fingernails to press the wraps close together. You can use pliers, but take care not to damage the wrapping wire. Never crush across the wrapping wires; use a gentle sideways pressure to the outer edge of the outermost wrap to push the wraps together.

20 Wrap three times around both inner and outer head frames on either side of the head. Then wrap the 30AWG (0.25mm) wire on each side only around the inner head frame. Add a 6mm bead using the criss-crossing method of wrapping wires through the bead as used to add in Step 15.

21 Continue wrapping twice more around the inner frame only on either side and then around both frames two or three more times (depending upon space) until you reach the bottom of the head frame. Do not cut the wire ends.

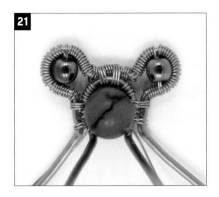

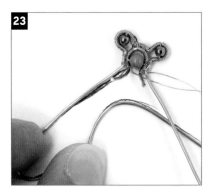

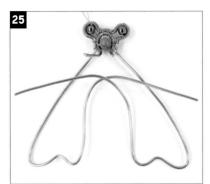

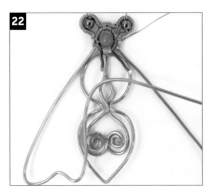

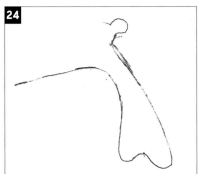

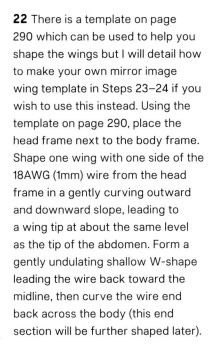

22 There is a template on page 290 which can be used to help you shape the wings but I will detail how to make your own mirror image wing template in Steps 23–24 if you wish to use this instead. Using the template on page 290, place the head frame next to the body frame. Shape one wing with one side of the 18AWG (1mm) wire from the head frame in a gently curving outward and downward slope, leading to a wing tip at about the same level as the tip of the abdomen. Form a gently undulating shallow W-shape leading the wire back toward the midline, then curve the wire end back across the body (this end section will be further shaped later).

NOTE: Cut the wire end to about 2¹/₂in (6cm) from the midline as shown in Step 25.

23 To make your own mirror-image template. The other wing needs to be formed; it is important that the wings are symmetrical. Press the wing frame shape firmly onto a sheet of plain paper placed on a spongy rubber mat to form an impression of the first wing.

24 Turn the sheet over and trace over the impression. This gives you a mirror-image template to form the other wing. (See also the template on page 290.)

25 Make the other wing using the template. Cut the wire ends so that they are at least 2in (5cm) long from the top of the inner side of the wing.

26 Hammer the wings only on a steel block to work-harden them without flattening them: don't hammer the wire ends or the head section.

27 Take a 4in (10cm) length of 18AWG (1mm) wire. Form a circle at the midsection of the wire using the base of one prong of your round-nosed pliers to start making an antenna component. The circle should fit onto the head section, so that the base of the circle fits at the base of the head where the end wires from the inner head frame project upward and the sides fit around the head frame passing inside the eye beads.

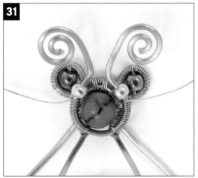

28 Thread two 3mm-diameter copper beads onto the circle, then bend the wire ends away from the circle. The wire ends should be 1³/₁₆in (3cm) long.

29 Curl the wire ends for the head antennae component from Step 28 (see page 27). Hammer only the spirals to flatten them. I would use pliers to straighten out the antenna a little on the right side to match the other side in this image.

30 Place the antennae component on top of the head section and use the 30AWG (0.25mm) wire ends from Step 20 to bind this component on using three wraps around the antennae component and the base of the head section.

31 Wrap the 30AWG (0.25mm) wire ends along each side of the antennae component until you reach

the base of the eye socket. Make sure the 3mm beads threaded on to this component are sitting at the base of the eye socket under the other eye beads already in place.

32 Wrap the 30AWG (0.25mm) wire ends on either side around both the antennae frame and the base of the eye socket twice to bind these components together. Pass the 30AWG (0.25mm) wire around the 3mm bead and bind the antennae frame to the top of the eye socket with wraps of the 30AWG (0.25mm) wire. The image above shows the upper eye on the lower side of the image at the stage where it should be ready to move on to the next step.

33 Wrap the 30AWG (0.25mm) wire from either eye in Step 32 along the antennae until you reach the base of the antennae where the two wires are closest.

Attach a 3mm round copper bead using a criss-cross attachment and the 30AWG (0.25mm) wires from the side through the bead. Continue wrapping up along the antennae for ¹/₄in (6mm). Cut the 30AWG (0.25mm) wire and tuck in the wire end neatly around the antennae section. Put this section to one side for the moment.

34 Take a 4in (10cm) length of 26AWG (0.4mm) wire and wrap around where the central wires touch in the abdominal frame space to join them together. Wrap six to seven times. Cut the wire on one side only and gently press flat. The side with the wire ends can be used to face the back of the cabochon so it will be hidden and won't catch on skin.

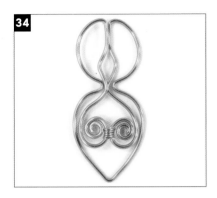

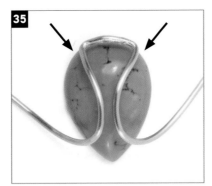

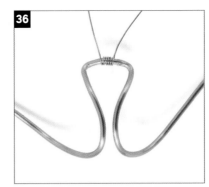

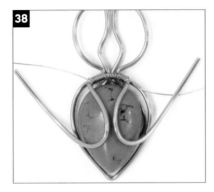

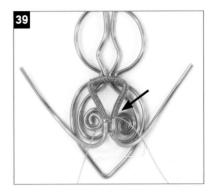

35 Take a 6in (15cm) length of 18AWG (1mm) wire and make a gentle curve about ³/₈in (10mm) long in the midsection of the wire. This curve needs to fit nicely around the top curve of the pear-shaped turquoise gemstone (see arrows in image). Bend the wire ends sharply up at an angle and press the wire ends with the heat of your fingers to curve over the gemstone. Place the gemstone on a rubber mat so this pressure does not crack it. The wire ends should splay away from the gemstone. They will be further trimmed and shaped later.

36 Take a 40in (1m) length of 30AWG (0.25mm) wire. Using the mid-section of this wire, wrap it around the gentle curve from the cabochon setting component made in Step 35, leaving long ends on either side for wrapping to either side.

37 Place this component over the top of the abdominal frame section from Step 34. Using the 30AWG (0.25mm) wire, bind the cabochon setting component to the frame at the midline and ¹/₄in (6mm) across from the midline on one side at the top of the pear-shaped part of the abdominal frame (see black arrows in image).

38 Continue wrapping the 30AWG (0.25mm) wire along the cabochon setting component across from the midline of the abdominal frame and bind at a third place to the setting ¹/₄in (6mm) along from the midline. I placed the pear-shaped stone in the setting to check that it fitted well before proceeding. Trim the 18AWG (1mm) wire ends from the cabochon setting component so they project about ⁷/₈in (22mm) from the side of the frame.

39 Remove the pear-shaped cabochon and continue wrapping along the sides of the cabochon setting component until they start to run closely together (see arrow in image).

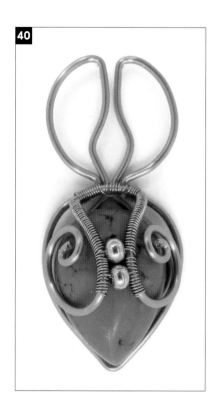

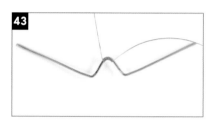

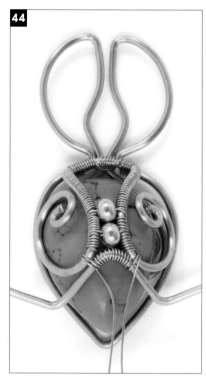

40 Attach a 3mm round copper bead using a criss-cross attachment of the 30AWG (0.25mm) wires from either side through the bead. Continue wrapping up along the sides of the cabochon setting component for six wraps. Add in another 3mm bead in the same way, then continue to wrap along the setting wires for another 1/8in (3mm). Cut the 30AWG (0.25mm) wire and tuck in the wire ends using the tips of chain-nosed pliers. Curl the wire ends for the cabochon setting (see page 27) to achieve a loose circular spiral. Press these into place along the side of the stone. I placed the stone into the setting so I could shape another cabochon setting component in the next steps.

41 Take a 4in (10cm) length of 18AWG (1mm) wire. Make a V-shape in the mid-segment of the wire with 1³/₈in (3.5cm) lengths of wire projecting either side of the V.

42 Don't cut the wire to size until you have checked the fit of the "V" properly. It should fit over the bottom third of the pear-shaped gemstone bisecting it at this level.

43 Take a 40in (1m) length of 30AWG (0.25mm) wire. Using its mid-segment, wrap along the tip of the V to about ³/₁₆in (4mm) along on either side. Make sure this wrap is far enough along the V so that you have reached a point where you can attach to the rest of the cabochon setting in the next step.

44 Using the 30AWG (0.25mm) wire ends from the V setting, attach them to the rest of the cabochon setting at two points where they touch with seven or eight wraps around both frame wires.

45 Continue to wrap along the V component until you reach a point ⁵/₈in (15mm) from the end of each 18AWG (1mm) wire. Cut the 30AWG (0.25mm) wire and tuck in neatly around the 18AWG (1mm) wire.

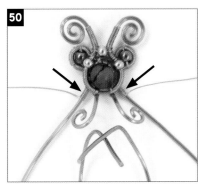

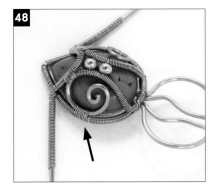

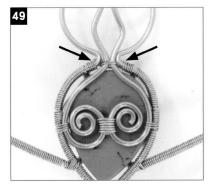

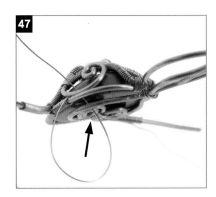

46 With the pear-shaped gemstone in place, attach a 40in (1m) length of 30AWG (0.25mm) wire at its mid-section to the tip of the pear-shaped setting. Start to wrap either side of the abdominal pear frame setting on either side. When you get to the point where the V frame touches the pear frame setting, bind around this three or four times on each side to securely attach it to the abdominal frame on each side. Carry on wrapping up the side of the frame until you reach a point on each side where the wire curls from the cabochon setting components touch the sides of the frame.

47 Bind the 30AWG (0.25mm) wire around the wire curls from the cabochon setting components and the curls at the backing of the cabochon setting to bind them all together four or five times. (See arrow in image.)

48 Bind just around the wire curls from the cabochon setting components and the sides of the abdominal frame for five to six more binding wraps (see arrow in image). Please also see image 49 showing the back of the cabochon setting to see where the binding wraps at the side of the frame also attach to the backing curls.

49 Continue to wrap along only the abdominal frame until you reach the top of the pear-shaped section where the cabochon setting frame has already been attached. Cut and tuck in the 30AWG (0.25mm) wire ends at this point on either side. (See arrows in image.)

50 Curl the ends of the wires projecting downward from the head and wing component that you were working on in Step 33 ready to form a cabochon setting over the lapis coin gemstone later. Attach a 40in (1m) length of 26AWG (0.4mm) wire to the base of the head at its mid-section. Wrap along the top edge of the wing from the base of the head for ¼in (6mm) until you reach a point where it would be ready to bind to the body abdominal section from Step 49 (see arrows in image).

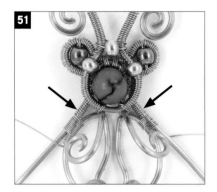

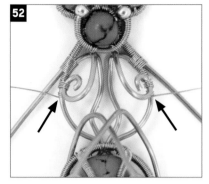

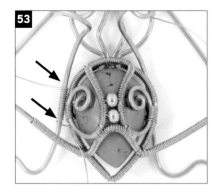

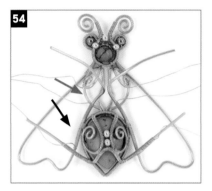

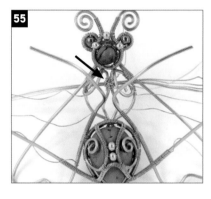

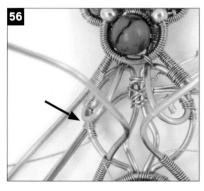

51 Using the 26AWG (0.4mm) wire ends from Step 50, bind to the top of the body section with about ten binding wraps across the top of both wings and the top of the body section on either side (see arrows in image).

52 Continue wrapping along just the sides of the circular section of the body frame for four wraps. Also wrap around the sides of the curls from the head section made in Step 50 for three or four wraps on either side to bind them to the abdominal frame. Then wrap just along the circular frame for one or two wraps (see arrows in image).

53 Take a 40in (1m) length of 30AWG (0.25mm) wire and wrap 4in (10cm) from the end of the 30AWG (0.25mm) wire with the shorter length projecting downward (do

not cut this wire end). Wrap up the inner edge of the left-hand wing with the lower edge of this wrap until about halfway along the pear-shaped gemstone setting (see arrows in image).

54 Wrap the upper end wrapping 30AWG (0.25mm) wire from Step 53 also around the pear-shaped setting where the inner edge of the wing touches against it about three-quarters up the pear-shaped setting from the tip. Wrap about eight times to bind the wing to the body frame on this side (see black arrow in image). Continue to wrap along the inner wing wire until you reach a point just past where it would cross the base of the circular body frame section (see red arrow). Do not cut the 30AWG (0.25mm) wire ends. Repeat Steps 53–54 for the other side.

55 Cut five lengths of 26AWG (0.4mm) wire, each 16in (40cm), and bundle them lengthways. Take an 8in (20cm) length of 26AWG (0.4mm) wire and bind the bundle of five wires at its midsection at the back of the coin shape setting with a few wraps around the back of the setting (see arrow in image). Do not cut the 26AWG (0.4mm) wires you have used to attach the bundle; you will use these to attach the brooch pin later. Direct them toward the back of the frame, ready to use to attach a brooch pin.

56 Bend the 26AWG (0.4mm) wire bundles outward and downward slightly on either side so they pass under the circular setting where you stopped wrapping in Step 52 (see arrow in image).

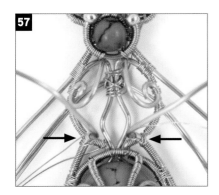

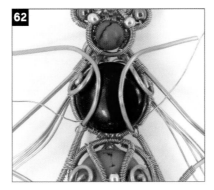

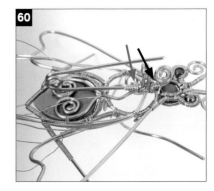

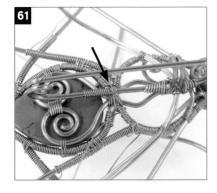

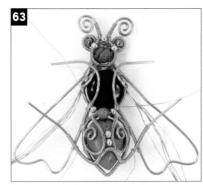

57 Bind the bundle to the back and side of this frame at these points on either side using binding wraps of the 26AWG (0.4mm) wire from Step 52. Continue to wrap along the circular frame on each side. Also bind and wrap the inside wing wires where they cross the circular frame with three or four binding wraps to attach them firmly in place (see arrows in image). They will form the bottom of the cabochon setting for the circular lapis gemstone later. Continue wrapping to the base of the circular frame. At this stage, there are a lot of wires projecting from the moth frame. We will use all of these wires later—they are all useful.

58 Make a brooch pin ready to attach to the brooch frame (see page 32).

59 Measure against the moth the length of the brooch pin you require so the fixing wires left in Steps 55 and 56 can attach near either end of the pin you are making. The total length of the brooch pin is 1⁹/₁₆in (4cm).

60 Start to secure the brooch pin to the moth brooch. Place the 180-degree loop end of the clasp against the back of the brooch at the base of the head where there are two 26AWG (0.4mm) wires projecting from Step 55. Bind the lower wire around the brooch pin just below the catch, around the back frame, and back to the pin. Wrap along the pin a few times, cut the 26AWG (0.4mm) wire, and tuck in the end neatly (see red arrow in image). Do the same with the upper 26AWG (0.4mm) wire just above the catch to secure the pin at this level (see black arrow).

61 Using the 26AWG (0.4mm) wires from Step 56, attach the lower end of the brooch pin in the same way as the upper section by binding with wraps around the waist section (see arrow in image). You can add decorative beads into the waist section either now or in Step 63.

62 Place the 15mm lapis lazuli coin in the setting, then curl the wire ends from the inner wings over the stone to lie either side of the base of the head.

63 Using the 30AWG (0.25mm) wire ends from Step 54, attach a 3mm copper bead, a 4–5mm diameter turquoise bead, and another 3mm copper bead to the base using a criss-cross bead attachment.

64 Wrap up either side of the cabochon setting using the 26AWG (0.4mm) wire ends from Step 63, attaching two 3mm copper beads a quarter of the way up the gemstone in the criss-cross bead attachment (see black arrow in image). Attach a single 3mm bead halfway up the setting where the two wires lying over the stone are closest to each other (see red arrow). Another two 3mm beads can be added three-quarters of the way up the setting. Then wrap along the wires until you reach a point where the wires cross over the outer edge of the frame at the base of the head (see blue arrow).

65 Curl the 18AWG (1mm) wire ends of the cabochon setting and press them into place carefully at the top of the setting at the base of the neck/head.

66 Bind the cabochon setting wire to the top of the cabochon setting using wires wrapped around the base of the neck ending up with the 30AWG (0.25mm) wires emerging from the central space at the base of the head (see arrows in image).

67 Add one 3mm bead into this space using a criss-cross attachment with the 30AWG (0.25mm) wire ends (see arrow in image).

68 Thread on a 3mm bead to each 30AWG (0.25mm) wire end projecting from the bead added in Step 67 (see arrows in image).

69 Pull tight to bring the beads into place. Attach the 30AWG (0.25mm) wires to the brooch pin or another easily hidden place at the back of the moth, then cut and tuck in the wire ends.

70 Thread on a 5mm-diameter antique bronze metal bead to all five 26AWG (0.4mm) wires projecting from the root of the wing on each side (see arrow in image).

71 Working on the left wing first, separate the five wires into a top group of two and a lower group of three. Thread three 3mm beads onto the top two wires. Then thread three beads only on the top wire and direct it across the mid-segment of the top wing edge. Thread ten 3mm beads onto the second lower wire and direct it toward the outer edge wing tip. Push the beads firmly onto the wires to reduce gaps and prevent the 26AWG (0.4mm) wire from sagging.

72 Wrap the 26AWG (0.4mm) wire ends from the first and second top wires around the wire frame. Pull them tightly and securely to attach them as tautly as possible without distorting the wing frame. Wrap the 26AWG (0.4mm) wires upward along the frame until you reach the attachment above, or the top of the wing. Cut the 26AWG (0.4mm) wire ends and tuck in neatly.

73 Thread three beads onto all three lower wires in the lower group from Step 71. Separate this lower group into an upper group of two wires and a lower group of just one wire. Then thread four

beads onto the upper group of two wires and four beads onto the lowest wire. Direct the lowest wire to the mid-segment of the lower wing edge to the lower edge of the frame wrap from Step 53. Thread three beads on each wire in the upper group and direct them to the middle of the lower wing edge and to the inner wing tip. Start to attach these wires to the frame with firm wraps to keep the beaded wires as taut as possible.

74 Wrap along the frame in a clockwise direction from each wire attachment until you reach the next wire attachment. Cut the 26AWG (0.4mm) wire ends and tuck in neatly. Repeat Steps 70–74 for the other wing, in mirror image.

75 Spiral curl the lower cabochon V-setting end wires from Step 45 into loose and symmetrical curled spirals lying over the beaded wings (see arrow in image).

76 Use the lower 30AWG (0.25mm) wire ends left over from Step 53 to wrap around the curls from Step 75 down onto the lower wing edge with several wraps around both frame and curls. Then wrap the 30AWG (0.25mm) wire around the frame in a well-concealed place just above the binding wrap. Cut and tuck in the wire ends on either side.

77 Pictured is the back of the brooch to show the finish and the brooch pin attachment. The resting moth brooch is now finished and ready to wear.

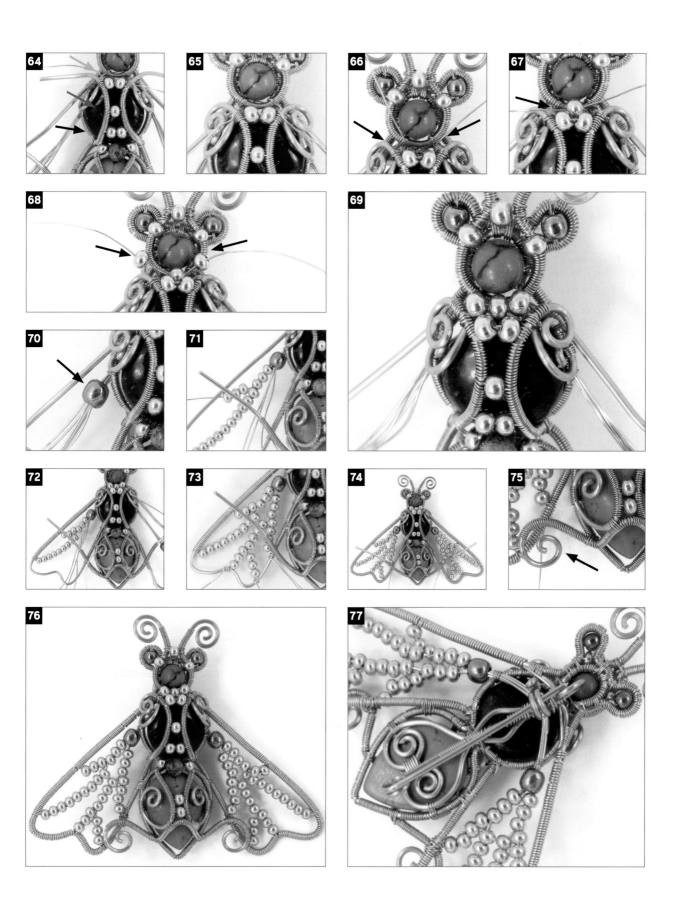

Crystal peacock brooch

This little peacock brooch is made with champagne gold-colored copper wire featuring freshwater pearls and Swarovski crystal details; but also looks wonderful made in copper with multi-colored crystals, as shown opposite.

Templates
See page 292 for the templates for this design.

Tools
General tools (see page 10)

Dimensions of finished piece
3¹/₄ x 2in (8 x 5cm)

Materials
18AWG (1mm-diameter) round champagne gold copper wire
(20AWG/0.8mm-diameter wire can be used in some components instead of 18AWG/1mm)
26AWG (0.4mm-diameter) round champagne gold copper wire
30 AWG (0.25mm-diameter) round champagne gold copper wire
(Copper, bare copper, silver or gold-plated wire will also work)
5 x Swarovski Aurora Borealis (AB) crystal bicone beads 6mm/48pk
9–13 x Swarovski AB crystal faceted round beads 3mm/48pk
8 x Swarovski AB crystal faceted round beads 4mm/48pk
1 x Swarovski AB crystal heart pendant 10 x 10.3mm
1 x white freshwater cultured pearls rice beads approx 5 x 3mm
5 x white freshwater cultured potato pearls approx 7 x 8mm
(Any flat-backed small heart-shaped cabochon will work in this design)

Alternative color
18AWG (1mm-diameter) round copper wire
(20AWG/0.8mm-diameter wire can be used in some components instead of 18AWG/1mm)
26AWG (0.4mm-diameter) round copper wire
30 AWG (0.25mm-diameter) round copper wire
8 x rose gold plate brass seed beads approx 3mm
1 x Swarovski Crystal Heart Pendant (style #6228) 10mm x 10.3mm, Bermuda Blue
5 x Swarovski crystal round beads (style #5000) 8mm, light turquoise
5 x Swarovski crystal, round beads (style #5000) 6mm, capri blue
7 x Swarovski crystal, round beads (style #5000) 4mm, emerald
8 x Swarovski crystal, bicones xillion (style #5328) 4mm, blue zircon

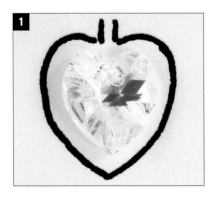

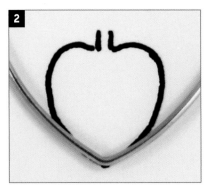

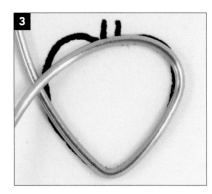

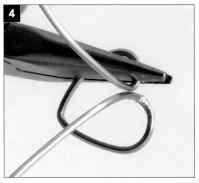

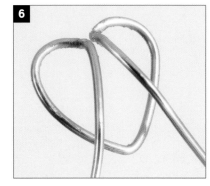

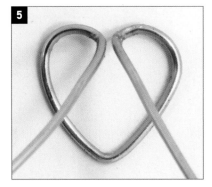

1 Make the setting for the cabochon. Draw around the heart-shaped Swarovski crystal (SC) with a $^1/_{32}$in (1mm) gap around it, to allow for wire-wrapping space in later stages. If your cabochon is different, draw your own heart template using this one as a basis. If you are using the same sized stone as listed, you can use the template on page 292.

2 Take a $6^5/_{16}$in (16cm) length of 18AWG (1mm) wire (better too much than not enough). Make a bend in the midsection of the wire to form the tip of the heart shape using the diagram in Step 1 as a template.

Tip
Don't make the bend too acute; use the wire's natural curve to form the heart shape.

3 Pull and shape the 18AWG (1mm) wire gently around one side of the heart shape with fingers and pliers so the wires cross at the top of the heart.

4 Bend the wire at the top of the heart sharply upward. Try to keep the main heart shape flat in one plane using pliers.

5 Do the same for the other side.

6 Grip the wires where they emerge from the top of the heart with the tips of the pliers (about $^1/_8$in/3mm width). Press the wires down so they will eventually lie flat over the heart-shaped stone. The $^1/_8$in (3mm) width will allow for the depth of the stone.

Tip
If your stone is a flat cabochon, do this on a rubber mat, pressing down on the stone to mold the wire over the stone. The rubber mat will prevent stone fracture.

7 This stone has a pointed cullet at the back and does not sit flat. Therefore, curve the 18AWG (1mm) wire tails slightly diagonally so they touch the sides of the heart frame. Make a very soft bend at this point (not too much, as you may need to reshape later). Here I placed the stone on my finger and am holding the frame around to show how it all fits together. The setting allows light to pass around the stone and is not a tight fit around the stone. Put this heart shape aside for the moment.

8 Shape the bird's head and body. You can use this template (reproduced at actual size on page 292) using the heart frame as a core shape. There are solid lines for the head, neck, inner tail feathers, and inner backing frame wires. There are dotted lines for the eye, face, head crest frame, shoulder, and outer tail feathers frame.

9 Shape the head, neck, and inner tail feather section. Take 20in (50cm) of 18AWG (1mm) wire and make a little beak shape. Make a little "V" in the wire first.

10 Form the bend to mark the base of the beak/start of the head. Squash either side of the beak with pliers to sharpen the beak angle.

11 Shape the head, neck, and body section using the diagram as a template. Form the top of the head and back of the neck first.

12 Make a little curve for the lower jaw, creating a bend at the base of the jaw.

13 Form the front of the neck and body. Do not shape the tail feathers yet.

14 Join the heart shape to the body. Take 80in (2m) of 30AWG (0.25) wire and wrap twice around the top of the heart (using the midsection of the 30AWG/0.25mm wire) to start to bind the top of the heart together.

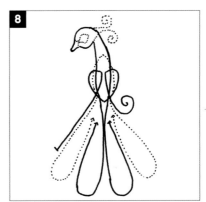

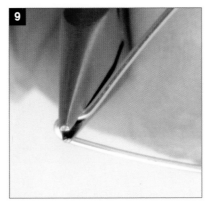

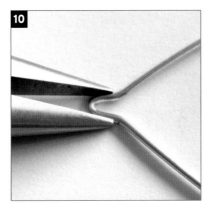

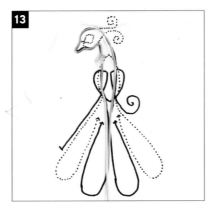

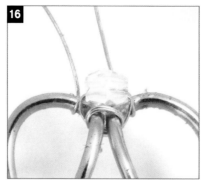

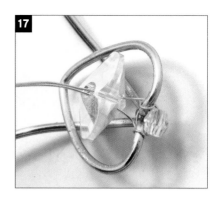

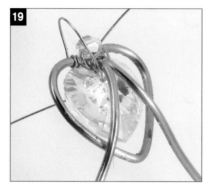

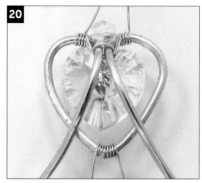

15 Bind on a 3mm Swarovski crystal (SC) to this point with a criss-cross bead attachment (see page 26): one wire through one side of the bead and the other through the other side of the bead.

16 Pull the 30AWG (0.25mm) wire ends to attach the 3mm SC into place and wrap either wire end around either side of the top of the heart.

17 Take your heart-shaped SC, turn the heart body setting upside down, and pass the 30AWG (0.25mm) wire ends through the hole in the top of the SC on either side.

18 Holding the stone level in the center of the heart setting, pass the 30AWG (0.25mm) wires back to the side of the top of the heart that either wire originally came from and bind around the heart frame.

19 Repeat this binding wrap on both sides to make this attachment stronger.

Tip

Make sure you don't bind the heart too tightly to the top edge of the frame. Try to bind leaving a $^1/_{32}$in (1mm) gap at the top edge of the stone and the heart frame and evenly on both sides so the heart is balanced.

20 Wrap along each side of the heart for about $^1/_8$in (3mm) until the wraps reach a level where they can be bound onto the main neck and head frame. Stop and check against the neck frame to gauge this level. Take another 40in (1m) of 30AWG (0.25mm) wire and wrap around the tip of the heart on either side until this wrap also reaches a level where it could be bound to the two wires leading down from the neck frame. You can now bind the heart frame to the head, neck, and body frame at four points.

21 Place the heart shape over the head, neck, and body frame (use the diagram from Step 8 to help site the placement). You will need to hold everything in place with one hand while making the binding attachments with the other.

MASTERING WIREWORK JEWELRY

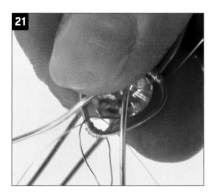

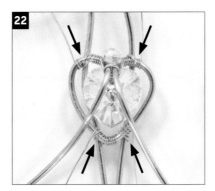

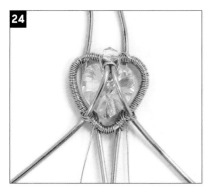

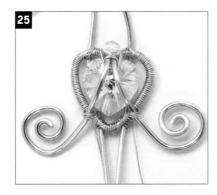

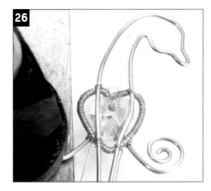

22 As you wrap around the heart frame, with the 30AWG (0.25mm) wrapping wire, bind the heart frame to the body frame at four points using three wraps at each level (see arrows in image). Continue to wrap around the heart frame for a few wraps. Wraps need to be mirror-image symmetrical and in the orientation shown. Do not let the wraps overlap and place them carefully into position.

23 Using chain-nosed pliers, make a little bend in the 18AWG (1mm) wires lying over the heart stone where they cross over the bottom edge of the heart frame.

24 Leave the 30AWG (0.25mm) wires at the bottom for a moment and work around from the top of the heart using the 30AWG (0.25mm) wire. Wrap around the heart frame. When you reach the point where the wires lying over the heart stone cross the frame, wrap the 30AWG (0.25mm) wires three times around the 18AWG (1mm) wires where they cross on either side. Wraps need to be mirror-image symmetrical and in the orientation shown. Wrap once or twice at the inside edge of the heart frame, then cut and tuck in the 30AWG (0.25mm) wire ends. Now cut the wire ends running over the heart stone from the edge of the heart to a length of $1^9/_{16}$in (4cm) on either side.

25 Spiral curl the wire ends (see page 27) to make loose spirals on either side to represent the peacock's wings. Keep the curls as mirror-image symmetrical as possible.

26 Hammer the back of the spirals on a steel block.

27 Now work on the eye, face, and head crest. Use the diagram from Step 8 to help shape the eye and face. Take 4³/₄in (12cm) of 20AWG (0.8mm) wire and form the eye section. Make one acute bend halfway along the wire and two bends a little further along to form the upper and lower eye. Then form a little diamond shape by making two outward bends at the other end of the diamond to form the corner of the eye.

28 From the corner of the eye, shape the 20AWG (0.8mm) wire over the diagram and head of the bird.

29 Cut the wire tails to a length of 1³/₈in (3.5cm) for the upper wire and 1³/₁₆in (3cm) for the lower wire, measured from beyond the limit of the head frame line.

30 Check this shape against the head of the bird. Make any adjustments so that the shapes fit each other.

31 Take 40–60in (1–1.5m) of 30AWG (0.25mm) wire. Bind around the corner of the eye three times at the midline of the 30AWG (0.25mm) wire, then wrap along the front of the face until you reach a point where you can bind onto the head frame.

32 Bind around the head and face frame at the two points shown (see red arrows in image) with several wraps around both frames.

33 Start a basket weave (see page 24) along the chin and forehead sections until you reach the top and bottom corners of the eye, halfway along the eye socket, making sure you have the 30AWG (0.25mm) wires wrapped to the eye socket at this level. Use a weave ratio of three wraps around the face relative to two around the eye frame as there is a relatively longer distance along the face frame.

34 Bind on a 4mm SC using a criss-cross attachment.

35 Continue the basket weave up to the corner of the eye top and bottom.

36 Wrap the top and bottom wires along the head frame without weaving, wrapping the bottom head wire over the head frame three times (see red arrow in image) so they meet in between the two head crest wires as shown (blue arrow).

37 Thread a seed pearl onto one or both of the 30AWG (0.25mm) wires, bind to the corner of the eye, and cut and tuck in the wire ends.

38 Curl the head crest as in Step 25 and hammer the back carefully.

Tip
Use a small-faced hammer to avoid damaging the rest of the design.

39 Start making the shoulder and outer tail section using the diagram from Step 8 to help shape this frame. Take 12in (30cm) of 18AWG (1mm) wire and bend in the middle, curving the sides running away from the bend into a leaf shape.

40 Using the main bird frame and the drawing from Step 1, bend the wires so they start to form the tail, but do not form the whole tail yet.

41 Make a brooch pin for the bird about 1⁹/₁₆in (4cm) in length (see page 32).

42 Cut the 30AWG (0.25mm) wire tails from Step 24 at the base of the heart. Wrap a 12in (30cm) length of 26AWG (0.4mm) wire around the brooch pin. Positioning the main frame over the shoulder and outer tail section, place the brooch pin beneath these other two frames. Bind the brooch pin, shoulder, and main bird frame together using the 26AWG (0.4mm) wire ends a few times around the inner and outer wire tails just beneath the heart tip, three times on each side (red arrows in images).

43 Thread on a 3mm SC to the 26AWG (0.4mm) wire on either side wrapping to the wing. Wrap along the wing curl on either side for eight to nine wraps, then cut and tuck in the wire ends around the wing curls.

NOTE: This step is fiddly until the binding wraps are firmly in place.

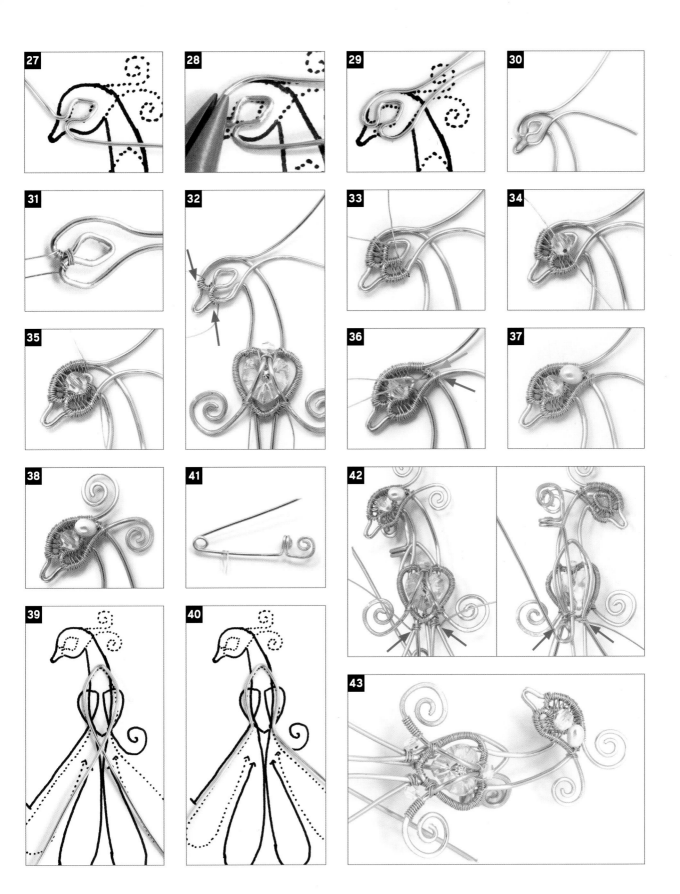

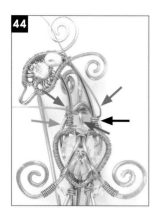

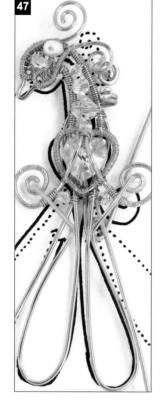

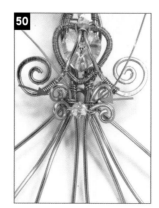

44 Decorate the neck section. Bind a 40in (1m) length of 26AWG (0.4mm) wire at the midsection around the base of the neck frame three times. Wrap up along the neck frame on that side, three to four times. Stop wrapping here for the moment (see green arrows in image). Turn the peacock over and wrap the other end of the 26AWG (0.4mm) wire around the brooch pin (see red arrow), in a similar way to the brooch pin attachment in Step 42. Hold the pin in place with one hand while you wrap with the other. Then, with that same 26AWG (0.4mm) wire end, wrap across to the other side of the frame, binding at the base of the other side of the neck frame three times (see blue arrow). Wrap up the neck frame three to four times. Do not bind to the shoulder section. Bind once around both the neck frame and the shoulder section where it crosses at the back of the neck section once (see black arrow).

45 Add a 6mm SC in a criss-cross bead attachment, and wrap up the neck to a level where you can add the next bead.

46 Add a 4mm SC in a criss-cross bead attachment, wrap up the neck frame again, add a 3mm SC with a criss-cross wrap, and wrap up to the jawline, cutting the 26AWG (0.4mm) wire tails and tucking in the wire ends neatly.

47 Shape the tail feathers, making four teardrop loops of wire using the template from Step 8 as a guide. Shape the inner two tail feathers (originally from the head and neck frame) from inside edge to outside edge, making a little bend in the wire tail (on the outside edge of the feather) about ⁵/₁₆in (8mm) below the tip of the heart.

48 Cut the wire tails to a length of ⁵/₈in (15mm). Shape the outer two tail feather frames using the wire tails from the shoulder section.

49 Make the bases of the wings slightly higher than the inner two feathers with a wire tail after the little bend you make at the base of the feather ¹³/₁₆in (20mm) in length. Carefully curl the wire tails using round-nosed pliers.

50 Bind a 4mm round SC to the central tail just under the wire curls, wrapping on one side around the two right-hand tail feather bases and around the two left-hand tail feathers on the other side. Bring the wire ends up the

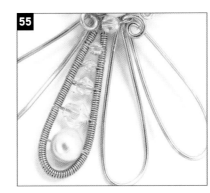

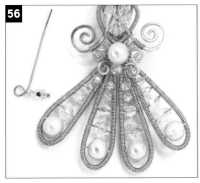

base of the tail so they project inside the two outer tail feathers but on the outside edge of the outer tail curls. Wrap one wire twice around all the base wires of the two outer tail feathers on that side (see red arrow in image) and the other 26AWG (0.4mm) wire around all the base wires of the two outer tail feathers on the other side (blue arrow). The wire tails should project out of the front of the base of the tail.

51 Bind on a 6–7mm pearl with a criss-cross bead attachment of the 26AWG (0.4mm) wire.

52 Wrap around the side of the tail to fix the pearl into place. Pass the 26AWG (0.4mm) wires to the back of the peacock and wrap them around the shaft of the brooch pin below the other two brooch pin attachments to make another anchor point for the pin.

53 Work on the tail. I started with one of the central feathers. Take 80in (2m) of 26AWG (0.4mm) wire and wrap at the midsection of the 26AWG (0.4mm) wire around the tip of the feather until you reach a point where you could add in a pearl with a criss-cross wrap.

54 Use a pearl reamer if the hole is not large enough, or use 30–28AWG (0.25–0.3mm) wire.

55 Continue in the same way, adding in a 6mm, 4mm, and 3mm SC working from the tip to base of the feather. Add in another 3mm SC if there is room. Cut and tuck in the 26AWG (0.4mm) wire ends at the base of the feather.

56 Repeat for the other tail feathers, making sure the additions of middle and side feathers look the same in mirror image.

57 It may be difficult to wrap around the bases of adjacent feathers, so just lift them slightly away from the others and then move them back after attaching the weaves. You don't have to wrap all the way to the base. This image shows the back of the bird.

58 Thread a 4mm and 3mm SC onto a ball headpin and attach with a wrapped loop to the tip of the peacock's beak. Gently adjust the tail feathers and wing swirls with your fingers. The brooch is now finished.

Egyptian cat brooch

The enigmatic and beautiful feline form is reproduced in many designs that people adore wearing. Here is a little Egyptian-style cat brooch made with copper wire featuring lapis lazuli and turquoise stone details.

Templates
See page 293 for the templates for this design.

Materials
18AWG (1mm-diameter) diameter round copper wire
(20AWG/0.8mm-diameter wire can be used in some components instead of 18AWG/1mm)
26AWG (0.4mm-diameter) round copper wire
30AWG (0.25mm-diameter) round copper wire
(Antique bronze, bare copper, silver or gold-plated wire will also work)
1 x Beadsmith 8/0 3mm-diameter gold-plated copper bead
2mm-diameter turquoise or turquoise color round beads
3–4mm-diameter turquoise or turquoise color round beads
3mm-diameter lapis lazuli round beads
1 x 22 x 16mm pear/teardrop-shaped gemstone or cabochon, no drill hole required (I used lapis lazuli)

Tools
General tools (see page 10)

Dimensions of finished piece
2⁹/₁₆ x 1⁹/₁₆in (6.5 x 4cm)

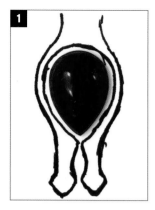

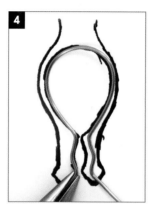

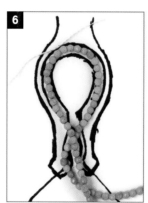

1 Draw around the pear-shaped cabochon, leaving a $1/32$in (1mm) gap around it to allow for wire wrapping space. Draw two front legs and a line around the first line you drew around the cabochon. If your cabochon is different, draw your own template based on this one, tracing over difficult shapes like the head, legs, and body in later stages. If using the same sized stone as listed, see the template on page 293.

2 Take a 50in (120cm) length of 18AWG (1mm) wire and start to shape around the cabochon frame at the 32in (80cm) point of the wire using the diagram as a template. The shorter length of wire needs to run to the right and the longer length to the left of the diagram as more of the cat in later stages is formed from the left-hand wire end. Form the pear shape first, crossing the wires at the base of the pear.

3 Sharply bend the wires where they cross, using chain-nosed pliers and the diagram as a guide. Take care to get this shape perfect for size around the cabochon; you will obtain a better fit when setting the cabochon later.

4 Shape the legs and paws with little bends of the wire.

5 Shape the wire ends back from the paws around the first pear-shaped outline.

6 Next, make the setting for the cabochon. The cabochon that I used was fairly deep; I spaced out the internal cabochon frame wire with 2mm round seed beads to add detail and give depth to the setting to help hold the stone in place. You can achieve this spacing with extra frame wires and/or weave spacing, but the seed beads add lovely detail. I laid the seed beads inside the drawing from Step 1. I drew the internal cabochon frame inside the first one as a green line allowing for the seed beads and a little channel down at the tip of the pear and two wire tails running down the legs and projecting from the paws by $5/8$in (15mm). There is a template for this on page 293 but this is just a guide and this internal shape will differ depending on the depth of your cabochon.

7 Cut one length of 18AWG (1mm) wire about $13/16$in (20mm) long. Shape it at the midsection around the drawing and place it over the cabochon to check it fits.

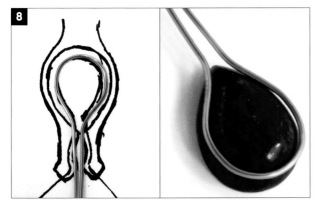

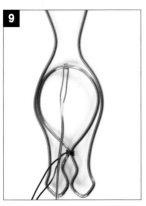

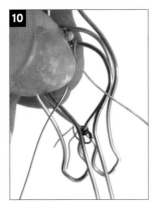

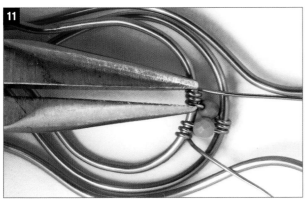

8 Bend the wires—not too sharply—at the tip of the inner pear shape on the drawing. Place over the cabochon again to check that the bend matches the cabochon point. This bend will differ if the cabochon is deep or shallow, so we will not make the final bend until after the cabochon setting has been 90% woven.

9 Check what wire diameter will fit through your seed beads. 26AWG (0.4mm) wire fits through the bead I am using, and this gives a stronger weave. If 30–28AWG (0.25–0.3mm) wire only fits through, you will have to use that and make more wraps and more traversing weaves to make the structure stronger. Take a long piece of 26AWG (0.4mm) wire (I used 60in/1.5m) and wrap in the midsection of the 26AWG (0.4mm) wire around the top of the main pear setting frame. I term this the middle frame in the following steps, as there is an outer frame of wire around it. I tied some scrap wire at the base of the setting to help hold it all in place.

10 Add a 2mm bead to each 26AWG (0.4mm) wire end and wrap across to the inner frame.

Tip

Do not pull the traversing weave wire too tight: you need to maintain spaces between the wires as you will use these to weave backing wire onto. Hold the frame wires apart with the fingers of one hand while weaving with the other hand to help achieve this spacing. It will become easier with more attachment weaves.

11 Use a figure-of-eight weave technique (i.e., if the wire is coming from the front of the outer frame wire, pass to the back of the inner frame wire) wrap around three times. Do the same with the other end of the 26AWG (0.4mm) wire so you secure the frames together at two points. Make sure the 2mm beads lie in between the frames, not above or beneath them. Wrap three times around the inner frame on either side. This part is fiddly, but things get easier after this attachment.

Tip
Neaten the wraps with gentle side-to-side squeezes with chain-nosed pliers so as not to damage the wire.

NOTE: If you are using 30–28AWG (0.25–0.3mm) weaving wire you may need more wraps around the frames before each traverse to keep creating the same weave spacing as if you used 26AWG (0.4mm).

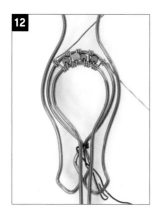

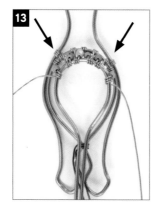

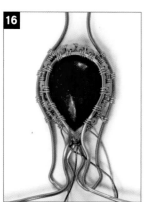

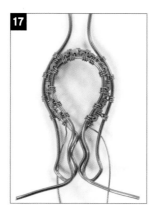

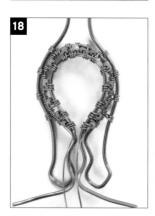

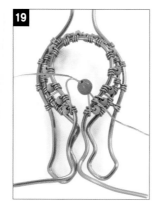

12 Centre this attachment at the top of the pear setting then weave back to the middle frame, but don't add a bead this time. Wrap three times at each side. Weave back to the inner frame, add a bead on each side, wrap three times around the inner frame then back to the middle frame.

13 Weave across to the outer frame with three wraps on either side without adding a bead (see arrows in image). Weave across to the middle frame, wrap three times, then weave across to the central frame adding a bead this time. You are creating a zigzag pattern by weaving up and down the three frame wires.

14 Do not pull the frames together too tightly when you are weaving. This will prevent the weave frame looking distorted and also allows gaps through which to pass binding wires for the tails, brooch pin, and cabochon backing frame later. Repeat Steps 13–14 until you reach the start of where you bent the inner frame wires.

15 Place the setting over the cabochon, all placed on a rubber bead mat to prevent damaging the stone when pressing down on it.

16 Bend the inner frame wires to fit down either side of the tip of the stone with enough space between the wire tails to allow a 3 or 4mm bead to sit in between, depending on your cabochon.

Tip

Make sure the 3–4mm bead you use allows two 26AWG (0.4mm) wires to pass through the drill hole.

17 Bend the wires around the inside of the forelegs. Trim the wire ends to ⁵⁄₈in (15mm) in length from the outside edge of the paws on either side. Remove the scrap wire.

18 Add one more 2mm bead on either side, and wrap toward the inner frame three or four times on either side.

19 Thread a 3mm turquoise bead (this is the bead that best fitted the setting for my cabochon) onto one 26AWG (0.4mm) wire from the previous step and thread the other 26AWG (0.4mm) wire through the bead in a criss-cross bead attachment.

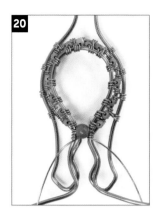

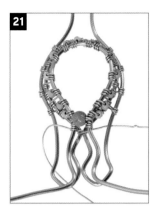

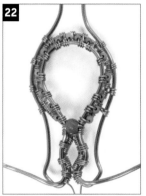

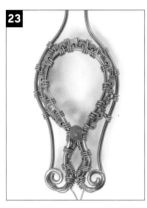

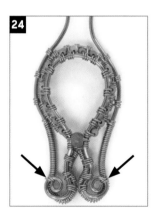

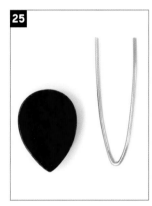

20 Pull the wires firmly to bring the 3mm bead down slightly above and between the 18AWG (1mm) frame wires. Wrap along the tail wires from the inner frame until you reach the same level as the tip of the middle pear frame.

21 Bind the 26AWG (0.4mm) wires around the join from either side.

22 Wrap along the inside leg three times on either side. Press the inner frame tails against the inside edge of the inside leg and wrap across both wires on either side, keeping the frame wires parallel. Then wrap only around the inside leg frame wire. Keep the wraps neat with side-to-side pressing from the tips of chain-nosed pliers. Wrap in this way down to near the inside edge of the paws.

23 Curl the 18AWG (1mm) wire ends at the base of the paws (see page 27). Keep the curls as mirror-image symmetrical as possible. Don't press the curls into the paws yet, and leave a little gap for wire wrapping the 26AWG (0.4mm) wire around the base of the paws.

24 Wrap the 26AWG (0.4mm) wire around the base of the paws, binding around the paw curls at one point (see arrows in image) on either side. Wrap along the outside edge of the legs and cut and tuck in the wire end neatly when you reach the top of the legs.

25 Make the backing frame for the cabochon. Take 2¹/₂in (6cm) of 18AWG (1mm) wire and bend in half with ¹/₈in (3mm) length ends.

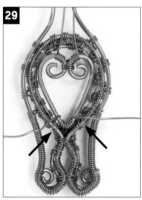

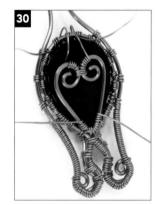

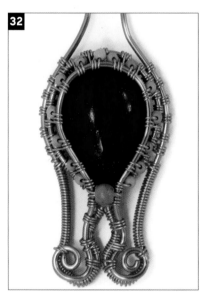

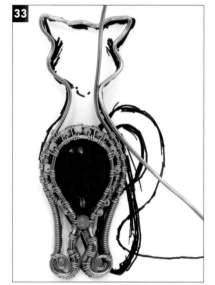

Then wrap along the side of the heart until you reach the points shown in the image.

29 Attach the heart shape to the back of the cat frame by wrapping the 26AWG (0.4mm) wire near the tip of the backing heart frame across to the bare wires at the tip of the main frame with two wraps on either side (see arrows in image). Bring the wires back again. Wrap up the heart frame for three or four wraps. Stop working at this end of the setting for the moment.

30 Place the cabochon into the setting, working over a soft surface (in case the stone falls out). Bind with the 26AWG (0.4mm) wires at the top of the heart backing frame across to the spaces between the weaves along the middle pear setting frame.

26 Curl the wire ends on each side to make a curly heart shape that fits on the back of the cabochon.

27 Hammer the shape on a steel block to flatten it slightly.

28 Using the midsection of a 32in (80cm) length of 26AWG (0.4mm) wire, wrap around the tip of the backing frame. Wrap another 32in (80cm) length around where the two heart curls touch a few times.

31 Pull the 26AWG (0.4mm) wires to hold the heart backing frame and the stone tightly in place in the setting. Work along the setting, wrapping around the heart frame from all four 26AWG (0.4mm) wire directions across to the outer pear frame at a few points where there are bare wires in between the weave wraps from Steps 13–24.

Tip

You need to find the space to pass the 26AWG (0.4mm) wires under and around the heart frame. You can kink the end of the wire and pull the end with pliers to help you wrap along the frame.

32 Wrap three times around the outer frame before each pass back to the heart frame. Once all the wires from bottom and top of the settings meet each other, cut the 26AWG (0.4mm) wires and tuck in the ends neatly at the back of the setting.

33 Shape the head, body, and tail outlines (see template on page 293). Use the wire end on the left side of the cat's body and shape the head, ears, rounded back, and shoulder.

34 Shape the tail, leaving a 1³/₁₆in (3cm) length wire end projecting from the side of the cat. Use round-nosed pliers to form the curve of the tip of the tail.

35 Grip the tip of the tail with one hand and pull the wire round in a curve to shape the side of the tail.

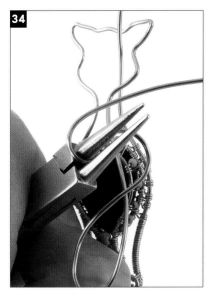

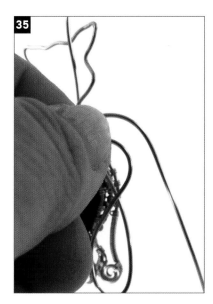

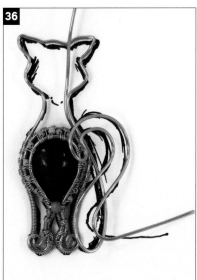

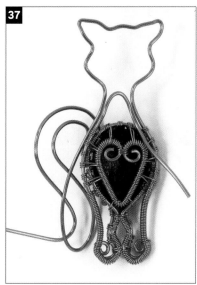

36 Do not cut the wire end from the right side as you will use this for neck features. Leave a wire tail about 1³/₁₆in (3cm) in length projecting from the side of the cat.

37 Shape the wire end from the right side over the line drawn in the template from page 293. The back view is pictured.

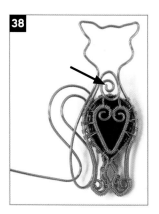

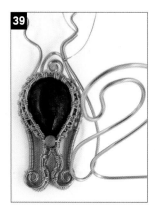

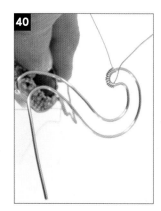

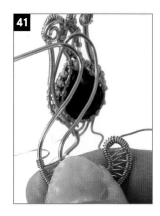

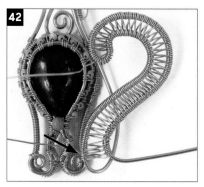

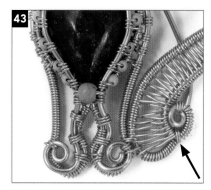

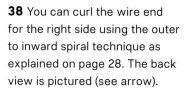

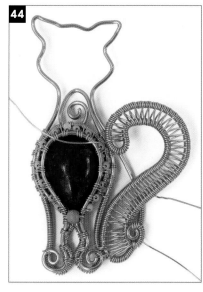

38 You can curl the wire end for the right side using the outer to inward spiral technique as explained on page 28. The back view is pictured (see arrow).

39 Bend the tail upward out of the plane of the cat to start work on it.

40 Take 80in (2m) of 26AWG (0.4mm) wire and wrap near one end of the 26AWG (0.4mm) wire at the end of the tail.

41 Start to weave in a figure-of-eight basic basket weave along the tail (see page 24). The first few weaves are two by two; as you move along the tail, the weave ratios need to change to allow for the longer distances along the outer frame relative to the inner frame. Use a four to two weave ratio with four weaves along the outer frame and two along the inner before each weave traverse. Return to a two by two ratio as one moves along the tail increasing to a two by three as the inner (left side) of the tail has a longer length relative to the right as you move toward the base of the tail. (Note that the brooch is upside down in the image.)

NOTE: Make sure you don't weave with too much tension or the tail wires will distort and pull together. It can be helpful to hold the frame wires with one thumb and forefinger to maintain width and separation while weaving with the other hand.

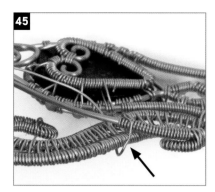

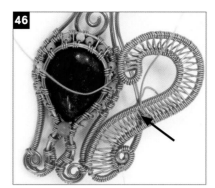

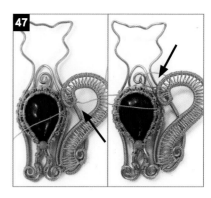

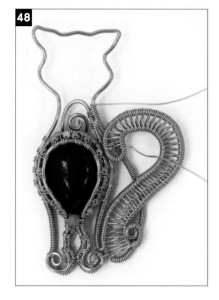

47 Cut the lower 26AWG (0.4mm) wire. Wrap the 26AWG (0.4mm) wire from the binding point at the lower edge of the tail to the body, wrapping only along the main frame of the back of the cat until you reach the upper edge of the tail where it crosses the body. Make another binding wrap here to the tail. See arrow on left image for the lower edge of the tail and arrow on right image for the upper edge of the tail.

48 When you reach the upper edge of the tail you will have two frame wires to wrap along up the back and neck of the cat. Use the three-by-three weave technique (see page 26), as used in Step 22 (along the inner leg), with three wraps around both frames and three wraps around the outer frame, workin along the base of the neck up to the top of the neck. Cut and tuck in the 26AWG (0.4mm) wire end.

49 Thread a 3–4mm round turquoise bead onto the cat's tail end wire from Step 39. Wrap the 26AWG (0.4mm) wire around the end of the tail. Do not cut the 26AWG (0.4mm) wire end—you will need it to bind on a brooch pin.

44 Take 40in (1m) of 26AWG (0.4mm) wire and wrap along the back of the cat. Start at the upper edge of the base of the tail, leaving a length of 26AWG (0.4mm) wire for later use.

45 Bend the tail out of the way to make wrapping along the back easier. When you have reached the lower edge of where the tail overlaps the back, bind around this frame wire (see arrow in image).

46 Wrap along behind the tail again along the back and also bind at the base of the tail (see arrow).

42 When you reach the level of the top of the paw nearest the tail, bind around this frame as well (see arrow in image). As you weave down the tail and finish the weave, make sure you end up near the paw ready to wrap along the bottom of the frame.

43 Wrap along the bottom of the frame and bind also to the main frame and the end of the tail wire (see arrow in image). Start to wrap along the tail wire end for ⁵/₁₆in (8mm). Trim the tail wire to ⁵/₈in (15mm). Curl this wire end, but do not press into place just yet.

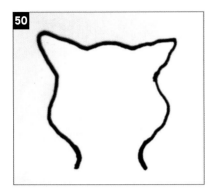

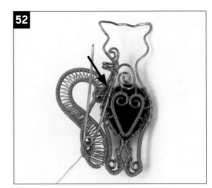

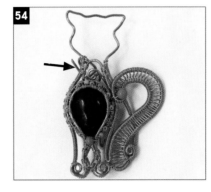

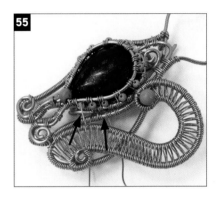

50 Press the head frame into a piece of paper over a rubber mat to make an impression of the head. You can draw over this to plan the head components. It is easier to do this now before attachment of the brooch pin. Draw several so you can use them if you make any mistakes while planning the face. There is also a face in the templates on page 293 if you prefer to use this.

51 Make a brooch pin to fit the back of the cat (see page 32).

52 Bind the brooch pin to the back of the cat. Use the 26AWG (0.4mm) wire ends from Step 39 first (from end of tail; see arrow in image).

53 Bend the brooch pin to curve around the cat frame.

54 Take a new section of 26AWG (0.4mm) wire and wrap onto the left side of the cat's neck, working up the neck and binding across to the neck curl in the same way. At the top of the neck, bind the end of the brooch pin onto the frame (see arrow in image) as well with the same length of 26AWG (0.4mm) wire. Cut and tuck in the ends of the wire.

55 Add a new section of 26AWG (0.4mm) wire at the tail end. Do this by wrapping wire around just the back of the brooch pin a few times (see arrows in image).

56 Wrap to the frame and then along the brooch pin a few times (see arrow in image). Cut both wire ends.

Tip
Pull the 26AWG (0.4mm) wire tight where it wraps around the cat frame to make it disappear between the wraps that are already there from previous wrapping stages.

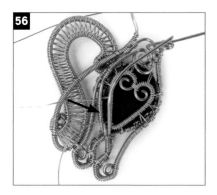

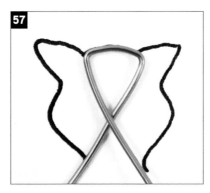

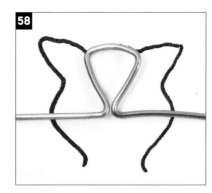

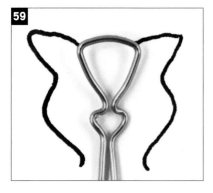

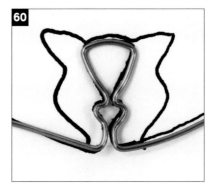

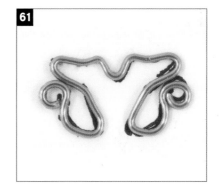

57 Make the face component using the template on page 293. Make a curve in the midsection of a 4³/₄in (12cm) length of 18AWG (1mm) wire about the same width as the head between the ears in the main frame. Bend the wire ends downward and inward to form a triangle about two-thirds the length of the face.

58 Make a little nose shape by bending the wire on either side to make a triangular shape where the wires crossed in the previous step. (See image 58 and 59.)

59 Bend the wires straight downward again from the lower point of the nose frame.

60 About ³/₁₆in (4mm) along from the base of the nose, curve the wires outward and slightly upward to make the lips of the cat. Trim the wire end to ¹³/₁₆in (20mm) on either side.

Tip

Because we are making a 3D shape, the face component needs to be ¹/₈in (3mm) longer than the flat face. If you find a 3D shape too difficult, make a flat shape to fit the cat's face frame.

61 Make the eye and inner ear component. I have drawn these components on the diagram from Step 50 and is more easily seen in the template on page 293 where the two face components are drawn in two colors so you can clearly see how they fit together. The eye and inner component is represented by the black line shapes within the cat's head, lying adjacent to the green line of the face component. Take a 3¹/₄in (8cm) length of 18AWG (1mm) wire and shape this component with V-shaped bends for the forehead and inner ears. Make a straight section running alongside the face frame to form the upper eye and then a sharp bend back on itself and downward to form the lower eye and a ³/₈in (10mm) wire tail on either side in mirror image. Curl the little wire end.

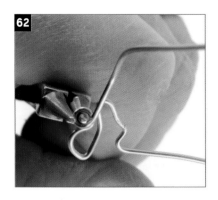

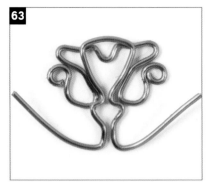

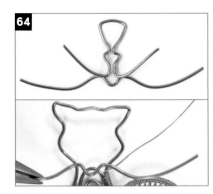

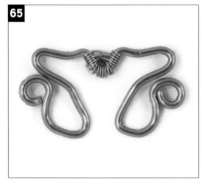

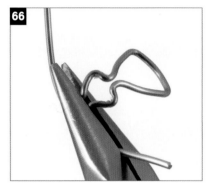

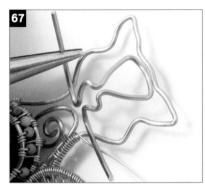

62 Use the diagram on page 293 as a guide and scrap wire to practice. If you find it easier, you can use 20AWG (0.8mm) wire for this section. Use the tips of fine-nosed chain-nosed pliers to make the shapes and to make little curls at the eye corners.

63 This image shows how this eye component fits over and around the face component made in Steps 57–60.

64 Make the chin component. Make a wiggly section with a short length of 18AWG (1mm) wire with a small U-shape for the chin with curving 1in (25mm) length wire tails. The image at the top shows where I have placed the chin component under the face component from Step 33. The image at the bottom shows the chin in proportion to the face frame.

65 Assemble the face. Use a short length of 30AWG (0.25mm) wire to make a two-by-two basket weave (see page 24) up the triangle shape in the eye/inner ear component. Work from base to tip. Cut the 30AWG (0.25mm) wire ends and tuck in.

66 Make the face shape into a 3D form. Bend the face component using chain-nosed pliers.

67 Bend the forehead section downward as a flat section. Keep the nose flat and facing forward and the lips bent downward below the nose.

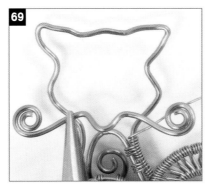

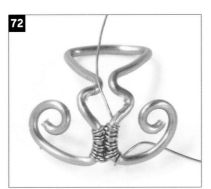

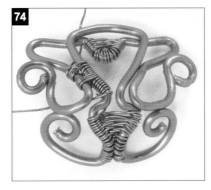

68 Curl the face shape wire ends.

69 Curl the chin section ends.

70 Hammer the wire ends.

71 Bend the inner ear eye shape with pliers so the ear triangles lie flat in the same plane as the forehead and the eyes are bent upward so they can lie next to the nose section from Steps 57–60.

72 Take the face component and a 40in (1m) length of 30AWG (0.25mm) wire. Use a two-by-two basket weave (see page 24) to join in the lips. Cut the wire end at the bottom of the lip.

73 With the 30AWG (0.25mm) wire at the top of the lip join, weave up the nose in a two-by-two basket weave. Cut the wire end and tuck in.

74 Start to bind the face and the eye component together. You need to shape the eye sections gently so they lie alongside the face nicely. Use 30AWG (0.25mm) wire and wrap along one side of the face, binding to the eye frame in a five to three ratio (three wraps around both).

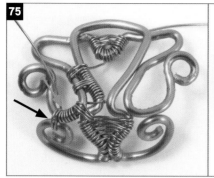

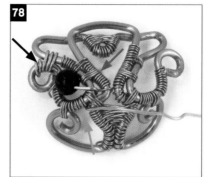

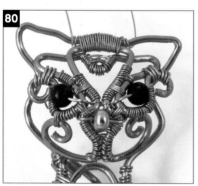

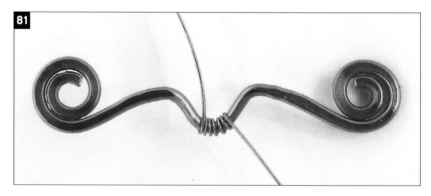

75 When you reach the corner of the eye, weave over to it, binding to the top corner of the nose (see blue arrow in image). Wrap along the base of the eye, binding to the lip curl where it lies close to the eye (black arrow). Stop when you reach the top of the eye and cut and tuck in the 30AWG (0.25mm) wire ends. Do not bind around the ear yet.

76 Repeat this step in mirror image for the other eye.

77 Take a short length of 26AWG (0.4mm) wire and wrap three times near one end of the 0.4mm wire near the outside of one eye.

78 Wrap one end of the wire two times around the outside eye loop (see black arrow), then cut and tuck in the wire. Thread on a 3mm lapis bead and wrap to the corner of the eye, and over it from front to back (see red arrow), bringing the 26AWG (0.4mm) wire up from the back at the top corner of the nose (blue arrow).

79 Thread on a 3mm copper bead and wrap across to the other side of the nose, threading the wire from front to back and then up between the nose and the lower corner of the other eye (see arrow in image). Thread on another 3mm lapis bead, wrap across to the upper corner of the eye, and wrap in the same way as on the other side in mirror image. Cut and tuck in the 26AWG (0.4mm) wire end.

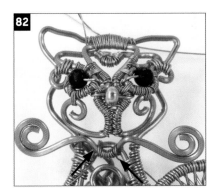

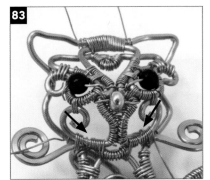

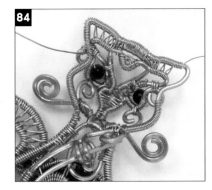

83 Wrap the 30AWG (0.25mm) wire from Step 82 around the base of the lips and the chin curls on either side a few times. Wrap along the lip curl (see arrows in image) and the chin curl. There is a little space below the lip that allows you to do this. Continue wrapping until you reach the cheek. Wrap around all three wires (chin curl, lip curl, and cheek) three times on either side. Wrap up the cheeks on both sides until you reach the base of the eye curl. Cut and tuck in the 30AWG (0.25mm) wires that you are wrapping with on either side. Do not cut the wires either side of the forehead attachment.

84 Weave along the ear frame using a six to three basket-weave (see page 24) ratio (i.e., six wraps) along the longer length of the top of the ear before each traversing weave to the inner shorter length of frame with three wraps around the inner ear wire. The image shows the back of the head.

85 Cut and tuck in the wire ends at either side of the back of the ear. Your beautiful cat brooch is now finished.

80 Bind the face section to the head. Take an 80in (2m) length of 30AWG (0.25mm) wire. Start to bind the top of the face and head sections together by wrapping around both frames over the foreheads at the center point of the 30AWG (0.25mm) wire with the wire ends left either side ready to wrap toward the ears. Make sure the face section lies slightly below the outer frame as you are binding so it does not end up over or above it.

81 Bind on the chin section to the face section using another length of 30AWG (0.25mm) wire. Wrap the wire around the midsection of the chin wire a few times.

82 Start by binding the base of the chin to the top of the chest curl. Wrap the 30AWG (0.25mm) wire around the base of the chain then bind to the chest curl on either side (see arrows in image), making sure the chin section lies over the chest curl.

Running horse brooch

Horses are noble and beautiful creatures: symbols of freedom, energy, and grace. This beautiful little running horse brooch features a natural stone cabochon forming the body shape.

Templates

See page 292 for the template for this design.

Materials

18AWG (1mm-diameter) round antique bronze-colored copper wire (20AWG/0.8mm-diameter wire can be used in some components instead of 18AWG/1mm)

26AWG (0.4mm-diameter) round antique bronze-colored copper wire

30AWG (0.25mm-diameter) round antique bronze-colored copper wire (Copper, bare copper, silver or gold-plated wire will also work)

1 x 4mm-diameter gold-plated copper bead

Beadsmith 8/0 3mm-diameter gold-plated copper beads

2mm-diameter antique bronze or gold-plated copper beads

1 x 24 x 18mm pear-shaped or teardrop-shaped gemstone or cabochon, no drill hole required (I used faceted black agate)

Tools

General tools (see page 10)

Dimensions of finished piece

Approx. 3^1/$_2$ x 2^3/$_4$in (9 x 7cm)

MASTERING WIREWORK JEWELRY

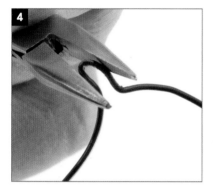

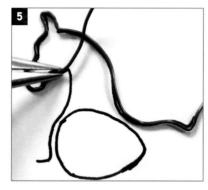

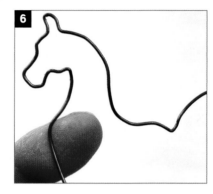

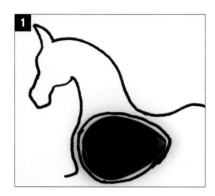

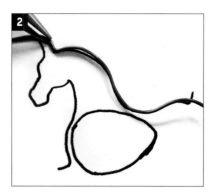

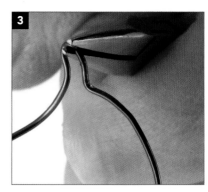

1 In the image above there is a diagram for you to shape the wire over. I have drawn around the pear-shaped cabochon so you can see how the cabochon frame section will fit into the horse shape. I have not shaped the whole of the horse yet, as the legs are complex to form with wire; if you have them in the wrong place after attaching the cabochon frame it can be difficult to reshape without damaging the wire. If your cabochon is different, draw your own template using this one as a basis. Trace over difficult shapes such as the head, legs, and body. Also please see page 292 where a full horse template is provided for you to use as a guide.

2 Take a 20in (50cm) length of 18AWG (1mm) wire and start to shape around the horse's head, ears, and back. Use your fingers and gentle plier-shaping

movements to shape the curves of the back and neck, using the diagram in Step 1 as a template. Make a small bend for the base of the tail and the start of the base of one of the ears.

3 Make a little bend at the shorter end to start forming the tail section about 4in (10cm) from the end of the wire. Gently reshape if required at the bends. Use small shaping movements with the tips of chain-nosed pliers to form the ears and face.

4 Clamp either side of the bend with chain-nosed pliers to make the tip of the ear bend sharper and also across both sides of the ear to shape this section further.

5 Shape around the muzzle of the horse, its chin, and the front of the throat.

6 Curve the wire using your fingers, and pliers if necessary, outward at the front of the horse to make the chest shape.

7 Make a soft bend using chain-nosed pliers at the base of the chest to mark where the front leg will be: do not make too sharp a bend yet. Check repeatedly against the template.

8 Add a tail wire about 3¹⁄₄in (8cm) long to the drawing in Step 1. Also please see page 292 where a full horse template is provided for you to use as a guide.

MASTERING WIREWORK JEWELRY

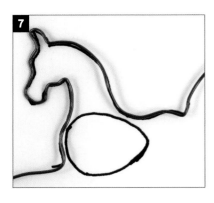

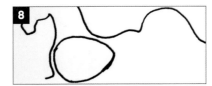

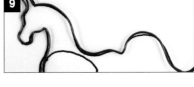

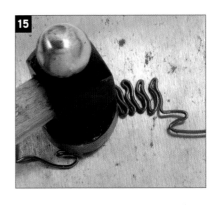

9 Take the wire frame from Step 2. Shape the tail wire over the template and cut the end of the wire to the same length as the template. The end of this wire will be curled later.

10 Make a mane, ear, forelock, back, and tail section. I drew the shape onto the template with a wavy mane. The forelock in front of the second ear should be about 1⁹/₁₆in (4cm) long. The upper tail section should be about 3in (7.5cm) long. The end of this wire will be curled later.

11 Take 20in (50cm) of 18AWG (1mm) wire and shape the back and tail section over the new line using your fingers and pliers. The base of the mane should be about 6in (15cm) from the end, with the shorter end forming the second tail wire.

12 Start to form the mane, using the template on page 292 as a guide. As you form each mane frond, gently shape the frond with chain-nosed pliers and fingers.

Tip

If you hold the tip of the mane frond with your fingers, you can pull the returning wire against the line of the outward frond wire. This helps to shape the frond to mirror the shape of the outward frond wire.

13 Make a side-to-side squeeze along the frond from tip to base with your pliers to bring the sides of the frond really close together.

14 Shape the next frond repeating these techniques. Press the mane flat with your fingers as you work along it. Place the mane against the diagram until you make enough curly mane fronds to reach up to the base of the first ear (between nine and eleven should do—you don't have to make the same number as in the diagram). Squeeze all the fronds at the bases. Make the ear and cut the forelock wire tail.

Tip

If you find the wire shaping difficult, practice with some scrap wire.

15 Hammer the mane shape (but not the rest of the shape) to give it a flat reflective surface. Hammer the back so that any marks appear on the back and not the front of the mane.

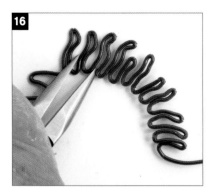

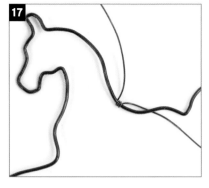

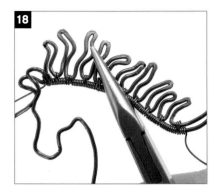

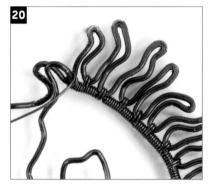

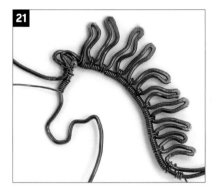

16 Reshape the mane with little squeezes at the bases of the mane fronds to fit along the back of the neck as the hammering will have splayed the shape. Check the mane shape against the main horse frame.

17 Bind the mane to the back of the horse's neck. Take a 40in (1m) length of 26AWG (0.4mm) wire and wrap around the base of the horse's neck three times.

18 Wrap around at the base of the bottom mane frond twice around the mane and main horse frame. Then wrap along the main frame until you reach the base of the next mane frond. Hold the mane and the main frame next to each other as you wrap so they don't overlap.

A gentle plier squeeze over the binding wraps for each frame will help this positioning and keep the mane and neck frames lying side by side.

19 A side-to-side squeeze of the 26AWG (0.4mm) wire wraps (gently so as not to damage the wire) with chain-nosed pliers will help to neaten up these wraps.

20 Wrap all the way along the back of the neck and mane until you reach the ears.

21 Make sure that you place the second ear formed from the top of the mane section behind the first ear formed on the main head frame. After binding the 26AWG (0.4mm) wire twice at the base of the ears in front of the top mane frond base, thread on a 2mm antique bronze or gold-plated copper bead. Wrap across the base of the ears (in front of the ears). Wrap around the base of the forelock wire tail and the forehead for two to four wraps. Then wrap the 26AWG (0.4mm) wire along the forehead only until you reach a level where you will need to bind on the eye section in later stages. Do not cut the 26AWG (0.4mm) wire.

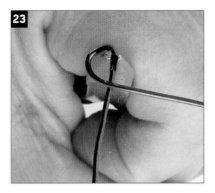

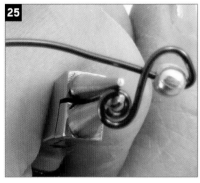

22 Plan the eye and muzzle detail section. I have drawn these details onto the template from Step 1. (See also the horse template on page 292.)

23 Make the eye and muzzle detail. Take 3¼in (8cm) of 18AWG (1mm) wire (use 20AWG/0.8mm wire if you find it easier to shape). Bend it in half with a straight length of wire at the base of the eye and an arching curve for the top of the eye.

24 The tail wire for the top wire should point downward over the tail wire for the bottom of the eye and project ¹³/₁₆in (20mm) (trim to this length with flush cutters). The tail wire for the base of the eye should project 1⁹/₁₆in (4cm) from the point where the eye wires cross. Thread a 4mm bead onto the base eye wire so it is trapped in the eye frame shape.

25 Curl and shape the wire ends projecting from the eye frame using round-nosed pliers to start the curl and fingers and pliers to finish (see page 27).

26 Curl the wire from the top of the eye upward and outward so it lies over the wire emerging from the base of the eye leading to the muzzle end, trapping the golden bead in place. Curl the muzzle end using chain-nosed pliers downward and inward. The wire curl from the upper curve of the eye forms an eye and muzzle detail.

27 Hammer only the muzzle detail on a steel block, hammering the back of the curl. Do not hammer where the wires cross, or you risk breaking the wires.

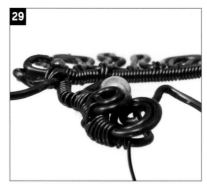

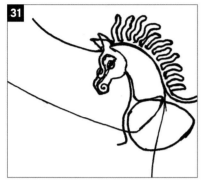

28 Attach the eye detail to the head. Hold the eye in position and bind the 26AWG (0.4mm) wire (from Step 21 from the ear section) around both the eye and the forehead, three to four times (see arrow in image).

29 Wrap only around the muzzle, not the muzzle detail.

30 Continue to wrap along the muzzle, binding to the eye/nostril section at a few more places (see arrows in image). Finish wrapping at the base of the jaw ready to bind to the neck panel.

31 Make the neck panel section. I added these to the diagram from Step 1. The neck panel forms part of the jawline and fills out the neck. (See also the horse template on page 292.)

32 Take 10in (25cm) of 18AWG (1mm) wire, bend it in half, and shape it over the diagram, leaving a 3in (7.5cm) wire tail from the front of the base of the neck and a 2¼in (5.5cm) length of wire from the back of the base of the neck.

33 Make sure the back of the neck is arched to match the arch of the back of the neck in the main horse frame. Form a curve for the back of the jaw, then bend and curve in a convex shape over the front of the neck. Bend the front neck wire inward to meet the back of the neck wire. Bend again to form the wire tails; these will form the covering for the cabochon in the horse's body later.

34 Weave the neck panel. Bind a piece of scrap wire around the base of the neck to hold it together for the first part of the weaving process. Take 80in (2m) of 26AWG (0.4mm) wire and wrap around the top of the neck section. Do not wrap around the tip of the neck section – leave it bare for binding wraps to the rest of the horse's frame later. Leave a 6in (15cm) 26AWG (0.4mm) wire tail at the top of the neck section ready to bind this to the horse. Start to weave along the neck section using the long end of 26AWG (0.4mm) wire. Use a standard figure-of-eight weave (see page 24) with two wraps of the wire around each frame side before each traverse to the opposite frame side wire, keeping the weave as tight as possible. As the back of the neck is slightly longer than the front, you may need to make three wraps around the back of the neck

  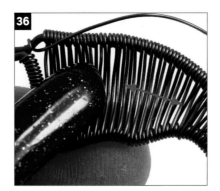 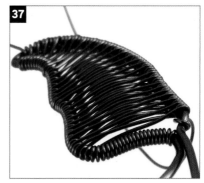

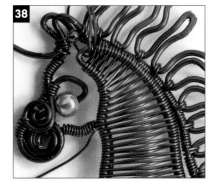 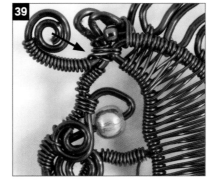 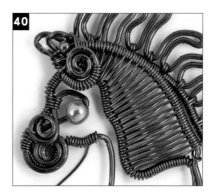

compared to the front of the neck so the weave stays parallel and does not start to travel faster down the front of the neck (which would result in a lopsided weave pattern). You will end up with a woven neck shape as shown in images 34 and 35.

35 Stop weaving at the base of the neck at the front (see black arrow in image). Remove the scrap wire. Wrap along the base of the neck section to bring the 26AWG (0.4mm) wire end back to the junction of the two neck section wire ends. Wrap across to the back and bottom of the neck section (see red arrow).

36 Add a little dimension to the weave by curving the neck segment. Using the rubber end of the plier handles, rub up and down at the back of the neck segment along the middle of its width to make the midline of the weave curve and bow outward at the front (see arrow in image).

37 This gives some shaping to the neck panel.

38 Bind the neck panel to the rest of the horse. Take the 26AWG (0.4mm) wire end from the top of the neck section and bind it to the back of the ear, wrapping around twice.

39 Bring the 26AWG (0.4mm) wire from the top of the neck panel to wrap around the front of the ear and the forelock (see arrow in image). Wrap along the forelock for $1/2$in (12mm), cut, and smooth in the 26AWG (0.4mm) wire end. Curl the end of the forelock wire (see page 27).

40 Take care not to damage the wire wrapped around the forelock. Bend the curl around over the forehead and gently press into place under the ears with your fingers.

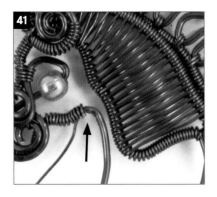

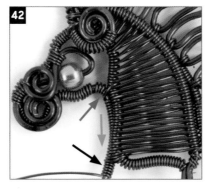

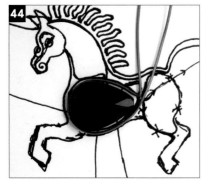

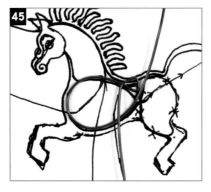

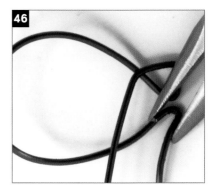

41 Bind the wire end at the base of the neck panel to the base of the mane (see arrow in image) with two binding wraps. Wrap around the small section of bare wire at the bottom right of the neck panel and cut, smooth, and tuck in the wire end neatly.

42 Make a third binding attachment for the neck section using the 26AWG (0.4mm) wire end at the base of the jaw (see red arrow in image). Wrap along the front of the neck (blue arrow). Make the fourth attachment for the neck panel at the base of the neck (black arrow).

43 Make a frame for the cabochon setting and the horse's rump panel. I have drawn this on the diagram from Step 1, see the template on page 292. I have outlined where

the top front and top rear legs will be, but you will not shape these yet. I have also outlined a multifunctional wire frame shape to outline the cabochon and form a rear rump panel and curl detail.

44 Take 14in (35cm) of 18AWG (1mm) wire and shape it around the pear/teardrop cabochon shape on the diagram. Make a sharp bend at the top end of the pear to mark the start of the pear shape.

45 Make a triangular shape at the top end of the teardrop. Make one bend $1/4$in (6mm) from the end of the pear shape and the next bend $1/4$in (6mm) further along to bring the top wire tail for the pear shape over the pear-shape frame near the top with a $2^1/4$in (5.5cm) wire tail. Trim the wire end to fit the drawing.

46 Make a sharp bend to start shaping the lower wire tail from the pear-shape frame setting downward.

47 Shape the wire around the rump panel until you return to the pear setting tip. Trim the wire tail to $2^1/2$in (6cm). This wire tail will curl over the rump later.

48 Wrap on a 40in (1m) length of 26AWG (0.4mm) wire from near one end of the 26AWG (0.4mm) wire along the top upper tip of the pear setting along the line of the blue arrow in the image. Bind around the top of the setting a few times to hold it all together (red arrow). Check the stone still fits nicely inside the setting with a small gap around it to allow wire weaving and binding around the stone later.

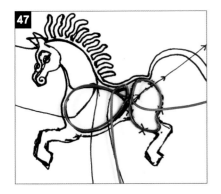

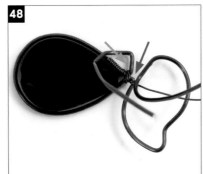

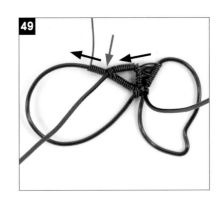

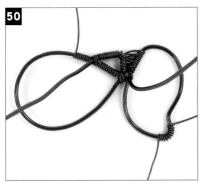

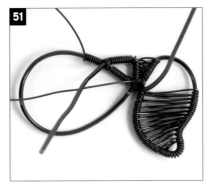

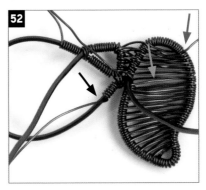

49 Weave up in a basket weave (two wraps on the left and three on the right) to the top of the shape; keep the weave loose, as you will need to work across and through this area when weaving the rump panel. Wrap along the top edge of the triangle frame until you reach where the wire tail crosses the pear/teardrop frame. Wrap around the teardrop frame three times (see red arrow in image). Then wrap along the teardrop frame for $^3/_{16}$in (5mm) (black arrows). Make sure the wire tail points upward ready to wrap over the cabochon later. Do not cut the 26AWG (0.4mm) wire you are working with.

50 Take a new 40–60in (1–1.5m) length of 26AWG (0.4mm) wire. Wrap around the bottom tip of the rump segment, near one end of the 26AWG (0.4mm) wire.

51 Cut the short 26AWG (0.4mm) wire end. Weave along the rump section with a basket weave. The shape you are weaving is complex; you will need to vary the weave ratio on either side as you progress up the section. At the base, use three wraps around the left side relative to two on the right. Stop when you reach the junction shown here. Start to wrap the 26AWG (0.4mm) wire up the wire tail at this point.

52 Add in a new long piece of 26AWG (0.4mm) wire at the top right side of the rump (see red arrow). Make sure the wire end at the top is to the right and top of the rump section (red arrow); you will need it to wrap the tail. Wrap along the top of the rump, then weave from the left-hand side top of the rump segment down (blue arrow in image shows the weave direction). Stop when you reach the weave from the bottom. As you weave down you will have to poke the weaving wire into the woven section from Step 49 on the left side of the weave. This can be fiddly, so it helps to keep the weave in Step 49 loose. Finish at the intersection of the wires. Pass the 26AWG (0.4mm) wire to the lower side tip of the pear frame. Wrap along for $^3/_{16}$in (5mm), then stop for the moment (black arrow).

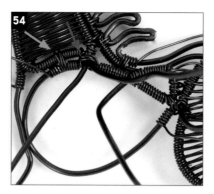

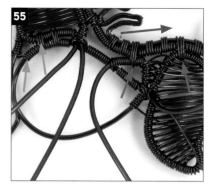

53 Press on the back of the rump segment with the rubber tips of your plier handles to give a rounded shape.

54 Fit the cabochon and rump frame to the main horse frame. Lay the frames over the template on page 292. Check the points where the frame will attach to each other and make sure everything is orientated correctly. Wrap along the top of the pear frame about ⅛in (3mm) with the 26AWG (0.4mm) wire from Step 49 until it is at the right level to bind around the wire tails from the neck panel. Bind around the two tails and the pear frame three times (see red arrow in image). Then wrap along the top pear frame for three to four wraps. Bind across to the base of the mane with three wraps, keeping them tight and neatly placed alongside each other (blue arrow). Continue along the pear frame with four wraps.

55 Wrap to the base of the mane with three wraps. Continue along the pear frame for seven or eight wraps and stop for the moment (see blue arrows in image). Wrap along the back of the horse using the same technique, with three wraps around the inner/lower back frame wire and three across both (red arrows). Keep the weaves neat, tightly packed, and even. Use side-by-side pushes with the plier tips and your fingernails to keep the weave even. At two points (see green arrows) wrap across three frame wires (the two back wires and the rump section) with three wraps; these attachments add strength to the structure. Do not cut the 26AWG (0.4mm) wire end; you will need it to wrap along the tail later.

56 Place the stone cabochon inside the setting. Press and shape the three 18AWG (1mm) wire tails (two from the mane frame and one from the pear setting frame) over the cabochon. Curve the wires around so they touch the edge of the pear setting for about ⅛in (3mm), then bend the wires upward and inward over the stone. The wire tails are numbered **1**, **2**, and **3**. You will curl them later to help hold the stone in place.

Tip

Place the horse and stone on a rubber mat (I use the Beadsmith sticky XL bead mat); this will absorb some of the force and the stone is less likely to fracture from any pressure from the wires being formed over it.

57 You will have two 26AWG (0.4mm) wires tails emerging from the horse: one from Step 42 (from the front of the neck) and the other from the top of the pear frame. Using the shorter wire, wrap down to just before the point where the foremost wire tail touches against the pear frame (see arrows in image). Cut and trim this wire, leaving the other 26AWG (0.4mm) wire for further wrapping. In this case, I cut short the wire running around the pear shape.

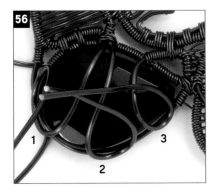

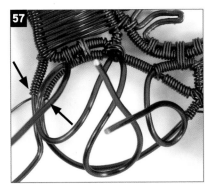

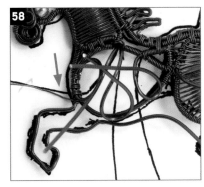

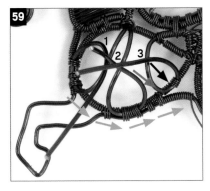

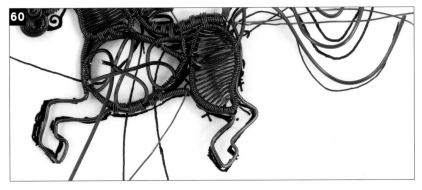

58 Wrap along the horse's chest, wrapping across outer frame, pear frame, and wire tail **1** (from Step 57) for three wraps. Wrap only around the outer frame for three wraps and then around both outer and the front of the pear frame in a three-by-three weave pattern (see page 26) until you reach where you would be shaping the upper front leg (see green arrow in image). In this picture, I have shaped the front leg, but you can see where the weave needs to go. It is easier to weave before shaping the foreleg. Return to the diagram from Step 43, and on page 292, and shape the upper front leg, tummy, and start to form the leading edge of the hind leg: don't shape the hind leg too much in case you need to reshape it after wrapping the foreleg and tummy section to the rest of the horse frame.

59 Following the template on page 292, work slowly with small movements of the pliers to make the little angles and shapes. Now, take the 26AWG (0.4mm) wire tail from the lower tip of the pear you were wrapping along in Step 52. Wrap along the pear and bind to wire tail **3** where it touches against the pear frame (see black arrow in image), stopping just before the pear shape touches the line of the tummy wire. Cut and tuck in the 26AWG (0.4mm) wire end (see red arrow). Now take the 26AWG (0.4mm) wire from wrapping along the chest and wrap along the inside of the upper front leg along pear frame.

When you reach the tummy section, use the same three-by-three weave wrap as in Step 58: three wraps across the pear and tummy frame and three around just

the lower pear frame, with wraps to wire tail **2** where they touch against the pear frame (see blue arrows). Hold wire tail **2** carefully in place over the cabochon frame and tummy frame as you bind to them to stop wire tail **2** slipping across the frame wires and making the setting too large for the stone. Make three wraps across all three, three wraps around the pear and tail **2**, and three wraps across all three. Continue with three around the pear frame and tummy, and three around just the tummy weave. Then wrap only along the tummy frame until you reach the start of the hind leg.

60 Shape and form the hind leg, rump, and tail wires following the template on page 292.

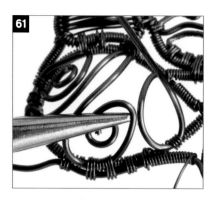

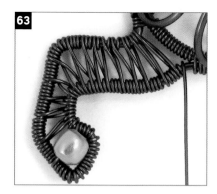

61 Curl the wires over the cabochon in an outer to inner spiral (see page 28). This technique will help you form spirals to fill the spaces over the cabochon setting. Press the spirals flat using pliers after you have formed them. The spirals should fill the space over the stone to hold it in place and add detail and a feeling of movement to the horse.

NOTE: I chose to spiral these wire tails after binding to the cabochon setting; this means you know exactly how much space you need to fill accounting for the curve over the stone setting.

62 Weave and attach beads to the top front leg. Take 40in (1m) of 26AWG (0.4mm) wire and start to wrap near one end of the 26AWG (0.4mm) wire around the base of the hoof and up either side of the hoof for ³/₁₆in (5mm). Cut and tuck in the shorter end of wire, leaving the longer length for weaving. Add a 3mm gold bead as you weave across to the other side of the leg frame with the longer end of 26AWG (0.4mm) wire from Step 61. Cut and tuck in the shorter length of 26AWG (0.4mm) wire.

63 Weave up the front fore leg using the simple basket weave as for the neck and rump panels. Here you will need to vary the weave ratio as you work up the leg. Use a weave ratio of six or seven to two (front to back) to help your weave keep up with itself as you work up the leg. This is due to all of the angles of the limb and the fact that the front of the leg has longer to weave up compared to the back of the fore leg. Once you reach the upper leg you might be able to revert to a two-by-two weave if the weave has evened up and the distances either side of the frame are the same. Then change to a four to two ratio (two upper to four lower in the upper foreleg. Study the weave ratios as one travels up the leg on the image. Leave a short length of wire at the end near the underside of the front leg ready to bind on another set of legs later.

64 Wrap the 26AWG (0.4mm) wire tail from Step 59 along the underside of the uppermost hind leg binding to the bottom of the rump panel a few times (see red arrows in image). Stop when you reach the inside back knee of the horse and cut and tuck in the 0.4mm wire end (see black arrow).

65 Taking a new 40in (1m) length of 26AWG (0.4mm) wire, weave up the top hind leg with the same techniques and the same weave ratio as in Step 63, adding a 4mm bead to the hoof space. Make sure your wire ends up at the back of the leg.

Tip

Bind a piece of scrap 26AWG (0.4mm) wire around the tail wires to help hold the back of the frame together. This makes it easier to weave the hind leg without distorting it.

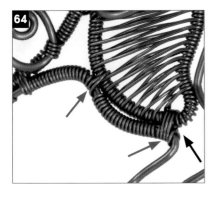

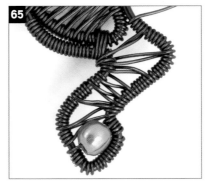

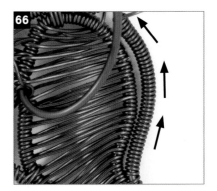

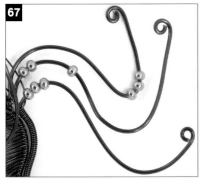

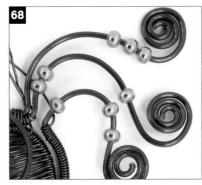

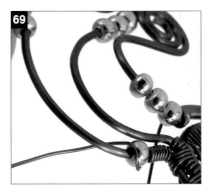

66 Remove the scrap wire from Step 65 at the base of the tail. Wrap the 26AWG (0.4mm) wire from Step 65 along the hindquarters of the horse, binding to the rump panel at the base, and wrap up to the base of the tail (see arrows in image). Do not cut the 26AWG (0.4mm) wire yet.

67 Work on the tail. Thread three 3mm gold metal beads onto each 18AWG (1mm) tail wire. Curl the ends upward so they don't fall off.

68 Make a tight spiral (see page 27) at the end of each tail wire, leaving about $1^{3}/_{16}$–$1^{3}/_{8}$in (3–3.5cm) of straight bare wire extending up to the spiral from the base of the tail. Arrange the tail wires neatly as shown in image. The lower tail wire has a slightly shorter bare section compared to the middle and upper tail wires. Hammer only the back of the spirals, so as not to mark the front of each spiral too much and create a lovely flat and reflective surface. Do not hammer the rest of the tail.

69 You should have three 26AWG (0.4mm) wires at the base of the tail, left over from wrapping the back, rump panel, and hindquarters. If these wires are too short, cut them, tuck in, and add new wire at the base of the tail. Starting with the top tail wire, wrap along the 18AWG (1mm) wire with the 26AWG (0.4mm) wire nearest to it. After about $^{1}/_{4}$in (6mm) of wrapping, bring a 3mm bead close to the wrap. Wrap around the bead with the 26AWG (0.4mm) wire, then continue wrapping along the wire to trap the 3mm bead in place.

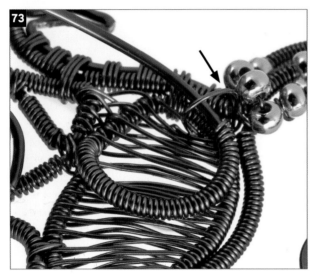

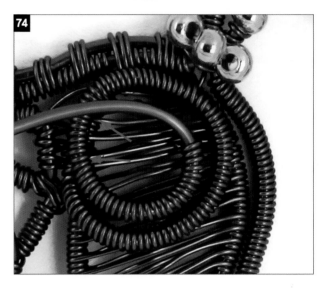

70 Wrap around another 3mm bead in the same way about ³/₈in (10mm) further along, and the third bead on this tail wire about ³/₈in (10mm) further along from the second. Continue to wrap up to the hammered spiral of wire at the end of the tail. Cut and smooth in the wire end with pliers. Repeat this step with the middle tail wire. Space out the beads so that they are not at exactly the same level as the beads on the tail wire above it.

71 Working on the lower tail wire, make a tight binding wrap of the last 26AWG (0.4mm) wire around the base of the tail. You can thread on a few 3mm beads to wrap around the tail base, if you like.

72 Wrap along the lower tail wire with the final 26AWG (0.4mm) wire here. Cut and tuck in the end once you have added all the beads.

73 Swirl the wire end from the rump section around toward the tail. Wrap the 26AWG (0.4mm) wire end from Step 51 along it until you reach the base of the tail. Bind around the top of the rump frame at the base of the tail to attach the wire end here (see arrow in image).

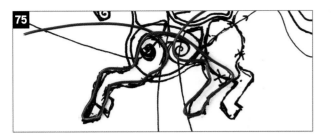

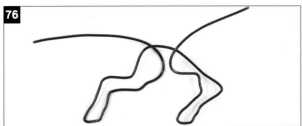

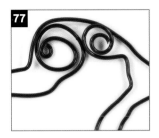

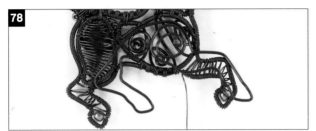

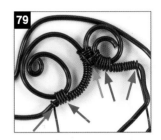

74 Press the wraps tightly together with chain-nosed pliers. Wrap along the wire end for ³/₈in (10mm) until you can bind to the other side of the top of the rump, binding at a minimum of two points (see red arrows in image).

NOTE: These attachments at the level of the red arrows are difficult to see, as they naturally concelaed within the wraps already in place in place, on the woven rump panel.

Curl the wire in an inward spiral and wrap the 26AWG (0.4mm) wire along until 1in (25mm) from the end. Cut and tuck in the wire. Spiral the 18AWG (1mm) wire end and press the spiral carefully into position over the rump using fingers or the rubber ends of your pliers.

75 Form the lower front and back legs and, with this frame, also form a backing plate for the cabochon setting. I have drawn the backing shape as a dotted line on the diagram from Step 43. Please also see the template on page 292. I placed a 12in (30cm) length of 18AWG (1mm) over the diagram to make the outline clearer.

76 Leave 1³/₁₆in (3cm) wire tails extending from the frames to make into spirals.

77 Shape the wire and make curls using the outer to inner spiral method (see page 27) to fill the space inside the shape.

78 I have laid the shape over the horse frame at the back so you can see how the shape will lie across it.

79 Take 20in (50cm) of 26AWG (0.4mm) wire and wrap around the midline of the shape where the two spiral ends touch (see blue arrow in image). Make sure the upper end of the 0.4mm (26AWG) wire crosses over the midline wrap, ready to wrap along one lower edge of the lower leg frame. The crossing wrap must be concealed, so make sure this is the side that faces the back of the cabochon. Wrap each 26AWG (0.4mm) wire end along either lower side of the first binding point. Bind across to the wire spirals where they touch against the wire you are wrapping along, to strengthen the backing frame (red arrows). Stop when you reach the attachment points where you will be binding the backing frame to the main horse frame later (green arrows).

NOTE: Make the back wraps as neat as the front ones, as both will be on view.

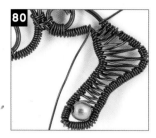

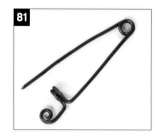

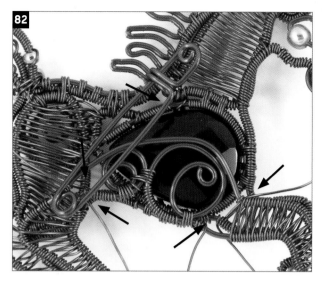

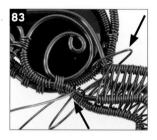

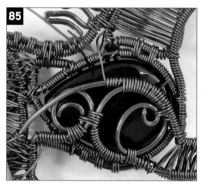

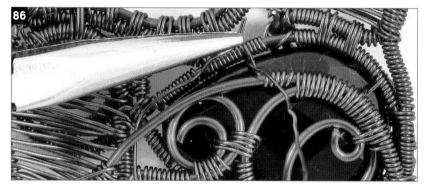

80 Weave the legs as in Step 62. Use 40in (1m) lengths of 26AWG (0.4mm) wire for each leg. Make sure the 26AWG (0.4mm) wire ends up at the upper edge of the top of the leg. This wire tail will be used to wrap along the top of the backing frame and to the main horse frame later.

81 Make a 1⁹/₁₆in (4cm) length brooch pin (see page 32).

82 Insert the cabochon into the frame by pressing it over a rubber mat to protect the stone from undue pressure. With the piece turned to look at the back, place the backing frame and pin into place to make sure the pin fits

across the back of the horse frame. Also plan fixing points (see arrows in image) to bind the backing frame and the brooch pin to the rest of the horse.

83 With the stone in place and working over a soft surface in case the stone drops out, place the backing frame over the back of the horse frame. Start by binding the 26AWG (0.4mm) wires at the upper and lower side of the foreleg. Bind two or three times around the corresponding upper and lower edge of the foreleg on the main horse frame (see arrows in image). Cut and tuck in the lower front leg edge wires.

NOTE: You may have two 26AWG (0.4mm) wires at the lower edge. You can trim one and work with the other.

84 Using the upper leg edge 26AWG (0.4mm) wire, wrap along the top edge of the backing frame and also around the loops of the backing frame where they touch the backing frame (see black arrows in image). Also wrap across to the cabochon frame (red arrow).

85 Wrap across to the cabochon frame just behind the neck with a traversing weave (see red arrow in image). Wrap around the cabochon frame and back again to the backing frame. Pull the wire tight

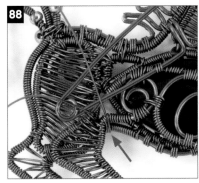

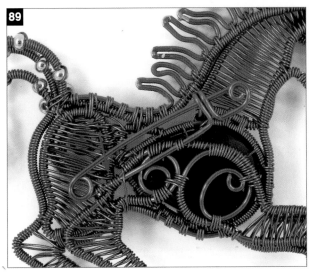

around the cabochon frame to click the 26AWG (0.4mm) wire tightly in between the weaves already there.

86 Hold the hind leg in position when you pull these weaves into place to stop you pulling the weaves too tight and moving the backing plate out of the ideal position. You may have to move the stone a little and wiggle the 26AWG (0.4mm) wire through the small gaps at the side of the cabochon frame. Use pliers to help you grab the wire end if your fingers cannot get into the small spaces.

87 When you get near a point where you can attach the brooch pin, wrap the 26AWG (0.4mm) wire from Step 84 around the straight portion of the brooch pin to attach it (see green arrow in image). Continue to wrap along the top of the backing frame if you have enough wire (if not, you will have to do this step with spare wire left after binding the back legs in Step 80). Again, pliers will help you grab the wire end. I stopped where I ran out of wire and have cut and tucked in the end (black arrow). Fold the brooch pin down a little to make this step easier. Bind to the other backing plate curl (red arrow) and the cabochon frame (blue arrow).

88 Use the two 26AWG (0.4mm) wire tails at the hind leg end of the backing plate. Bind the lower 26AWG (0.4mm) wire around the base of the top of the hind legs a few times (see red arrow in image).

89 Bind the upper wire around the brooch pin and the cabochon frame a few times. I also bound the lower 26AWG (0.4mm) wire across to the brooch pin. Wrap around the brooch pin only a few times and cut and tuck both 26AWG (0.4mm) wire ends neatly (red arrow in image).

90 Your beautiful running horse brooch is finished.

Indian elephant necklace

This Indian elephant design with dreamcatcher tassel drops makes a lovely pendant. The cabochon setting can be used on its own to mount stones without placing an elephant on top, so that the stone can be seen.

Templates
See page 290 for the templates for this design.

Materials
18AWG (1mm-diameter) antique bronze coated copper round wire
(20AWG/0.8mm-diameter wire can be used in some components instead of 18AWG/1mm wire)
26AWG (0.4mm-diameter) round antique bronze-coated copper wire
30AWG (0.25mm-diameter) round antique bronze-coated copper wire
(Antique bronze, coated copper, bare copper, silver, or gold-plated wire will also work)
4mm-diameter bronze-colored/coated metal or hematite beads
3mm faceted smoky quartz beads (can be 4mm)
2mm round antique bronze colored metal or seed beads
1 x 70 x 50mm oval cabochon, no drill hole required. (I used dyed turquoise howlite; turquoise, dyed or natural howlite, amazonite, lapis, or jasper would also work well. Try searching for "palmstone" on the Internet to find a cabochon of suitable size.)
Seven headpins
10mm-diameter turquoise howlite rounds

Tools
General tools (see page 10) plus:
Gizmo tool with a 1mm-diameter mandrel (or you can hand-wind directly onto 18AWG/1mm wire)

Dimensions of finished piece
With dangles: 4 x 3in (10 x 7.5cm)
Without dangles: 3¼ x 3in (8 x 7.5cm)

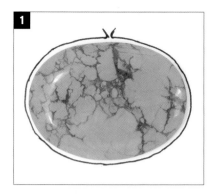

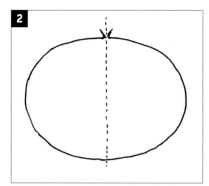

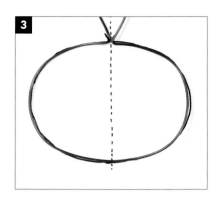

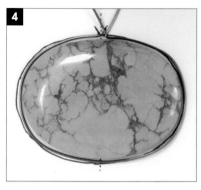

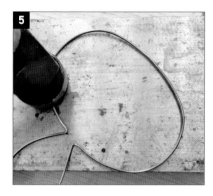

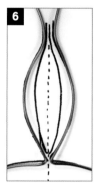

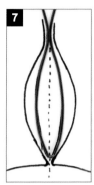

1 Draw around the cabochon with a 1/32in (1mm) gap around it to allow for wire wrapping space later.

2 I drew a midline dotted line, as shown in the image, to help me plan the rest of the design later.

3 Take a 40in (1m) length of 18AWG (1mm) wire. Start to shape around the cabochon frame at the midpoint of the 18AWG (1mm) wire using the diagram from Step 1 as a template. Form the oval shape first, crossing the wires at the top of the oval. Sharply bend the wires where they cross using chain-nosed pliers, using the diagram as a guide.

4 Try to get this shape perfect for size around the cabochon so you obtain a better fit when setting the cabochon later.

5 Hammer the oval frame section gently to work-harden but not flatten. Do not hammer the bale wires.

6 Work out the bale size you need by drawing on the diagram from Step 1. I drew a bale approx. 13/16in (20mm) wide and 1 13/16in (4.5cm) long with an internal bale wire frame (see template on page 290). Take the wire frame made in Step 3 and shape the bale on either side. Use fingers to make a gentle curve and pliers to fine-tune the shaping and make the bend at the end of the bale. Leave wire tails about 2 3/4in (7cm) long at the end of the bale.

7 Take another section of 18AWG (1mm) wire, about 10in (25cm) long, and bend in half to make a V-shape. Shape either side of the V along the inner bale frame shape on the diagram in Step 3, or use the template on page 290. Use the techniques used to shape the bale and clamp either side of the V with chain-nosed pliers to sharpen the bend.

8 Start to weave the bale, see page 24. Take 100in (2.5m) of 26AWG (0.4mm) wire and bind around the base of the bale with a figure-of-eight pattern to join the bale together at the base. Bring the wire ends up at the back of this attachment ready to wrap up the sides of the bale. Wrap up either side of the bale for 1/8in (3mm) so you are ready to bind to the inner bale wire frame.

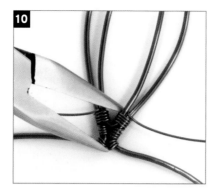
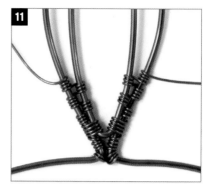
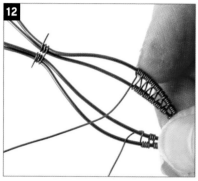

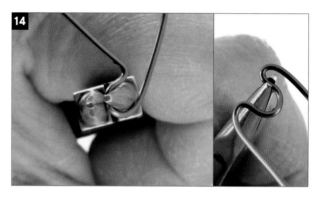

9 Wrap the 26AWG (0.4mm) wires around the outer and inner bale wires four times on each side of the bale, then once around just the outer bale wires. I bound some scrap wire around the top of the bale to help hold the bale frames in position during wire weaving (see arrow in image).

10 Use pliers to press the wraps tightly into position.

11 Use 30–26AWG (0.25–0.4mm) wire for this step. I chose 26AWG (0.4mm) for strength and weave density, plus speed of weaving as you cover more distance in the time and use a shorter wire length. Wrap along the outer bale wires for three wraps. Now start a basic basket weave technique (see page 24). Use three wraps of the 26AWG (0.4mm) wire around each inner

frame side before each traverse to the outer frame side wire with four wraps around the outer frame wire.

12 The weave ratio has been chosen as the outside of the bale frame is slightly longer than the inside: more wraps are required along the outer bale wire so the weave stays parallel and does not start to travel faster on the inside of the bale (which would result in a lopsided weave pattern.) Keep the weave tight with fingers and pliers.

13 Weave up both sides of the bale. As you reach the end of the bale, where the side bale wires run closely together, wrap four times around each side. Stop weaving at the end of the bale. Do not cut the 26AWG (0.4mm) wire ends. Put this section to one side for the moment.

14 Make the front frame for the cabochon and loops for the tassels. I have drawn a number of loops on the template (see page 290). You may have a cabochon that is a different size and you can alter the number of loops accordingly. Take a 40in (1m) length of 18AWG (1mm) wire and start to make loops. Use round-nosed pliers to make the loops and chain-nosed pliers to make the sharp bends on either side of the loops.

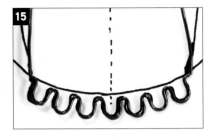

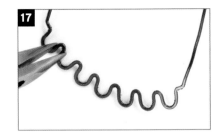

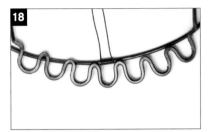

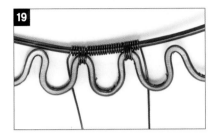

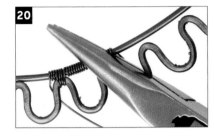

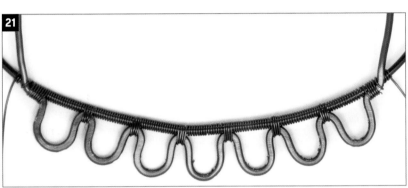

15 Keep checking against the diagram for size and spacing of the loops. I made seven little loops and then a little bend sideways and upward at the end of the row of loops. Curve the looping setting a little to match the bottom curve of the cabochon setting. Leave a 12in (30cm) length of wire tail either side of the loops.

16 Hammer the loops but not the rest of the wire.

17 If the shape has splayed a little, squeeze either side of the bends between the loops with chain-nosed pliers to move them closer together, checking the diagram for spacing.

18 Attach the loops to the cabochon setting. Take 80in (2m) of 30AWG (0.25mm) wire and start to wrap along the cabochon frame at the midline bottom of the frame using the midsection of the wire.

NOTE: 26AWG (0.4mm) wire is fine to use instead of 30AWG (0.25mm) wire. Wrap a width as wide as one of the loops ready to bind onto either side of the middle loop.

19 Bind both sections together at the base of the middle loop with three to four binding wraps of the 30AWG (0.25mm) wire. Make sure the wire ends of the loop section are placed over the cabochon setting but the loops lie below the bottom line of the cabochon setting.

20 Take care to center the loops on the setting, using the template to help you. A gentle squash of the pliers over the binding wraps will help to neaten them up and keep the loops lying below the cabochon setting, not behind or in front of it.

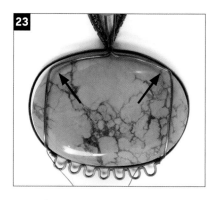

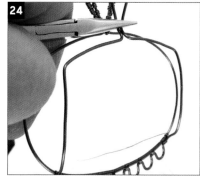

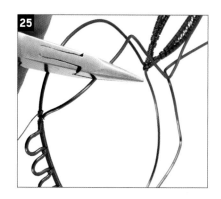

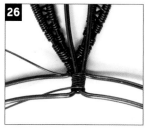

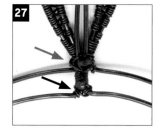

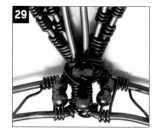

21 Bind along the bottom of the cabochon setting, wrapping around the bases of the loops where they touch against the cabochon setting. When you reach the sides of the loops where the wires point straight upward, bind around both cabochon and loop settings for seven wraps. Then wrap along the cabochon setting only for three wraps.

22 I have drawn a front cabochon frame setting guide on the template (page 290). Place the cabochon into the setting and mold the loop wire ends over the cabochon. Use chain-nosed pliers to shape the wire, especially at the bottom and top of the gemstone.

23 Bend the 18AWG (1mm) wire ends inward about ¼in (6mm) below the top edge of the cabochon setting (see arrows in image).

24 Bend the wires sharply upward and downward again at the midline of the bale, down over the stone and then about ¼in (6mm) along the downward sweep of these midline wires. Bend them both again upward so they lie flat in the same plane as the bale (so they lie along the front and midline of the bale).

25 This image shows some extra shaping I did for the wires so they lie over the curve of the cabochon.

26 Take 12in (30cm) of 26AWG (0.4mm) wire (30AWG/0.25mm will also work at this stage). Bind around the midline of the cabochon front wires where they descend over the top of the cabochon setting with a small tail at either end.

27 Bind on a 2mm antique bronze bead to the base of this attachment using the 26AWG (0.4mm) wire you are working with. Cut and tuck in the wire end after a few wraps (see black arrow in image). Wrap the other 26AWG (0.4mm) wire end around the base of the bale to bind the top of the cabochon cover

to the base of the bale with a few wraps, adding in a 3mm faceted smoky quartz or a 3mm bead of your choice over this binding wrap. Wrap above and below the smoky quartz (like an eye shape). Wrap along one side of the main cabochon setting for a few wraps, then cut and tuck in the 26AWG (0.4mm) wire end (red arrow).

28 Add a new 80in (2m) length of 26AWG (0.4mm) wire to the base of the bale and wrap along the back of the bale for two or three wraps on either side.

29 Thread two 2mm antique bronze metal or seed beads onto the 26AWG (0.4mm) wire. Weave up to the front/top of the cabochon frontal wire and wrap with three wraps along the front of the setting. Do this for either side. Pass the wire to the back of the setting using the basic basket weave technique as in Steps 10–13, this time without adding beads.

30 Repeat Step 29 until you reach the top corner of the frontal cabochon setting. Check the fit against the cabochon setting. Make sure the back of the setting is not distorted but nice and flat.

31 You can continue weaving along the sides adding in beads, as I have done in this alternative design. First, weave 30AWG (0.25mm) wire from Step 21 a few times across the connection at the base of the setting in a basket weave (three times around both sides) and cut and tuck in the 30AWG (0.25mm) wire (see arrow in image).

32 Study the image to see the pattern I have built up along the sides:

Add a 3mm faceted smoky quartz and 2mm metal bead in the first side row.

Then a row of three 2mm metal seed beads, then a row of 3mm faceted smoky quartz, and two 2mm metal beads.

Then a row of four 2mm seed beads.

Then a 4–5mm metal bead, 3mm smoky quartz, and 2mm seed bead, followed by a row of four 2mm seed beads.

Then a 4–5mm metal bead, 3mm smoky quartz, and 2mm seed bead, followed by a row of four 2mm seed beads.

Then a 4–5mm metal bead, 3mm smoky quartz, and 2mm seed bead, followed by a row of four 2mm seed beads.

Then 3mm smoky quartz and 2mm seed beads, a row of four 2mm seed beads, one 3mm smoky quartz, and finally a 2mm seed bead.

Wrap the 26AWG (0.4mm) wire to the front of the setting and cut and tuck in the wire at the back of the frame wire.

33 Repeat in mirror image for the other side. Check the fit over the cabochon.

Tip
You could add a hammered wire shape to the side as an alternative to adding beads.

34 Plan a gemstone setting along the bale. Take some gemstones that would look lovely set into the bale and place them into the bale space to see whether they would fit. Place the largest-diameter stone in the middle, flanked by smaller gemstone; e.g. 6mm blue howlite rounds, 4mm blue howlite rounds, antique bronze 4mm metal beads.

35 Using the 18AWG (1mm) wire tails from the front frame you started to make in Step 14, shaped in Steps 23–25 to send wire tails along the midline of the bale, make a wavy shape in mirror image along the bale to form spaces to fit the gemstones into. Use chain-nosed pliers to gently form the shapes, keeping them as mirror image as possible.

36 Form these wavy shapes along the bale. Check that the stones you have chosen fit in to the spaces with a little gap around them to allow for weaving of 30AWG (0.25mm) wire along this frame later.

37 Attach 80in (2m) of 26AWG (0.4mm) wire at its midline to the base of the bale. Start to wrap up along the wavy sides until you reach the widest point/middle of the first circular space.

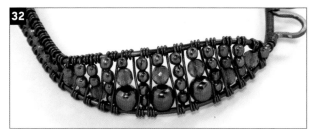

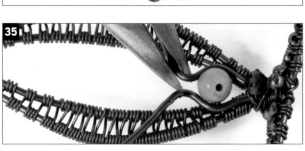

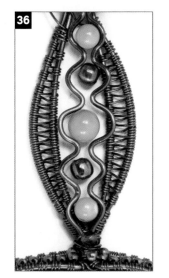

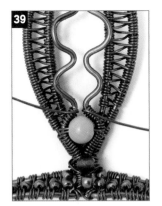

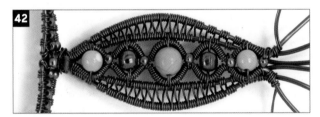

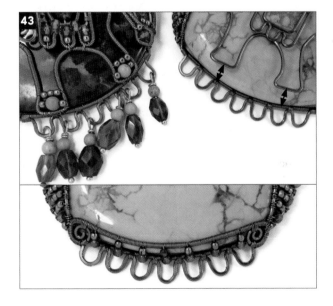

38 Thread one 26AWG (0.4mm) wire through one side of a 4mm blue howlite round and the other 26AWG (0.4mm) wire through the other side of the bead in a criss-cross bead attachment (see page 26).

39 Pull the wires tightly to pull the bead into place. Wrap the 26AWG (0.4mm) wire around the side of the wavy shape. Continue to wrap the 26AWG (0.4mm) wire along the bale until you reach the "waist" in between two bead space shapes.

40 At the waist, bind each of the 26AWG (0.4mm) wires around once or twice, binding on a 2mm bead as you do this. Weave up to the next frame space ready to attach another bead.

41 Bind on a 4mm round antique bronze metal bead in a criss-cross bead attachment. Pull the wires tightly to pull the bead into place. Wrap the 26AWG (0.4mm) wire around both the side of the wavy shape and the inner frame of the bale to attach these sections together.

NOTE: At this level, there is more space to pass the 26AWG (0.4mm) wire through weave spaces between the inner and outer bale wires (the lower space won't have as much space, so I did not wrap to the bale there).

42 Repeat the techniques in Steps 37–41 using the 026AWG (0.4mm) wire that was bound onto the bale in Step 37, adding a 6mm howlite, another 4mm antique bronze bead, and a 4mm blue howlite into the spaces and 2mm antique bronze beads at the waist points until you reach the top of the bale. You may not be able to bind to the side bale wires in the last gemstone space, but you can wrap the 26AWG (0.4mm) wire ends around the end of the bale for a few wraps on each side, after removing the scrap wire. Do not cut the 26AWG (0.4mm) wire ends yet.

43 You have two options now. If your cabochon is shallow, you will be able to wire the elephant's feet directly onto the bottom of the setting. See option on the left in the image. If the cabochon is deeper, you may have to add an extra plinth section to the bottom of the setting so you don't have to bend the legs over the stone too much. There is a gap marked by arrows in the setting on the right in the image.

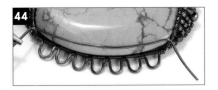

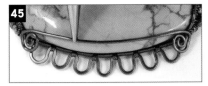

44 Take a section of 18AWG (1mm) wire about 4³/₄in (12cm) long. Gently curve the central section of the wire around the base of the stone while temporarily placed in the setting. Bend either end of the wire downward and trim each tail to 1in (2.5cm).

45 Curl the ends of the wire tails loosely and hammer the curls only.

46 Take the stone out of the setting. Using 40in (1m) of 30AWG (0.25mm) wire, wrap along one side of the curl about 8in (20cm) from the end of the 30AWG (0.25mm) wire, also binding across to the lower edge of the cabochon setting.

47 Wrap the short end of the 30AWG (0.25mm) wire end along the bottom of the curl. Bind to the base of the setting or the side of the first loop and then along the base of the curl. Cut and tuck in the short end of the 30AWG (0.25mm) wire. Bind the longer end of the 30AWG (0.25mm) wire along the top of the curl across the inner spirals of the curl where they touch the top of the curl for five wraps. Wrap along the straight section of 18AWG (1mm) plinth wire. Repeat Steps 46–47 in mirror image for the other curl of the plinth wire.

48 Weave along the base of the setting using the same techniques as in Steps 31–32 adding in 3mm faceted smoky quartz and 2mm beads as you go, depending on the amount of space you have in your setting. This is an opportunity to use different colors of beads,

even to create a pattern if you wish. I chose to weave down with the beaded wire to the midpoint of each loop to add detail to this feature of the pendant. Use one end of the 30AWG (0.25mm) wire, working along the setting as far as you can (if you run out, start from the other end). Cut and tuck in both 30AWG (0.25mm) wire ends where they meet.

49 Check the fit of the setting over the cabochon.

NOTE: I chose a gemstone that would stand alone on display in this setting without an elephant design on top. You can skip straight to Step 110 if you want to set your stone this way.

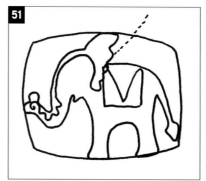

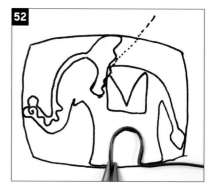

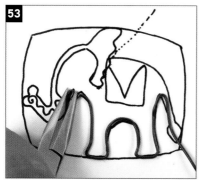

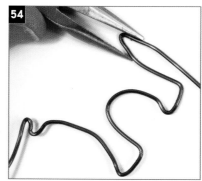

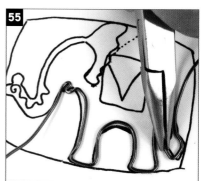

50 Plan the elephant design. Take the cabochon setting and measure the space you have within the setting for the elephant shape. Remember the stone is curved, so the height required for the elephant is a little larger than you think. Also your gemstone may have a different thickness, so every elephant will be a slightly different size. It may help to press the front of the setting into blank paper over a rubber mat and trace over the impression to gauge the size space you need to work with.

51 As you can see in the image, I have drawn an outline of the elephant shape I am going to make. If you scan the drawing (also on page 290) and print out different sizes, cut around the outlines, and lay them over your setting you can get a good idea of the size of elephant you will need to make. This diagram will be added to later, adding in other wire frame elements. I left them off this one so it won't be too confusing to shape the elephant frame.

52 Take 40in (1m) of 18AWG (1mm) wire. Start to shape in the midsection of the wire around the lower tummy and legs of the elephant using the diagram as a guide. Please see also the templates on page 290 for a scale drawing to work over.

53 Use small movements of the 18AWG (1mm) wire with the tips of chain-nosed pliers. Use side-to-side squeezes around bends if you need to make them tighter. Form the fore and hind legs. Form the lip and mouth with plier squeezes to sharpen up the bend and to point that wire end out of the way for the moment.

54 Now concentrate on the back end and the tail. Make a sharp bend at the top of the hind leg to form the inside edge of the tail, firming up the bend with clamps of chain-nosed pliers.

55 Form a little diamond shape for the tail (enough to fit a 2mm bead inside the diamond shape) with little clamping movements of the pliers. Bring the returning tail wire up to run parallel with the downward inside tail wire edge.

Tip

Use the diagram on page 290 to help you form the shapes, and don't make too many reshaping movements on a single wire point in case of breakage. Practice with scrap wire before making the elephant so you are more confident with these little shaping movements.

56 Form the back and inner blanket shape carefully with an internal triangle shape and a wire end 1in (25mm) in length. Bend the wire tail vertically upward for the moment.

57 Form the trunk with the sides gently bent and curved.

58 The bow-shaped tip is formed with movements of round-nosed and chain-nosed plier tips.

59 Use side-to-side squashes with pliers to neaten the tip.

60 Form the forehead. The ear is formed with a crinkly edge along the trailing edge.

61 Form the front of the ear taking the 18AWG (1mm) wire closely under the forehead frame section.

62 Form the crinkly trunk detail. This is fiddly: small movements of pliers are needed. If you find it too difficult, just form a small curl at the base of the trunk above where the tusk will lie. After forming the crinkly trunk section, leave a ³⁄₈in (10mm) wire end.

63 Curl the ³⁄₈in (10mm) wire end into the end of the trunk using round-nosed pliers.

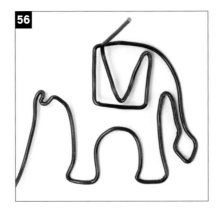

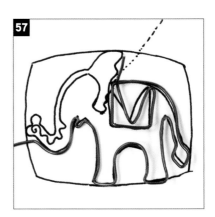

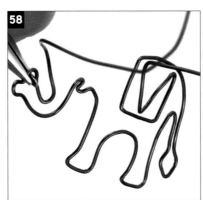

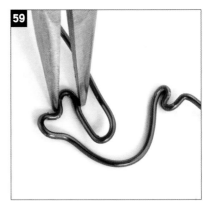

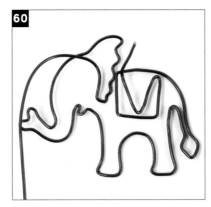

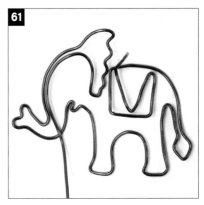

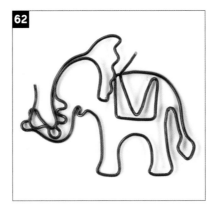

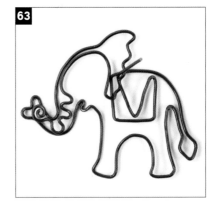

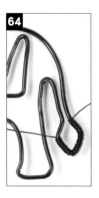

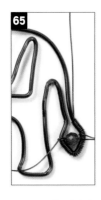

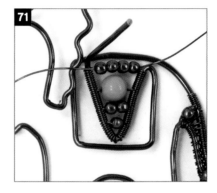

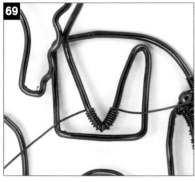

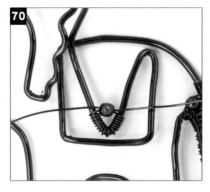

64 Weave the elephant tail. Take 40in (1m) of 30AWG (0.25mm) wire and wrap around the tip of the tail, leaving a 3¹⁄₄in (8cm) length of wire at the top of the tip of the tail. Wrap around the tip with the longer wire end until you reach three-quarters the way around the tip to the widest point of the tail.

65 Thread on a 3mm faceted smoky quartz. Wrap around to the other side of the tail tip, passing the 30AWG (0.25mm) wire back to the side you started from behind the 3mm bead. If possible, pass the 30AWG (0.25mm) wire through the bead again to add strength to the attachment.

66 Wrap up to the base of the tail tip.

67 You will have two 30AWG (0.25mm) wires, one long and one short. Using the long end of 26AWG (0.4mm) wire, weave up along the tail using a standard two-by-two figure-of-eight basket weave (see page 24). Change the weave ratio to make three wraps around the rearmost tail frame in the upper third of the tail (this a longer length of wire compared to the innermost tail frame). From the base of the tail, wrap up to the top of the tail base, threading on a 2mm bead. Wrap along the rump for ¹⁄₄in (6mm), then stop for the moment (do not cut the 30AWG/0.25mm wire end).

68 Thread a 2mm bead onto the short 30AWG (0.25mm) wire end at the bottom of the tail weave, just at the top of the diamond-shaped tip of the tail. Wrap on with a binding wrap, cutting and tucking in the 30AWG (0.25mm) wire

once the bead has been securely attached. Cut and tuck in the 30AWG (0.25mm) wire ends neatly.

69 Make the blanket triangle. Take 40in (1m) of 30AWG (0.25mm) wire and wrap around the tip of the triangle (at the midsection of the 30AWG/0.25mm wire) for about ¹⁄₈in (3mm) on either side.

70 Add in a 2mm metal bead with a criss-cross bead wrap attachment.

71 Wrap up either side of the triangle, adding a row of two 2mm beads with a criss-cross bead wrap attachment a little further up the triangle. Then add a 4mm blue magnesite bead. Wrap up to the top of the triangle and add a row of three 2mm beads with a criss-cross bead wrap attachment.

MASTERING WIREWORK JEWELRY

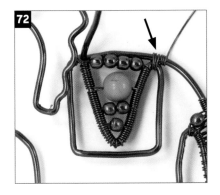

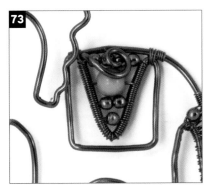

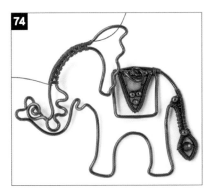

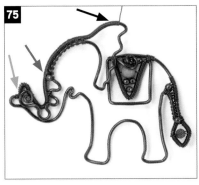

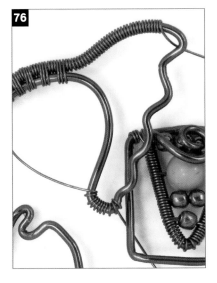

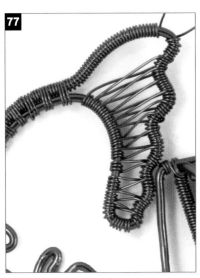

72 Bind the 30AWG (0.25mm) wire around the back frame wire and the triangular shape to bind this area together. Make sure to bind around the wire tail on the left (see arrow).

73 Cut the 30AWG (0.25mm) wire ends on either side and tuck the ends in. Curl the little wire tail at the top left of the blanket section. Press it into place over the top of the beaded blanket using your fingers, nylon pliers, or the soft end of your plier handles so as not to damage the wire curl or the beads below.

74 Work the top of the ear, forehead, and trunk. Take about 40in (1m) of 30AWG (0.25mm) wire and wrap with a three across both wires and three wraps around the outer frame wire only in a repeating pattern along the forehead, with 1/3 of the 30AWG (0.25mm) wire left to wrap along the ear and the rest to wrap up the trunk.

75 Wrap along the top edge of the ear with the short 30AWG (0.25mm) wire end from Step 70. Cut and tuck in the 30AWG (0.25mm) wire when you reach the top corner of the ear (see black arrow in image). With the long end of wire from Step 74, bind on a 2mm antique bronze bead (see purple arrow). Start to wrap along the upper edge of the trunk, wrapping across to the bends in the wavy trunk section where they touch against the upper trunk frame. Stop when you reach the tip of the trunk: this is a point where you will be binding to the cabochon setting later (see blue arrow). Cut the 30AWG (0.25mm) wire at the tip of the trunk but not at the top of the ear.

76 Weave the ears. Take 80in (2m) of 30AWG (0.25mm) wire and start to wrap along the lower edge of the ear near one end of the 30AWG (0.25mm) wire with the short end of wire left at the bottom left-hand corner of the ear and the long end of wire at the bottom right-hand corner of the ear.

77 Start a basic figure-of-eight basket weave (see page 24) with the long end of 30AWG (0.25mm) wire. Use a weave ratio of four wraps around the outer ear and two wraps around the inner (left side) of the ear as the distance is much longer along the outside of the ear.

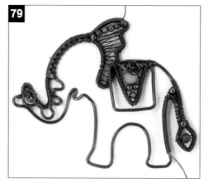

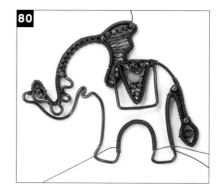

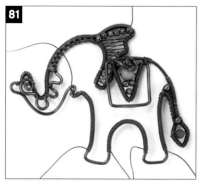

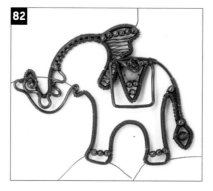

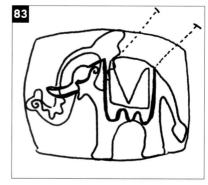

78 On the last pass, weave back from the top right corner of the ear. Thread on five 2mm beads to add detail to the top of the ear and compensate for any problems in getting the weave to fit the top of the ear without gaps. Tuck the 30AWG (0.25mm) wire in at the inner top section of the ear after a few wraps around the frame. You can also cut and tuck in the short 30AWG (0.25mm) wire end at the base of the ear.

79 Work on the feet and legs. Take 16in (40cm) of 30AWG (0.25mm) wire and wrap from the base of the tail down to the ankle of the elephant's rear leg. Cut the 30AWG (0.25mm) wire end leading towards the base of the tail, sliding the cut coil of wire firmly up to the tail to ensure a close fit of the wraps to the base of the tail.

80 Take 40in (1m) of 30AWG (0.25mm) wire and wrap from the midpoint of the 30AWG (0.25mm) wire around the base of the abdomen down the front of the back leg (down to the ankle) and down the back of the leg (also down to the level of the ankle).

81 Wrap 60in (1.5m) of 30AWG (0.25mm) wire along the front of the elephant, stopping at the top end at the top of the mouth (do not cut the 30AWG/0.25mm wire) and also stopping the wrapping once the ankle is reached.

82 Thread two or three 2mm beads onto one 30AWG (0.25mm) on one side of the hind leg ankle and thread the other 30AWG (0.25mm) wire through it in a criss-cross bead wrap attachment. Wrap down to the front and back of the hind foot but not all the way across the base as the

base wrap will be used to attach the elephant to the frame later. Make another criss-cross bead wrap attachment of three 2mm beads at the ankle, with the 30AWG (0.25mm) wire at the back of the forefoot. End up with two 30AWG (0.25mm) wire ends at the front and back of the foot ready for attachment to the cabochon frame later.

83 I have drawn a blanket detail, eye, and tusk on the diagram from Step 51. Please also see the template on page 290 if you want to use it to help you shape the wire. The eye space should be large enough to fit a 4mm bead inside. You can use 20AWG (0.8mm) or 18AWG (1mm) wire to make this section. Use the diagram to shape this complex form. Starting with the blanket section, make three loops. Squeeze the bases of the loops to make them fit along the bottom width of the blanket frame. Make the straight sides of the blanket fit around the panel you have already made. Leave a 1in (2.5cm) wire tail at the back of the blanket.

84 Make the top of the eye.

85 Make the little tusk.

86 Make the underside of the eye, with a little curl at the inside corner of the eye fitting against the side of the ear.

87 Curl the wire tails at the base of the eye to fit under the eye and at the back of the blanket to fit over the rump. Check the fit against the elephant and check the eye bead fits into place. Hammer the loops at the bottom of the blanket, and the base of the eye and the back of the blanket. Do not hammer the rest of this shape. Reshape the hammered sections to fit as they will splay slightly with the hammering.

88 Weave the tusk. Take a short length of 30AWG (0.25mm) wire and weave along the little tusk with a basket weave (see page 24), making two wraps on either side before each pass. Cut the 30AWG (0.25mm) wire near the tip of the tusk and tuck in the end. Wrap up and along the base of the tusk and cut and tuck in the wire.

89 Attach the blanket detail. Take 80in (2m) of 30AWG (0.25mm) wire. Wrap at the midsection of the 30AWG (0.25mm) wire around the tip of the blanket triangle and

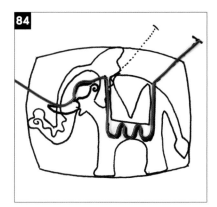

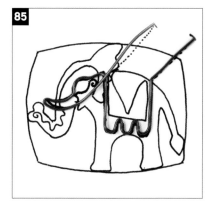

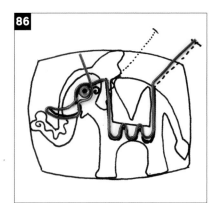

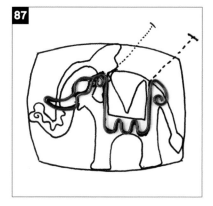

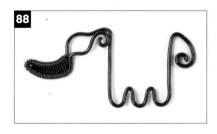

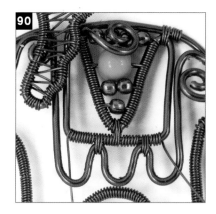

the bottom edge of the blanket frame three times, and then four times around the blanket frame only on either side.

90 Place the blanket loop detail into position. Make binding wraps also to the bases of the central loop on either side with three wraps. Wrap along the base of the blanket frame only until you reach the bottom corners of this shape.

  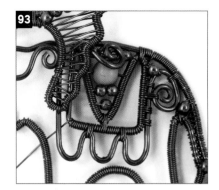 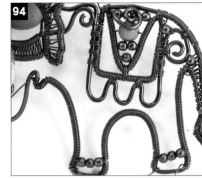

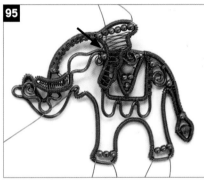 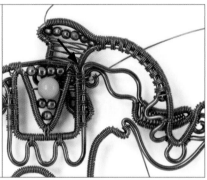 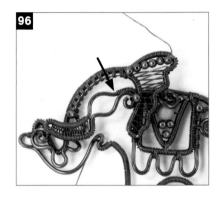

91 Weave up the rear side of the blanket using the same weave as in Step 74 for the elephant's forehead. (three across both and three around the inside blanket frame). Bind also to the rump curl where it touches against the blanket frame (see arrow in image).

92 Stop just before you reach the top of the blanket and wrap on a 2mm bead into the slightly widening space between the blanket and rump curl. Then wrap up to the rump frame (see arrow in image).

93 When you reach the rump curl, perform the same weave used for the blanket side. Cut and tuck in the wire end when you reach the wrap from the tail from Step 64.

94 Weave up the left (front side) of the blanket with the same weave as in Step 93. Stop when you reach the top of the elephant's back.

95 Pull the ear into place over the elephant. If it helps, make a temporary binding wrap of the tusk to the frame. Bind the end of the 30AWG (0.25mm) wire from the blanket section in Step 93 around the eye curl (see arrow in images) at the back of the head. Use three binding wraps and pull the 30AWG (0.25mm) wire firmly to pull the wire in between the ear wraps and hide them so they are invisible. I added a 2mm bead into the wraps at this point. At this stage, you can change the elephant's expression, character, and appearance with different placements of the ear,

tusk, and eye. You can also create a 3D appearance to the ear by bending it upward or forward a little.

96 Cut the 30AWG (0.25mm) wire at the base of the eye and tuck in the end at the back (see arrow in image).

97 Remove the scrap wire binding the tusk as you need a bit of mobility for the next stage with and around the eye. With a new 24in (60cm) length of 30AWG (0.25mm) wire, wrap around the back corner of the eye at the midsection of the eye. Wrap each end along the top and bottom of the eye frame. Stop halfway along at the widest point of the eye frame ready to attach the eye bead.

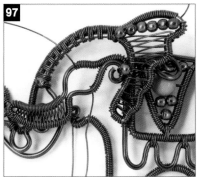

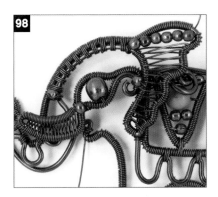

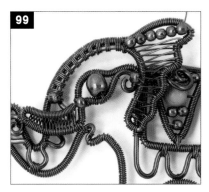

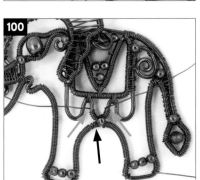

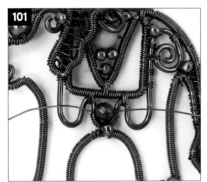

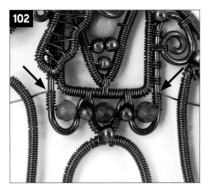

98 Attach a 4mm antique bronze bead with a criss-cross bead wrap attachment, then wrap each 30AWG (0.25mm) wire down to the corner of the eye. Cut and tuck one end of the wire in and wrap on a 2mm bead (if possible, thread the wire twice through the bead). Then cut and tuck in the other 30AWG (0.25mm) wire end.

99 Attach the tusk and wrap along the trunk. Take the upper 30AWG (0.25mm) wire end from Step 81 and bind the lower edge of the tusk into place over the top lip/base of the trunk with several binding wraps of the 30AWG (0.25mm) wire passed through the weaves of the tusk. Pull tight to ensure the binding wraps are hidden within the weave.

Wrap the 30AWG (0.25mm) wire along the trunk up to a level where it can be used to make a binding wrap to the cabochon frame.

100 With a 20in (50cm) length of 30AWG (0.25mm) wire, bind around the base of the middle blanket loop and the tummy of the elephant three to four times, adding in a 2mm bead with these wraps. Pull the 30AWG (0.25mm) wire firmly to click it into place between the wraps that are already there (see black arrow in image). Wrap either side of the middle blanket loop until you reach the level of the blue arrows in the image. This attachment will add strength to the whole elephant form and prevent it distorting with the pressure of holding in the cabochon.

101 Bind a 3mm faceted smoky quartz into the middle blanket loop space using a criss-cross wrap of the wire ends from Step 100 across the middle loop.

102 Add on a 2mm bead to either end of the 30AWG (0.25mm) wire and wrap to the side loops. Add on a further 3mm faceted smoky quartz to either side loop, then wrap the 30AWG (0.25mm) wire up either end of the side loops, passing them into the blanket space (see arrows in image). Wrap on a 2mm bead to either side. This will prevent the beads from slipping about in the loop spaces and add more detail.

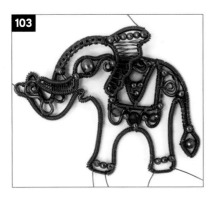

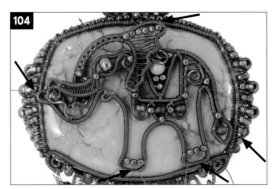

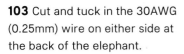

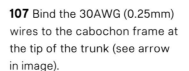

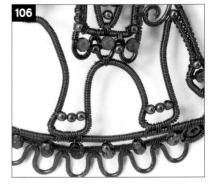

103 Cut and tuck in the 30AWG (0.25mm) wire on either side at the back of the elephant.

104 Attach the elephant to the frame. Place the elephant over the frame with the cabochon temporarily in place. There are four to five points of attachment using 30AWG (0.25mm) wire ends left from previous stages:
• base of the forefoot
• base of the hind foot
• leading edge/tip of the ear
• tip of the trunk
You might also be able to attach the tail to the setting (see arrows in image).

105 Remove the cabochon and start to bind the feet to the top of the plinth wire first. Bind with the longer of the two 30AWG (0.25mm) wires (you can use the other one if the one you are using breaks), using the same three-by-three weave (see page 27) as in Step 74 across the forehead. Use three wraps around the feet and plinth and three wraps around the feet along the base of the feet.

106 Cut and tuck in the 30AWG (0.25mm) wire ends when you reach the wraps created from the opposite 30AWG (0.25mm) wires.

107 Bind the 30AWG (0.25mm) wires to the cabochon frame at the tip of the trunk (see arrow in image).

108 Wrap around the tip of the trunk and cut and tuck in the 30AWG (0.25mm) wires really well here. If there is space, add a 2mm bead to the tip of the trunk with a little binding wrap. Bind the 30AWG (0.25mm) wire at the top of the ear with a few wraps to the cabochon frame where they touch. Cut and tuck in the 30AWG (0.25mm) wire at the back of the elephant (see red arrow in image).

109 In my setting I was able to bind the tail against the cabochon setting as well. I added in 30AWG (0.25mm) wire to do this, binding to the frame and tucking in the 30AWG (0.25mm) wire (see arrow in image).

110 Make the cabochon backing frame. Place the stone into the setting and mold it to fit the stone with your fingers, as there may have been some distortion during the work to attach the elephant.

111 Turn the setting and stone over. Take a 16in (40cm) length of 18AWG (1mm) wire and make an oval shape

over the back of the cabochon with two spirals that touch each other. You don't have to make the shape symmetrical but you can if you want to. Hammer the shape to slightly flatten it and also work harden the shape.

112 Take 80in (2m) of 30AWG (0.25mm) wire. Wrap at the midsection of the 30AWG (0.25mm) wire along the midline bottom of the heart shape for ⁵/₁₆in (8mm) with equal lengths of 30AWG (0.25mm) wire ready for wrapping on either side. This wire is for wrapping to the loop section, which has been wrapped with 30AWG (0.25mm) wire so it blends in more easily. Take another 80in (2m) length of 26AWG (0.4mm) wire. Wrap using the midsection of the 26AWG (0.4mm) wire around the midsection of the oval a few times to join the top of the heart together. Pass both

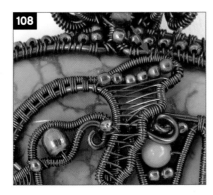

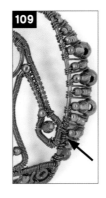

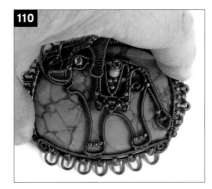

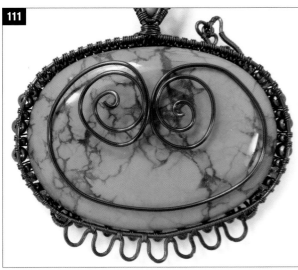

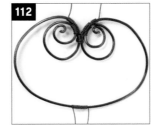

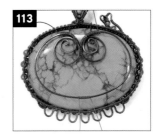

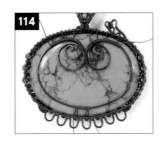

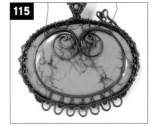

wires along each side of the top of the oval, wrapping along each side for ⁵⁄₁₆in (8mm) ready to bind to the main cabochon frame. The 26AWG (0.4mm) wire is for wrapping to the sides and top of the cabochon frame where 26AWG (0.4mm) wire has been used for wrapping already.

113 Now attach the cabochon backing frame to the rest of the frame to secure the cabochon into the setting. You can work without the cabochon in place for this step but I have put it in so you can see the connections more easily in the photo. First attach the backing frame to the top of the cabochon setting by binding the 26AWG (0.4mm) wires at the top of the

backing frame across to the top of the cabochon frame. Wrap around the frame twice and return the 26AWG (0.4mm) wires back to the backing frame, ready to wrap along the backing frame. Make sure there is an equal length to each binding wrap on either side—about ³⁄₈in (10mm) from frame to frame at this point.

114 Now work on this step with the cabochon in place inside the frame. Wrap the lower 30AWG (0.25mm) wires from the base of the oval across to the bottom of the cabochon at points near where the 3mm smoky quartz are bound into place, about the midline of each loop, to start to fix the cabochon

into position. This attachment should be virtually invisible from the front. Pull this fixing tightly to draw the backing frame and the cabochon frame together.

115 Work your way around the back of the cabochon frame, wrapping along it with the 30AWG (0.25mm) wire on either side. Work along the bottom first, as the 30AWG (0.25mm) wire may snap if not enough connecting points are in place and if too much tension is placed on them by the 26AWG (0.4mm) wrappings around the rest of the cabochon. Stop when you reach the end of the plinth section and cut and tuck in the 30AWG (0.25mm) wire ends.

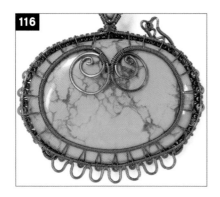

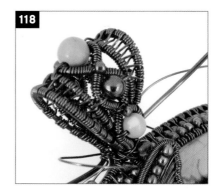

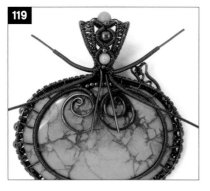

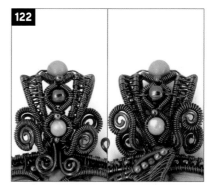

116 Using the same methods as in Step 114, use the 26AWG (0.4mm) wires at the top of the pendant back to bind around the pendant frame to the backing frame. When the 26AWG (0.4mm) wires at the top and sides of the backing frame meet the 30AWG (0.25mm) wires at the lower sides of the frame, cut the 26AWG (0.4mm) wires and tuck in the ends, smoothing them around the backing frame wires. The cabochon is now fixed into place.

Tip

Use your pliers to grab the weaving wire ends if your fingers cannot get into the gaps.

117 Bend and form the bale and wrap and shape the bale end wires. Bend the two outer bale wires outward and the inner bale wires downward. Take a 5mm-diameter mandrel or pen and use

the pressure from your fingers around the mandrel to gently bend the woven section of bale on either side into a bale shape (teardrop-shaped if seen from the side). Bend the woven section forward a little at the base (front) then around and downward. Press the end of the woven section against the base of the front of the bale.

118 Use some of the 26AWG (0.4mm) wires left over from weaving the bale in Step 11 to bind the front to the back of the bale with a few wraps on either side. Try to poke the 26AWG (0.4mm) wire ends through small spaces in as concealed a place as possible. Do not cut the 26AWG (0.4mm) wire ends yet.

119 There are six 18AWG (1mm) bale wires and four 26AWG (0.4mm) wire ends left from the weaving

steps. Trim the outer and middle bale wires to $1^{13}/_{16}$in (4.5cm) and the inner two bale wires to 1in (25mm). Wrap one 26AWG (0.4mm) wire along each of the longer bale ends. Trim the 26AWG (0.4mm) wires, leaving $5/_8$in (15mm) of bare wire at the ends of the wires.

120 Curl the bale wires (see page 27).

121 Use your fingers (rather than pliers) to manipulate any wrapped sections of bale end wire.

122 Press the outer bale wires over the front of the bale as shown—the middle bale wire at the back and sides of the bale and the inner bale wires over the back of the pendant. The images show the back and the front respectively.

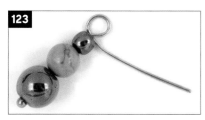

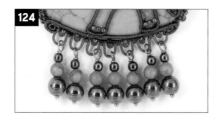

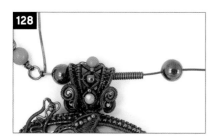

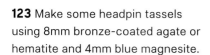

123 Make some headpin tassels using 8mm bronze-coated agate or hematite and 4mm blue magnesite.

124 Add these to the loops at the base of the pendant using wrapped loop attachments. Your beautiful elephant pendant is finished.

125 Now make the necklace. I made a rosary link chain link necklace and clasps using the methods on pages 20–23.

126 Start to make the bale hanging section. Make a short length of Gizmo coil from 18AWG (1mm) wire coiled onto a 1–1.6mm-diameter mandrel (see page 29).

127 Cut the coil to the width of the bale you have made.

128 The bale hanging section is made from a long length of 18AWG (1mm) wire with a wrapped loop at one end; one side of the necklace is attached to this first wrapped loop. Thread on a 10mm round bead, then the length of Gizmo coil made in Step 126. Thread on the pendant to sit over the Gizmo coil. Push the beads and coils against the wrapped loop you have made, and thread on another 10mm round bead to trap the pendant in place onto the bale.

NOTE: Make sure you push everything firmly against the wrapped loop already made, ensuring there is no "play" or gaps between the beads and coils.

129 Make the second wrapped loop at the other end of the bale hanging section. If you are able to, make the wrapped loop in an opposite direction so the wire ends end up in mirror image. You can then make a lovely detail of the coils over the end bale section beads. Attach the rest of the necklace.

130 Your beautiful necklace is now finished and ready to wear.

Golden-eyed owl necklace

Here is a beautiful golden-eyed owl pendant with an amethyst cabochon, embellished with gold-coated hematite, amethyst, and metallic beads.

Templates

See page 296 for the templates for this design.

Materials

18AWG (1mm-diameter) antique bronze-coated copper round wire
(20AWG/0.8mm-diameter wire can be used in some components instead of 18AWG/1mm)
26AWG (0.4mm-diameter) round antique bronze-coated copper wire
30AWG (0.25mm-diameter) round antique bronze-coated copper wire
(Antique bronze, coated copper, bare copper, silver or gold-plated wire will also work)
2 x 6mm-diameter faceted golden or bronze-coated hematite
2 x 4mm-diameter bronze-colored/coated metal or hematite beads
2mm faceted amethyst beads
4mm round faceted or plain round amethyst beads
2mm round antique bronze-colored metal beads
1 x 22–25 x 15–16mm pear/teardrop-shaped gemstone or cabochon, no drill hole required (I used amethyst; labradorite would also look wonderful)

FOR THE NECKLACE
10mm bronze-coated hematite rounds

Tools

General tools (see page 10) plus:
Gizmo tool with a 1mm-diameter mandrel (or you can hand-wind directly onto 18AWG/1mm wire)

Dimensions of finished piece

Approx. 4 x 2in (10 x 5cm)

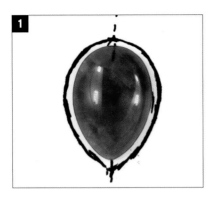

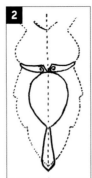

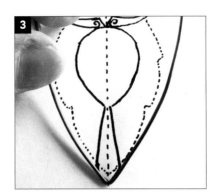

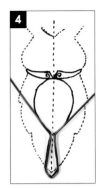

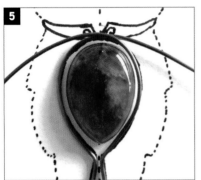

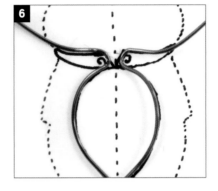

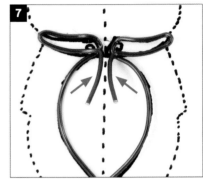

1 Draw around the pear-shaped cabochon, leaving a $^1/_{32}$in (1mm) gap. This gap is to allow for wire-wrapping space later. Draw a dotted vertical line down the midline of the outline shape so you have a line of symmetry to keep both sides of the owl in as perfect mirror image as possible.

2 Here I have drawn an outline of the basic owl shape to fit around the cabochon to use as a basis for planning the design. The dotted line marks the main outline frame and the solid line marks the cabochon frame, central tail feather, and chin feathers (see template at actual size on page 296).

3 Take a 20in (50cm) length of 18AWG (1mm) wire. Start to shape around the cabochon frame at the midpoint of the 18AWG (1mm)

wire using the diagram in Step 2 as a template. Form the central tail feather shape first at the midpoint of the wire, as shown.

4 Make little bends using the diagram as a guide to make a "tie" shape wider near the tip and tapering together toward where the tip of the cabochon setting will be.

5 Form the pear shape around the cabochon, again using the diagram as a guide, crossing the wires at the top of the pear. The image shows where I have placed the cabochon into the shape I am starting to form to ensure it fits well.

6 Sharply bend the wires out to each side where they cross using chain-nosed pliers. Take care to get this shape perfect for size around the cabochon so you obtain a better

fit when setting the cabochon later. Check the cabochon frame against the diagram with the cabochon in place to make sure it fits with a $^1/_{32}$in (1mm) gap; you may not be able to reshape it later if the fit is not perfect. Make a gentle bend first, check against the diagram, and either reshape or make the final bend after this check: if you make repeated sharp bends in the same piece of wire you risk overworking and fracturing it. Shape the wire ends with little bends using chain-nosed pliers to form the midline of the chin feathers $^1/_4$in (6mm) apart along the wire. Then gently curve the wire over the shape of the top edge of the chin feathers.

7 Make a sharp bend towards the midline on each side to form the tip of the chin feathers where they cross the dotted edge of the

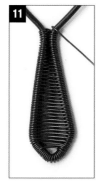

owl frame shape. Bend the wire downward at the midline again and trim the wire end to ⁵/₈in (15mm) long. Bend the midline wire tails upward and frontward slightly (see arrows).

Tip

Use chain-nosed pliers to help shape sharp bends by clamping either side of the bend. Use the tips of your chain-nosed pliers to make the bends sharp. Clamp either side of the outside of the bend to bring the bent wires even closer together.

8 Hammer the wire gently on the tail feathers and cabochon frame only to work-harden this section and not flatten it.

NOTE: Do not hammer the wires leading from the chin feathers as they have not been shaped yet. Do not hammer where the wires cross the midline or you will break them.

9 Weave along the midline tail feather. Take a 40in (1m) length of 30AWG (0.25mm) wire and attach it to the base of the tail feather with a figure-of-eight basket weave wrap (see page 24), leaving a 4in (10cm) tail for use later. Pull the base wires for the feather tightly together.

10 Start to weave along the base of the midline feather using the long end of 30AWG (0.25mm) wire. Use a standard figure-of-eight weave with two wraps of the wire around each frame side before each traverse to the opposite frame side wire (passing from front to back and back to front in

a figure-of-eight pattern). You will end up with a woven feather shape. Stop weaving about ³/₁₆in (5mm) from the tip of the feather.

11 Use the 30AWG (0.25mm) wire tail to finish the feather tip (see page 25). Cut and tuck in the wire end neatly at the tip.

12 Weave the chin feathers using the same weave technique, this time working from tip to midline (it is easier to weave from narrower into wider frame spaces). Leave a 4in (10cm) wire tail at the tip of the chin feather for attachment to the main frame later. Wrap around the feather tip.

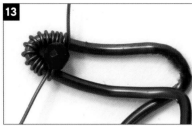

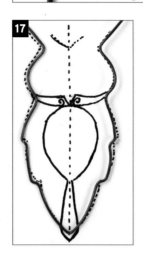

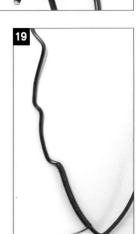

13 Add on a 2mm amethyst round bead in the first weave across the feather.

14 Weave towards the midline along the chin feather using the techniques from page 24. The lower edge of the feather may be slightly longer than the top edge: an extra wrap every so often around the lower edge, before the next weave traverse, will help the weave stay even and not lopsided. When you reach the midline, where the wire end for the feather base crosses the cabochon frame, wrap around these two wires to secure them together. Make another traversing weave to the top edge of the feather, then leave the 30AWG (0.25mm) wire end for the moment.

15 Weave the other chin feather in the same way in mirror image.

16 When you reach the midline, after wiring the end wire to the cabochon frame, bind the setting together with a few wraps across the midline (see blue arrow in image). Leave a wire tail at the same level on the other side (red arrows).

17 Plan and shape the head and body frame. Returning to the template from Step 2, take 32in (80cm) of 18AWG (1mm) wire and start to shape an owl body outline. Make the first bend at the tip of the tail, and make little bends in the wire to mark levels where layers of woven feathers will be attached later. Shape the wires upward and slightly inward with a gentle curve to form the owl's upper wing and shoulders. Make a bend at the level of the neck at the same level as the chin feathers, then shape the side of the owl's face. Curve the

side face wire, then bend the wire diagonally upward and outward. This final tail should be about 6in (15cm) long and will later form the bale and the owl's ears. Do this for both sides.

18 Hammer the owl shape only but not the bale wire tails, as these have not been formed or woven yet.

19 Attach the cabochon setting to the main owl frame. Take 20in (50cm) of 30AWG (0.25mm) wire and wrap along the lower tail section of the main owl frame on one side. Work from the first side notch down to a level where you can start to bind to the midline tail feather about $^3/_{16}$in (5mm) from the tail tip.

20 Use some scrap wire to bind the chin feathers to the owl frame with a few temporary wraps to hold this

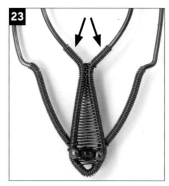

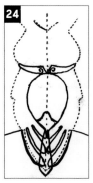

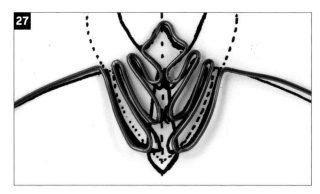

in place. This will be removed later (see red arrows in image). Bind the lower 30AWG (0.25mm) wire from the previous step to the side of the tail feather with a couple of wraps, wrapping carefully in between the weave already in place along the tail feather, making sure the tail feather lies over the owl frame (black arrow).

21 Thread on a 2mm antique bronze bead, a 3mm amethyst round bead, and another 2mm antique bronze bead to the 30AWG (0.25mm) wire and bind across to the other side of the tail frame.

22 Wrap up the other side of the tail to the same level as on the other side. Cut the 30AWG (0.25mm) wrapping wires on each side at this level. Cut the wire at the base of the owl.

23 Attach a new length of 30AWG (0.25mm) wire at the base of the midline feather and wrap up on either side for ⁵/₁₆in (8mm) (see arrows in image). Cut and tuck in the wire ends.

24 Make the lower row of tail feathers. This will also form part of the cabochon setting and the feet of the owl with the end wires. I have drawn an outline for the tail feather frame on the diagram from Step 2 for you to use as a template (see also page 296 for template).

25 Take 16in (40cm) of 18AWG (1mm) wire and make a "V" in the middle, squashing it slightly and making a small bend in its V-shape (see arrow in image).

26 Start to make the little rows of feathers on each side. Use the tips of your chain-nosed pliers, with

small careful movements to shape, using the template as a guide. After checking that each little bend is in the right place, clamp either side of the bend to help sharpen up the bend and keep the feathers lying closely together.

27 Hold the feather shapes in position as you shape the one below to make sure they end up long enough. Leave a 2in (5cm) wire tail on each side. Try to make the feathers as mirror image as possible and make sure they don't cover the beaded section at the tip of the midline feather. The feather lengths are: upper ³/₈in (10mm), middle ¹¹/₁₆in (17mm), and lower ⁷/₈in (22mm). These measurements are approximate, as each feather frame has different lengths for the upper and lower edges; just make sure they reach the midline, as in the diagram.

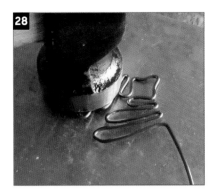

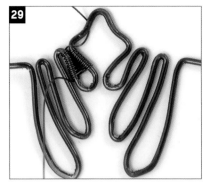

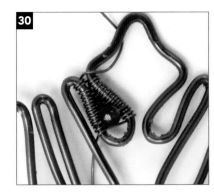

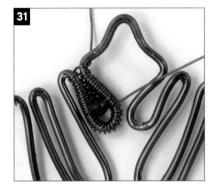

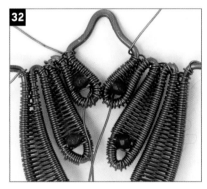

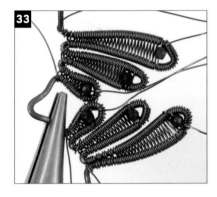

Tip

If you are making your own owl shape and not using the template, draw one half of the tail feather first. Using the dotted line should help you avoid oversizing the feathers across the midline. Make the wire shapes for the feathers on one side. Press this shape (flipped over) over the other blank side of the tail diagram over a rubber mat to make an impression. Draw over the impression. This is a way of creating a symmetrical mirror-image shape.

28 Hammer the V-shape to flatten it and hammer the feathers more gently only to work-harden; don't hammer the wire tails, as they have not been shaped yet.

29 Now it is time to weave along the tail feathers. You can use 30–26AWG (0.25–0.4mm) wire; I chose 30AWG (0.25mm). Start to weave along the base of the inside feather using 16in (40cm) of 30AWG (0.25mm) wire. Pull the base wires for the feather tightly together. Use a standard figure-of-eight weave with two wraps of the 26AWG (0.4mm) wire around each frame side before each traverse to the opposite frame side wire (passing from front to back and back to front in a figure-of-eight pattern). See also page 24. As the outside of each feather may be slightly longer than the inside, you may occasionally need to make three wraps around the outside edge of the feather compared to the inside so the weave stays parallel.

30 About ¹⁄₄in (6mm) from the tip, thread on a 2mm amethyst and incorporate it into the weave.

31 You will end up with a woven feather shape.

32 Stop weaving at the base of the feather. Wrap along the tip of the feather, then cut and tuck in the 30AWG (0.25mm) wire end at the tip. Use another length of 30AWG (0.25mm) wire and weave along the middle feather on one side. Repeat Steps 29–31 to weave down the outside feather and all the feathers on the other side of the tail. Leave 30AWG (0.25mm) wire tails at each end of the feather for attachment to the rest of the owl in later stages. However, cut the 30AWG (0.25mm) wire ends at the base of the middle feather. You should have five wire ends for attachment in later stages.

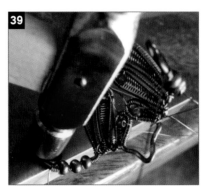

33 Make the first shape for the cabochon cover detail. Take chain-nosed pliers and bend the triangular shape in the middle of the lower tail feather shape forward and upward a little at the level of the base of the inner feather (so it will be easier to fit over the cabochon later).

34 Bend the side tail wires for the feather section upward so you can make the feet section.

35 Anchor a new section of 30AWG (0.25mm) wire at the base of the outer feather on one side with a few wraps across the base of the feather. Wrap along the 18AWG (1mm) tail wire for $^{3}/_{16}$in (4mm).

36 Thread on three 3mm antique bronze or antique copper metal beads (the drill hole is large enough to thread onto 18AWG/1mm wire) and wrap the 30AWG (0.25mm) wire around each bead in turn to trap them in place. Wrap along the 18AWG (1mm) wire for another $^{1}/_{8}$in (3mm).

37 You can trim the 30AWG (0.25mm) wire you added in Step 35 if it is shorter than the wire at the base of the inner feather; you will use only one of these wires at a later stage and it does not matter which you use, but the longer wire will be easier to work with. I cut the 30AWG (0.25mm) wire at the base of the inner feather on that side. Do the same for the other side.

38 Now curl the wires (see page 27).

39 Hammer these two little curls. I have a small-faced hammer that fits into the spaces without damaging the wrapping wire. If you have a larger hammer, unwrap the 30AWG (0.25mm) wire leading to the beads and hammer, then rewrap the wire again. Make sure you hammer the curl from the back, so any marks are hidden at the back of the curl (you are folding the curl over so the back becomes the front). Don't hammer wrapped wire or you will break the wrapping wire.

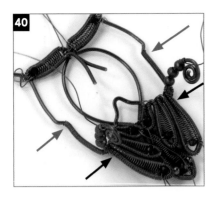

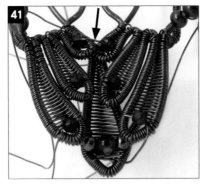

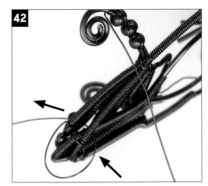

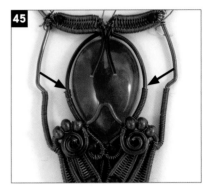

40 You will have a lot of 30AWG (0.25mm) wire ends emerging from your design. Use these to attach the feather section to the main owl frame. First wrap the outer upper feather base 30AWG (0.25mm) wires around the owl frame at the frame notch three times around the feather frame tail wire at the bend and the frame. See black arrows. Then wrap up along the owl frame, cutting the wire when you reach the next notch up. See red arrows. Perform this step for both sides of the owl.

41 Pull the feathers together slightly to see how they lie. The smallest inner feathers may be lying over each other. Cut the feather tip wire for the feather lying beneath the other, then bind using the feather tip wire for the overlying inner feather through the gap at the tip of the other feather, through the middle

feather weave, and back up through the gap at the tip of the overlying feather. This can be fiddly; try using chain-nosed pliers to pull the wire ends through small spaces (see arrow in image). Do this a couple more times for strength. Then cut and tuck in the 30AWG (0.25mm) wire in a hidden space at the back of the owl.

42 The lower two feathers also have 30AWG (0.25mm) wire ends at the tips. Use these to bind to the side of the midline feather three times (see arrows in image).

43 Press the side feathers down into place front to back before binding. Make sure the binding wraps don't overlap: Position your fingernail in front of previous wraps to help the new wrap slip into the right place, as shown.

44 Cut and tuck in the 30AWG (0.25mm) wire out of the way so it does not catch. Your owl should now resemble the image.

45 Fold the feet inward and backward to lie over the section over the front feathers, using a rubber bead mat to press on so you don't damage this section. Carefully move the curls under the row of 3mm antique copper beads that you threaded onto the feet wires in Step 36 and away from the 2mm amethyst at the bases of the innermost wing tip. Press them into place at flat as you can. Use the 30AWG (0.25mm) wire ends you have at the base of the inner wing tip to wrap around the claws just beyond the antique bronze beads and the V-shape for the feather section and the cabochon frame three times. Then wrap along the cabochon frame until you reach a

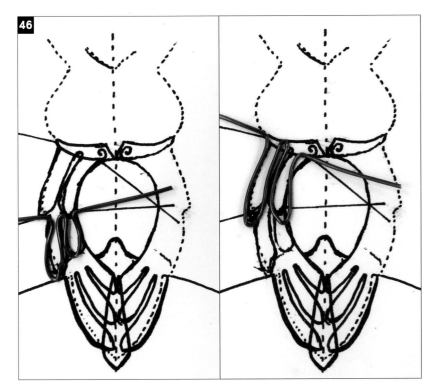

46

47

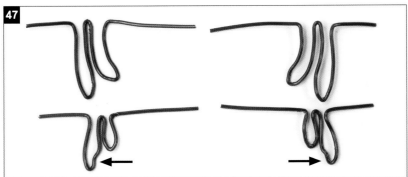

48

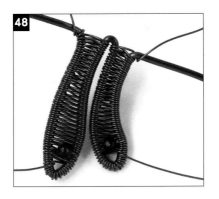

in length for the upper set and ⁵/₈ and ³/₈in (15 and 10mm) in length for the lower feather layer. The tail on the left of the feather component (which will form a curl at the side of the body later) is ⁵/₈in (15mm) long; the wire tail on the right is 1in (25mm) long. Take a 7in (18cm) length of 18AWG (1mm) wire and form the wing feather shapes using the template and the techniques from Step 25 when you formed the wing feathers.

47 Make a little notch in the outer lower feather that will fit around the feet beads later (see arrow in image). Make another set in mirror image. Use the same diagram for the other side but turn the wire over afterward to form the set in mirror image.

48 Weave the feathers. Using the same techniques as Steps 10–12, use 31in (80cm) of 30AWG (0.25mm) or 26AWG (0.4mm) wire to weave the feathers from base to tip using a two-by-two figure-of-eight basket weave. Leave an 8in (20cm) length of 30AWG (0.25mm) wire at the base and tip of each feather after weaving. About ³/₁₆in (5mm) from the tip of each feather you can add in a 2mm-diameter amethyst bead to add detail to the feather. After adding the bead, wrap around the end of the feather, leaving the 30AWG (0.25mm) wire tails near the tip of each feather.

level with the next notch up (see arrows in image). I have also placed the cabochon into the setting to make sure it fits well at this stage.

46 Make the wing feather frames using the template on page 296 as a guide to help you form the shapes. I made two layers of feathers on either side, although only one side is drawn here. The upper feather layer shapes are slightly larger than the lower layer. They are ⁷/₈ and ³/₄in (22 and 18mm)

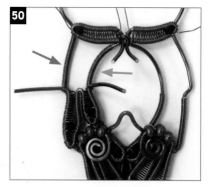

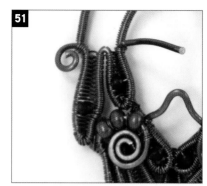

49 Attach the feathers to the body of the owl. Remove the scrap wire from the chin feather tips attached to the frame (see red arrow in image). Take the smaller pair of feathers and attach to the owl using the four 30AWG (0.25mm) wire ends left over from weaving the feathers. Bend the wire tails frontward. The inner top 30AWG (0.25mm) wire can be bound around the cabochon frame at the same level as the kink outward in the body side made in Step 17 with a couple of wraps around the top inner feather wire tail and the cabochon setting (blue arrow).

NOTE: The feathers need to be attached over/in front of the main owl frame so the side frame wires are hidden behind the feathers.

50 Wrap the 30AWG (0.25mm) wire up to 1/8in (3mm) below the level of the chin feather (see blue arrow in images 49 and 50) and cut and tuck in the wire end. The outer top 30AWG (0.25mm) wire can be bound around the outer upper wire tail and the owl frame a couple of times at the level of the frame wire kink outward on the owl body (green arrow in image 49).

Wrap the 30AWG (0.25mm) wire end up to the level of the chin feather at the bend for the neck and cut and tuck in the wire end (green arrow in image 50 above). The outer lower 30AWG (0.25mm) wire end can be bound around the frame and the tip of the lower outer wing feather a few times. Then cut and tuck in the wire end (purple arrow in image 49).

Find a spot to bind around either the feather or the owl frame once, then cut and tuck in the

wire ends neatly. The inner lower 30AWG (0.25mm) wire can be bound around any spot you can find to get the wire through around the base of the upper inner tail feather and cut and tuck in the wire end (red arrow in image 49).

51 Curl the upper outer wing feather frame wire tail (see page 27), making the curl as small as possible.

52 Bend this curl inward and downward. First use chain-nosed pliers, then use fingers to press the curl into position over the base of the outer lower wing feather.

Tip
Hold the feather in place as you press the curl to prevent distorting the frame and binding wraps.

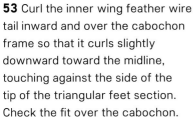

possible under the wing tip—and tuck it in neatly. This is fiddly; the wing needs to be pressed tightly onto the rest of the frame to stop it lifting up and to avoid a gap forming.

The lower inner 30AWG (0.25mm) wire needs to be wrapped twice around the inner upper wing tip and the base of the cabochon frame curl formed in Step 53. Then find a space to wrap in a hidden spot and tuck in the 30AWG (0.25mm) wire end (black arrow).

Tips

If there is a gap between the upper and lower wing feather layers, move the wing curl from Step 52 gently up into the space to fill it.

Use pliers to help direct the wire through smaller spaces.

56 Curl the upper outer wing feather tail down over the base of the chin feather (see red arrows in image). Do not curl the inner tail wire yet. Repeat Step 56 for the opposite side in mirror image with the other pair of upper wing feathers. Check the inner tail wires are the same length; trim to length if necessary (blue arrow).

53 Curl the inner wing feather wire tail inward and over the cabochon frame so that it curls slightly downward toward the midline, touching against the side of the tip of the triangular feet section. Check the fit over the cabochon.

54 Do this for the opposite side in mirror image with the other pair of smaller wing feathers.

55 Take the larger set of upper feathers and attach them to the body. As in Step 49, there are four 30AWG (0.25mm) attaching wires for one set of the upper feathers. The upper outer 30AWG (0.25mm) wire needs to be wrapped twice around the upper outer feather frame tail, the chin feather tip, the base of the owl's neck, and then three times around along the owl's face. Stop wrapping but do not cut the wire. The chin feather

tip wire end can also be wrapped around at this level as well. This is a temporary attachment; do not wrap too tightly here as you will unpick this when you attach the owl's face frame (see red arrow in image).

The other feather attachments are permanent and will not be unpicked. The upper inner 30AWG (0.25mm) wire needs to be wrapped twice around the inner upper feather frame tail then along the upper cabochon frame (where the cabochon frame wire has been left bare from the previous wraps along the cabochon frame) for a couple of wraps (blue arrow). Cut the wire end and tuck in.

The lower outer 30AWG (0.25mm) wire needs to be wrapped around the outer frame at the outer kink/bend in the frame wire (green arrow). Find a place to wrap the 30AWG (0.25mm) wire around a single frame—in a hidden spot if

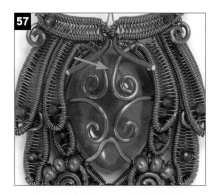

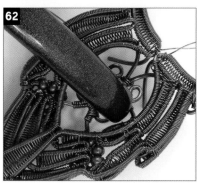

57 Curl the inner tail wires outward so the curl touches against the wire curls formed from the lower set of feathers. (See arrow in image.)

58 Check the fit over the cabochon.

59 Now bind the front of the cabochon setting together. Take 16in (40cm) of 26AWG (0.4mm) wire and bind around the tip of the triangular feet section for three to four wraps. Bind to the curl from the lower set of wings on either side for three wraps on either side, making sure they lie side by side and do not overlap. Make three further wraps along either side of the binding wraps to the other curl, wrapping along the triangle shape only. Cut and tuck in the 26AWG (0.4mm) wire ends at the back on either side.

60 Take another 16in (40cm) length of 26AWG (0.4mm) wire and bind twice around the top two curls over the cabochon (formed from the top wing sections), adding in a 2mm antique bronze metal seed bead with each binding wrap. The seed bead can sit in between the two curls of wire. Bring the two wire ends up either side ready to bind both curls on either side together.

61 Wrap with four to five binding wraps around both curls on each side (see black arrows in image) to join them together. Make sure they lie side by side with no overlap. Wrap along the side curl on either side for three wraps and cut and tuck in the 26AWG (0.4mm) wire ends at the back on either side.

62 Use the rubber handle end of any pliers to press (against a hard surface) the wire ends flat at the back of the setting to make it smooth.

63 Place the cabochon into the setting to check it fits. Shape the curved setting at the front by pressing into it with your fingers to help the cabochon fit into place. The image shows the back of the owl setting, curved, frontwards ready to fit around the stone and the finish of the wirework that will sit against the stone when it is set in later stages. Trim any 26AWG (0.4mm) wire ends, leaving the owl frame free of any residual wire ends at this stage. Bend the wire ends from the chin feathers into a curl over the front of the setting.

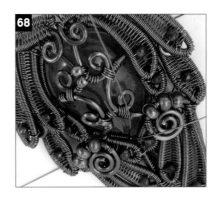

64 Make the backing frame for the cabochon. Take 3in (7.5cm) of 18AWG (1mm) wire and make a heart-shaped backing frame as for the Egyptian Cat Brooch (page 78). Check the shape fits over the cabochon back. Hammer the shape to slightly flatten it and also work harden the shape.

65 Now take 31in (80cm) of 30AWG (0.25mm) wire (or 26AWG/0.4mm wire if you are using that to make up the owl). Wrap at the midsection of the 30AWG (0.25mm) wire along the tip of the heart shape for a few wraps on either side of the tip, leaving equal lengths of 30AWG (0.25mm) wire ready for wrapping on either side. Take another 31in (80cm) length of 30AWG (0.25mm) wire and wrap using the midsection of the 26AWG (0.4mm) wire around the midsection of the heart a few times to join the top of the heart

together. Pass both wires along each side of the top of the heart, wrapping along each side for $^5/_{16}$in (8mm) ready to bind to the main owl frame.

66 Attach the backing frame to the top of the cabochon setting in the main owl frame. Bind the 30AWG (0.25mm) wires at the top of the backing frame across to the top of the cabochon frame, wrapping around the frame twice and returning the 30AWG (0.25mm) wires back to the backing frame, ready to wrap along the backing frame. (See arrows in image.)

67 Repeat this attachment for strength, then wrap along the backing frame for about $^1/_8$in (3mm) ready to make another attachment. Make sure there is an equal length to each binding wrap on either side of about $^1/_8$in (3mm) from frame to frame at this point. (See arrows.)

68 Place the cabochon into the frame. Wrap the lower 30AWG (0.25mm) wires from the tip of the heart across to the bottom of the cabochon to start to fix the cabochon into position. Thread the 30AWG (0.25mm) wires through just above the fixings for the feet shape and wrap back through the space between the gemstone and the cabochon frame (see red arrow).

NOTE: The red arrow doesn't show the wire in position. This attachment should be virtually invisible from the front.

69 This is fiddly; you will have to wiggle the 30AWG (0.25mm) wrapping wire through tiny spaces around the cabochon frame.

70 Pull the fixing tightly to draw the backing frame and the cabochon frame well together.

71 Work your way around the back of the cabochon frame, wrapping along it with the 30AWG (0.25mm) wire on either side. Wrap across to a few points along the owl frame to help secure the cabochon in place, pulling the wire firmly each time you traverse to the main frame and back. Try to conceal these fixings behind the feathers, wrapping only around the cabochon frame if you can. This might be difficult nearer the top of the heart frame. When the 30AWG (0.25mm) wires are at the bottom of the heart frame, meet the wires at the top of the frame, cut the wires and tuck in the ends, smoothing them around the backing frame wires. The cabochon is now fixed into place.

72 Make some of the face components (following the green lines on the template on page 296) that will fit into the head frame section of the main owl body you have assembled so far.

73 Take 16in (40cm) of 18AWG (1mm) wire and start to form a crescent shape in the middle using about $1^{13}/_{16}$in (4.5cm) of wire.

74 Using the diagram as a template, make a bend inward following the curve of the first curve you made to form a "lying down" moon shape toward the midline at either side. At the midline, bend both wire ends straight upward for about $^3/_8$in (10mm). Make the upper forehead frame using the diagram as a guide, leaving 2in (5cm) lengths of wire tails extending from the "forehead" at the midline. You can gently hammer this shape to work harden it, but do not hammer the wire tails extending from the forehead.

75 Take four 32in (80cm) lengths of 26AWG (0.4mm) wire and start to weave from tip to midline of each lobular shape. Leave a 6in (15cm) tail of wire at each end of the weave uncut for the moment. Use a simple figure of eight basket weave (see page 24) as for the feathers. As the lower edges of the moon/banana shapes are longer than the upper curve, use a weave ratio of two wraps around the upper edge to three wraps around the lower edge of the shape before each traverse. Make sure the 26AWG (0.4mm) wire ends at the midline in both moon shapes end up at the base. Leave a space at the lower edge of the upper frame shapes for attachment to the main owl frame.

76 Take the 26AWG (0.4mm) wire ends from the midline of the upper shape and thread a 4mm faceted amethyst and a 5mm bronze-coated hematite (gold-coated will also work) onto both wires.

77 Slide the beads into the midline space. Bind the 26AWG (0.4mm) wires across and around the 18AWG (1mm) wires projecting upward at the top of the shape to join the shape together at the top. Separate the top projecting wires a little, then wrap up the 18AWG (1mm) wires for $^3/_4$in (18mm) on either side. Cut and tuck in the 26AWG (0.4mm) wire ends neatly around the 18AWG (1mm) wire.

Tip

If your chosen beads will not allow two 26AWG (0.4mm) wires through it, you can cut the 26AWG (0.4mm) wire ends you were going to use. Add in a new length of 30AWG (0.25mm) wire to the bottom of the upper half-moon shape, add the beads in, and bind up the end wires using the 30AWG (0.25mm) wire instead.

78 Join the face frame to the rest of the owl body. There are five points of attachment: **(A)** the midline of the chin feathers/top of the cabochon setting; **(B)** and **(C)** either side of the chin feather tips; **(D)** and **(E)** either side of the top face frame. (See arrows in image.)

79 Take the attachment made for the upper feathers and chin tip feather in Step 20 and unpick them. You should have fixed this loosely; however, if the wire breaks, add new 30AWG (0.25mm) binding wire.

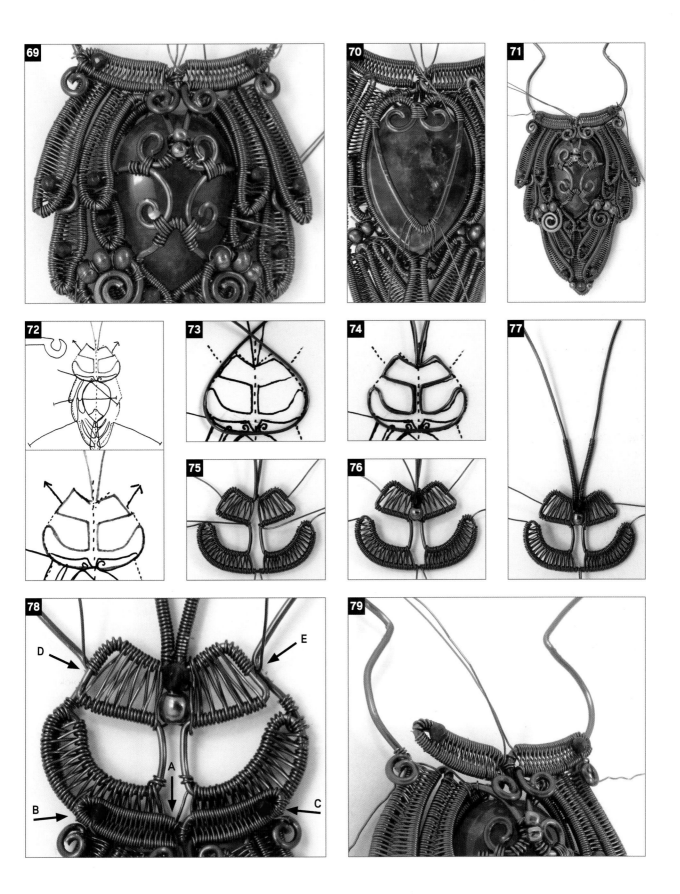

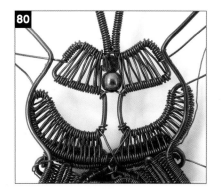

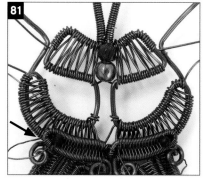

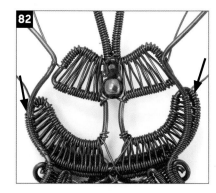

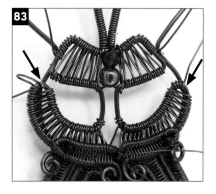

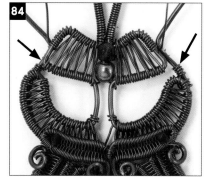

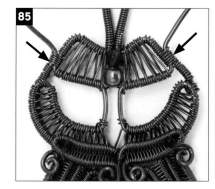

80 Bind the top feather attachment to the owl frame and bend the chin feather frontward slightly. Place the face frame section *behind* the chin feathers and line up the face and owl frame head wires. Take the two 26AWG (0.4mm) wires at the midline base of the face section and bind to the top of the cabochon section. Pass the 26AWG (0.4mm) wire ends that you were binding at the midline of the face section back under the chin feathers and back to the base of the face section, wrapping here. Then cut and tuck in the 26AWG (0.4mm) wires neatly. This is fiddly; try to conceal the wrap as much as you can. You might have to pass the 26AWG (0.4mm) wires to the midline of the face section to find an attachment point. I crossed the wires over to strengthen the attachment.

NOTE: This image shows the *back* of the owl.

81 Bind the 30AWG (0.25mm) wires from the tips of the chin feathers to the main owl frame and the side of the face frame (see arrow in image).

82 Wrap up the main owl frame until you reach a level where you will need to attach the next level of the face frame. Cut and tuck in the 30AWG (0.25mm) wire just below the level for the attachment (see arrows in image). Do this for both sides.

NOTE: This image shows the *back* of the owl.

83 Take the 26AWG (0.4mm) wires at either tip of the lower half-moon shape and bind to the side of the face frame wires on either side.

84 Wrap up base of the top shape of the face frame component and cut and tuck in the 26AWG (0.4mm) wire ends (see arrows in image). Make sure the main owl face frame lies *behind* the face frame component.

85 Bend the upper $\frac{1}{4}$in (6mm) of the main owl face frame inward toward the midline so it touches against the edges of the upper face frame shape. Bind these points together with the 26AWG (0.4mm) wires from the face frame shape a few times. See black arrows. Cut and tuck in the 26AWG (0.4mm) wires after a few wraps along the main owl frame below the face frame shape you have just attached. Reshape the bend for the bale if needed. This time, make sure the frame points lie side by side and not over each other.

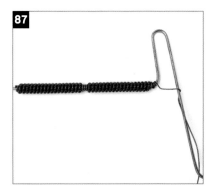

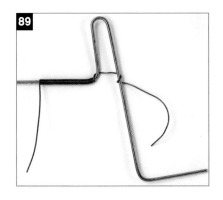

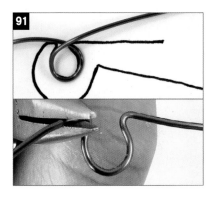

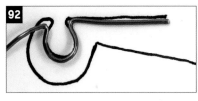

86 Make the eye component. Hand-wind two 2³/₄in (7cm) lengths of coiled wire made from 30AWG (0.25mm) wire coiled around a length of 20AWG (0.8mm) wire. A professional Gizmo with a 0.8mm-diameter mandrel can be used instead to make the coils. However, a 1mm-diameter mandrel (the smallest-diameter mandrel in a deluxe Gizmo) will be too large for these coils. This will take time, but is worth it if you are hand-winding and do not have a Gizmo mandrel small enough.

87 Work-harden and straighten a piece of 20AWG (0.8mm) wire. You can hand-wind or clamp in a professional Gizmo mandrel. Coil this coil again using a 1mm-diameter mandrel in a professional or deluxe Gizmo tool, using 2³/₄in (7cm) length 30AWG (0.25mm)

wire coils threaded onto 20AWG (0.8mm) wire as the core wire to make coiled Gizmo coils. I coiled two 2³/₄in (7cm) coils in sequence onto the same mandrels with some 20AWG (0.8mm) bare wire coils in between. Please refer to pages 29–30 for more Gizmo technique.

88 Cut the coils apart to gain two coiled coils of 30AWG (0.25mm) wire onto 20AWG (0.8mm) wire on a 1mm mandrel. These coiled coils need to be 1in (25mm) long.

89 Hand-coil more 26AWG (0.4mm) wire onto a 1mm Gizmo mandrel. If you don't have one, you can hand wind the 26AWG (0.4mm) wire onto some work hardened 1mm wire.

90 Cut the coil into ¹³/₁₆in (20mm) lengths, as shown.

91 Take a 4in (10cm) length of 18AWG (1mm) wire and wrap at the midsection of the 18AWG (1mm) wire loosely around a thin pencil, a 5–6mm-diameter knitting needle, or a Gizmo mandrel to obtain a circular shape. Using the eye component template on page 296 as a guide, size the circular shape of the eye first onto the template and then bend the wires sharply with chain-nosed pliers to form the edges of the shape.

92 Cut the wire on the right (top) to ⁷/₈in (22mm) long.

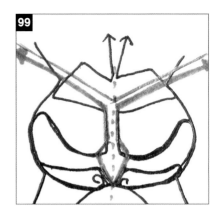

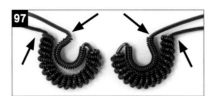

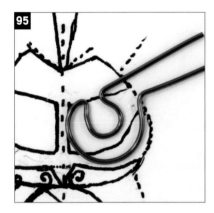

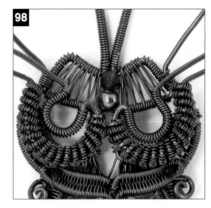

99 Make the beak component using the template on page 296 as a guide. I have drawn a beak shape in green on the template to help you size the beak relative to the face component.

93 Curve the longer end of wire to the left of the inner circular shape around the diagram to make an outer semicircular shape with a ³/₁₆in (5mm) gap between the two circular lines.

94 Bend the 18AWG (1mm) wire at the end of the outer semicircular shape and cut the wire tail to 1¹/₄in (3.2cm).

95 Repeat this step to make the other eye frame.

96 Thread the coiled coils from Steps 86–88 onto the outer semicircular shape and the short length of simple coil from Steps 89–90 onto the inner circular shape.

97 Both coils will need gentle handling, especially the simple coil, so as not to damage the delicate structure. Use gentle nudges with fingertips with a slight rotation to push the coils together if they start to separate. Grip the short wire tail with chain-nosed pliers to get more purchase and push the coil on with the other hand. Trim the coil if it is too long. Bend the bare wires at the outer edge of the upper and lower coils to trap the coils in place (see arrows in image).

98 The eye shapes should fit over the face component as shown. Put the eye components to one side for the moment.

100 Take 20in (50cm) of 18AWG (1mm) wire and bend it in the middle to form a V-shape. Clamp either side of the bend a few times with chain-nosed pliers to make the bend sharper. Shape the beak frame with chain-nosed pliers using the template on page 296 as a guide, with curving wire tails of 4in (10cm) on either side.

101 Take 40in (1m) of 26AWG (0.4mm) or 30AWG (0.25mm) wire (I used 30AWG/0.25mm) and weave from the tip to the widest point of the beak using a two-by-two basic basket weave (see page 24). Leave the weave wire tail at the base of the beak and cut the weave wire at the top of the beak.

102 Make a gentle curve in the beak (front to back) using pressure from your fingers. If you have nylon-coated pliers you can use these to curve the beak—ordinary pliers may damage the woven 26AWG (0.4mm)

MASTERING WIREWORK JEWELRY

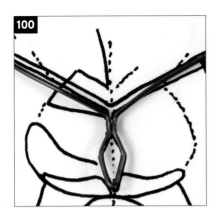

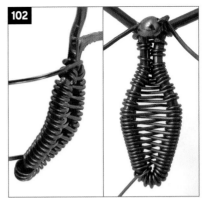

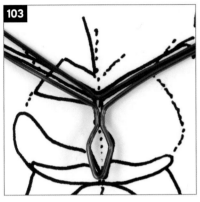

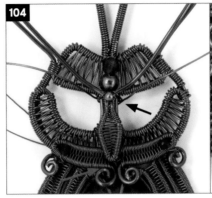

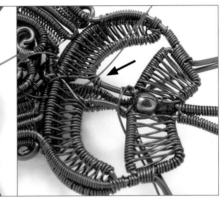

wires. Take a new 60in (1.5m) section of 26AWG (0.4mm) wire and wrap on a 2mm antique bronze bead to the top of the beak, leaving equal 26AWG (0.4mm) wire tails on either side. Put this piece a side for the moment.

103 Make the eyebrow component. Take 14in (35cm) of 18AWG (1mm) wire and bend in the middle with a little V to match the shape of the V at the top of the beak component. This image shows the eyebrow component placed above the beak component on the template. (See also the templates on page 296, where the eyebrow component is drawn in red.) The wire tails need to be about $6^5/_{16}$in (16cm) long.

104 Join the face together. Take the beak section from Step 103 and attach to the face section with binding wraps around the midline (see black arrow in the image above showing the front and back respectively). Leave the 26AWG (0.4mm) wire ends free. Bind the 30AWG (0.25mm) wire at the beak tip (left from Step 103) either to the base of the lower moon shape, the top of the cabochon frame, or the chin feather (see red arrow in image). These attachments can be fiddly; use pliers to pull the wire ends through the little gaps. Cut and tuck in all the 30AWG (0.25mm) wire ends after attachment.

Tips

Curve the wire tip to help you feed it through the space at the back of the owl so you can grab it with your pliers.

Make sure the beak lies in front of the chin feathers and is centered nicely.

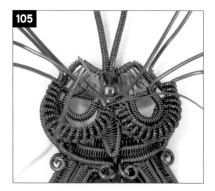

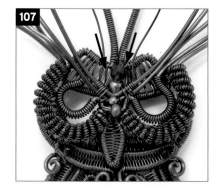

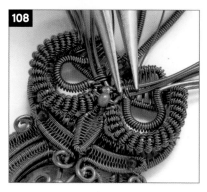

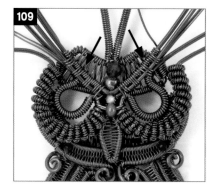

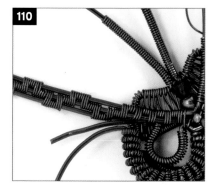

105 Take one eye frame and hold it close to the beak frame on one side. Wrap the 26AWG (0.4mm) wire around the inner upper eye space just above the Gizmo coil and the coiled coil. Attach to the midline of the face component (blue arrow) with a criss-cross bead wrap attachment (see page 26) and a 3mm antique bronze/copper bead.

106 Pull the attachment firmly into place, making sure the eye frames lie in front of the beak, not to the side of it. Pass each 26AWG (0.4mm) wire around the midline beak frame again. Pass the wire end up either side of the midline frame above the 3mm antique bronze bead. Wrap around the eye frame above the first attachment between the Gizmo coils (blue arrows). Pull firmly into place.

107 Take the eyebrow component from Step 103. Wrap one 26AWG (0.4mm) wire tail from Step 106 around one side of the eyebrow frame, the beak tail wire, and the upper inner eye frame corner. Then wrap twice around the brow and beak tail wire, and three times only around the brow wire. Do the same for the other side of the face. This part is fiddly; make sure all beads and frames are symmetrical and balanced (see arrows in image).

108 Push the wraps together with plier tips to space them neatly.

109 Wrap along the brow and beak tail wires on both sides of the face using three across both wires and three around the brow wire pattern only. Keep both wires parallel until you reach the outer edge of the inner eye circle where you can bind around this section as well with

three binding wraps (see arrows in image). Use pliers to neaten up wraps with a side-to-side push. Working from the level of the arrow in the image, make another two cycles of three wraps around the brow and beak tail wires and three wraps around the brow wire only to lock the eye attachment wrap into place.

NOTE: There are a lot of 18AWG (1mm) wire frame tails to organize over the face. The placement of wires from top to bottom are: brow wire, beak tail wire, bale wire (from main owl frame), short eye frame tail, and longer eye frame tail. These need to be the same on both sides so the face stays balanced. You should have reached the base of the bale by this point; if not, make a few more wraps along the brow wire.

MASTERING WIREWORK JEWELRY

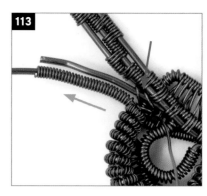

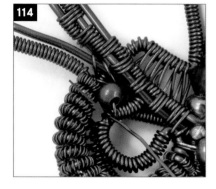

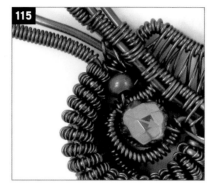

110 Now you will weave the bale with the long 26AWG (0.4mm) eyebrow weaving wire ends. If you have run out of 26AWG (0.4mm) wire, add some more to weave the bale. You will need 60in (1.5m) for each side. A zigzag pattern will be used to weave along the bale. You have three wires to weave along: upper, middle, and lower from the eyebrow, beak, and main owl frame. Do not weave around the eye tail wires; they will be dealt with later. First wrap the 26AWG (0.4mm) wire end around both upper and middle wires three times.

- Wrap around upper wire three times.
- Wrap around upper and middle wires three times.
- Wrap around middle wire three times.
- Wrap around middle and lower three times.

- Wrap around lower three times.
- Wrap around middle and lower three times.
- Wrap around middle three times. Repeat these steps until you have woven along 1⁹/₁₆in (4cm) of bale.

111 Place the weaves neatly. Press the wires together as you weave to make sure there are no big gaps. Squash the weaves and frame wires flat with gentle plier squeezes so as not to damage the 26AWG (0.4mm) wires; this neatens up the weave and makes sure the bale wires lie flat alongside each other. Make sure your weave wires do not overlap.

112 Repeat for the other side of the bale in mirror image.

113 Add beads to embellish the sides of the beak, eyes, brows and add detail to the ear feather tufts. Take 31in (80cm) of 26AWG (0.4mm) wire and wrap around the side of the ear tuft twice, leaving a long end to wrap over the face and a shorter end to wrap along the longer ear tail wire (see red arrow in image). Wrap along the long ear tail wire for ⁵/₈in (15mm), leaving a ⁵/₈in (15mm) length of bare wire. See the direction of the blue arrow. Cut and smooth down this wire end, leaving the longer 26AWG (0.4mm) wire tail for wrapping.

114 Thread on a 2mm antique bronze bead and wrap across to the eye inner pupil frame socket frame in the direction of the red arrow once, ready to add on the pupil bead.

115 Thread on a round of 6mm faceted gold- or bronze-coated agate or hematite beads, wrapping across to the other side of the eye inner pupil frame space in the direction of the blue arrow.

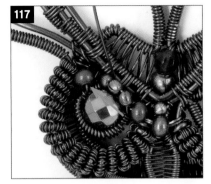

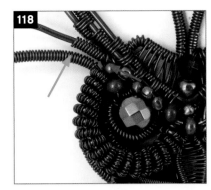

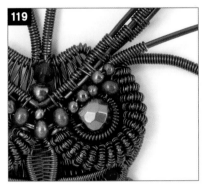

116 Thread on a 3mm antique copper/bronze bead across to a tiny space between the eyes next to the 2mm nose midline bead and pull firmly into place (see red arrow in image). Bring the 26AWG (0.4mm) wire up into the eye socket space under the 3mm bead added in the previous step.

117 Thread on three 2mm antique bronze beads. Wrap across to the top of the inner pupil frame space, pulling firmly to bring the little beads in place over the 6mm pupil bead in the direction of the blue arrow. Wrap once around the pupil socket on that side, bringing the 26AWG (0.4mm) wire upward again ready to add more beads.

Tip
You have a lot of fiddly spaces to poke 26AWG (0.4mm) wire through in between frame sections and wire weaves. Wiggle the wire end to push it through. If the wire end is frayed, cut it a little to obtain a clean end. Use pliers to grab the end of the wire if your fingers cannot grip it as it passes through spaces.

118 Thread on two more 2mm antique bronze beads in the direction of the red arrow. Wrap across to the upper short eye tail wire and wrap along it for ¼in (6mm). Cut and smooth down the 26AWG (0.4mm) wire end (see blue arrow).

119 Repeat Steps 113–118 in mirror image for the other side of the face.

120 Add a beak detail bead. Using 20in (50cm) of 26AWG (0.4mm) wire, attach a 4–5mm antique bronze bead to the upper center of the beak, wrapping the 26AWG (0.4mm) wire around the Gizmo coil adjacent to this area (see arrows in image).

121 The arrows in this image show the wrapping wires exiting from the back of the owl.

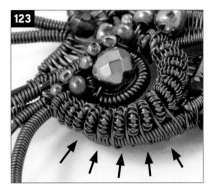

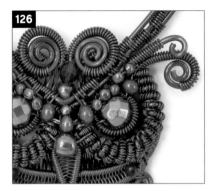

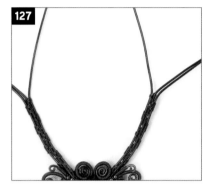

122 Pull the wire tight to hide it among the coil wraps. Cut and tuck in the wire at the back of the owl's face.

123 Take a short length of 26AWG (0.4mm) wire. Make a binding wrap around the outer edge of the eye (in between the coiled Gizmo coil coils) where it crosses the face frame a few times, then wrap around the face frame just above the outer upper wing feather curls. Carry on wrapping around the face frames and the gaps between the coils until you reach the wire curls at the base of the neck. Cut and tuck in the wire ends neatly. Do this for both sides. The arrows in the image show these binding wraps in between the Gizmo coils binding to the face frames.

Tip
Gripping the wire end with pliers helps you exert more pulling power and stops the wire slipping through your fingers.

NOTE: This binding step helps fix the eye components in position and stops them potentially flapping loose at the base and sides of the face.

124 Curl the wires at the top of the head (see page 27). Trim the wires to 1¹³/₁₆in (4.5cm). Hammer the unwrapped wire curls.

125 Press the curls into place at the top of the head. Use your fingers to curl the wire that has been wrapped with 26AWG (0.4mm) wire; using pliers risks damaging the wire.

126 Curl the eye wires at the side of the head using the techniques in the previous step.

Tip
Bend the lower eye wire tail slightly out of the way when working on the shorter upper eye wire tail.

127 Bend and form the bale wire ends. Bend the two outer bale wires outward and the inner bale wire downward.

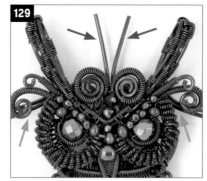

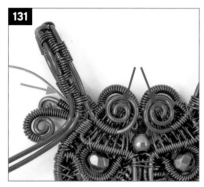

128 Take a 5mm-diameter mandrel or pen (or use your fingers) to gently bend the woven section of bale on either side into a bale shape (this is teardrop-shaped if seen from the side). Bend the woven section forward a little at the base (front), then around and downward. Press the end of the woven section against the base of the front of the bale.

NOTE: The bale should follow the line of the brow nicely at an angle; it should not point straight up from the head.

129 Curve the inner bale wire with your fingers at the back of the owl's head. Also see image 130 showing the inner bale wires at the back of the owl. Cut the end so about 1in (25mm) of wire tail projects above the edge of the head (see red arrows in image). Project the other two bale wires from the side of the head (blue arrows).

130 Add in a new length of 26AWG (0.4mm) wire to the end of the bale weave on one side (the black arrow in the image shows where the attachment is to be made). Bind the bale base together with a few wraps of the 26AWG (0.4mm) wire around at the inside edge of the bale at the level of the black arrow in and the inner bale wire. Bend the ear curl forward if it makes it easier to do this; press it back into place afterward. Wrap the short 26AWG (0.4mm) wire end along the inner shorter bale wire for $5/16$in (8mm) and cut and tuck in the 26AWG (0.4mm) wire around the bale wire (see red arrows).

NOTE: The outer bale wires will be woven later.

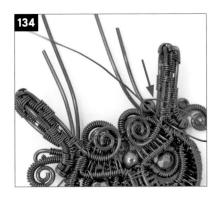

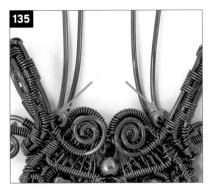

131 Finish with the longer 26AWG (0.4mm) wire end wrapping around the outer two bale wires ready to wrap along them in direction of the blue arrow. Curl the wire ends from the inner bale wires at the back of the head (see red arrows).

132 Weave along the remaining middle and outer bale wires using three across both and three around the outer (upper bale wire) only for ⁵/₈in (15mm) on either side in the direction of the red arrow. The image shows the back of the owl.

133 Pull and bend the woven sections from Step 132 around the base of the bale in the direction of the blue arrows so the edge of the woven section lies at the inner edge of the base of the bale.

134 Trim the bale wire ends to 1in (2.5cm) for the upper (originally outer) bale wires and 1³/₈in (3.5cm) for the middle bale wire ends. Thread a 4–5m bronze-coated hematite round onto the 26AWG (0.4mm) wire from Step 130 and bind the wire to the bale wire at the back of the head a few times (see red arrow). Cut and tuck in the wire end at the base of the bale.

135 Do this for both sides (see blue arrows in image).

136 Finish the face and bale details. Curl the bale wires. Your beautiful owl pendant is finished.

137 See pages 20–23 for details on how to make the necklace; it is very similar to the Indian Elephant Necklace (see page 106).

138 Make the bale hanging section to join the necklace onto. Take 8in (20cm) of 18AGW (1mm) wire and make a wrapped loop 3¹/₄in (8cm) from one end. Thread on one bead, a ³/₁₆in (5mm) length of Gizmo coil made with 20–18AWG (0.8mm–1mm) round wire on a 1.6mm mandrel the width of the bale on that side, then three to four 10mm beads. Thread the bale hanging wire through the

other side of the bale. Thread on another ³/₁₆in (5mm) length Gizmo coil and another bead. Make sure all the beads and coils are tight up against the other wrapped loops with no play in the beads. Make another wrapped loop at the other end. Leave ¹³/₁₆in (20mm) wire tails at either wrapped loop end and curl these tails over the end beads. Attach this section to the rest of the necklace.

Leaping dolphins necklace

This beautiful leaping dolphins necklace features amazonite, apatite, and hematite gemstones embellished with silver beads. Additional swirls and beads wired to the dolphin frames will help you work with different gemstone sizes and shapes.

Templates

See page 291 for the templates for this design.

Materials

18AWG (1mm-diameter) silver-plated round copper wire
20AWG (0.8mm-diameter) silver-plated round copper wire
26AWG (0.4mm-diameter) silver-plated round copper wire
4mm round hematite gemstones
2mm-diameter round apatite gemstones (I used a 2–4mm graduated apatite strand of round gemstones with plenty of size variation to choose from)
10 x 5–6mm fancy silver-plated copper round beads for necklace dangles
12 x 6mm blue quartz faceted rounds for necklace links and clasps
1 x 18mm x 13mm oval cabochon, no drill hole required (I used amazonite; lapis lazuli, sodalite, sea glass, or quartz will also work)
Ball-headed headpins

Tools

General tools (see page 10) plus:
Gizmo tool with 1.6mm, 3.2mm and 5mm-diameter mandrels

Dimensions of finished piece

Necklace length approx. 18in (45cm)
Each dolphin 3¼ x 1⅜in (8 x 3.5cm)

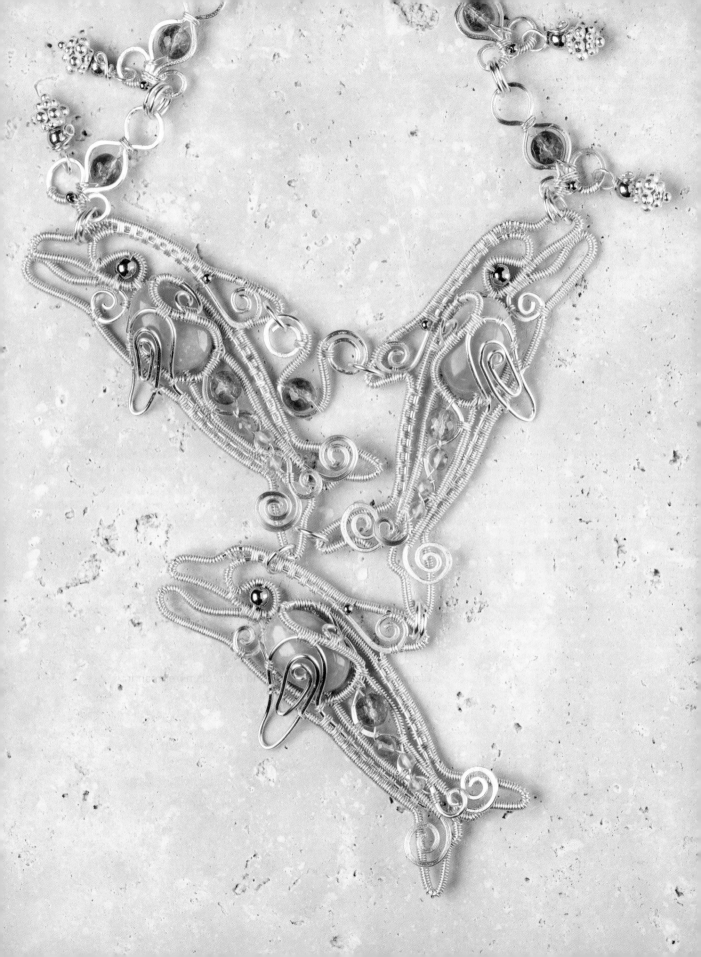

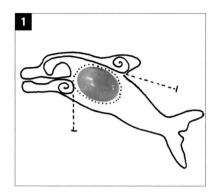

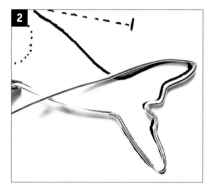

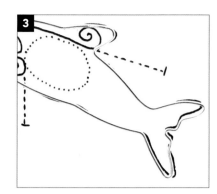

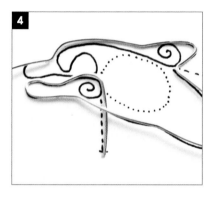

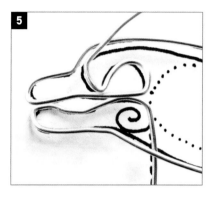

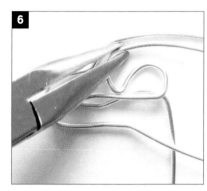

1 Here I have drawn an outline of a dolphin for you to use as a template, showing how the eye sections and lower jaw sections are formed from the same length of wire. I have also placed the cabochon I am using onto the template and drawn around it with a dotted line $^1/_{32}$in (1mm) larger than the stone. The dotted lines extending from the back (1in/25mm long) and lower jaw ($^3/_4$in/18mm long) of the dolphin are used to make wire tails ready to form body detail curls in later stages. If you want to make a larger or smaller dolphin, scan in this image, scale it up or down, then print it out to check whether it fits the stone you are using. It may take a few attempts to get the shape right. See also the template on page 291, where there is a scaled drawing for the same size cabochon for you to use as a guide.

2 Take a 20in (50cm) length of 18AWG (1mm) wire (or 20AWG/ 0.8mm if making a smaller dolphin brooch). Begin to form into a dolphin shape, starting with the tail and bending first at the central point of the wire.

3 Shape the wire, forming the sweep of the tail and upper/ dorsal fin shape carefully. I used chain-nosed pliers and my fingers to do this with small, gentle shaping movements. Use the template in Step 1 to lay the wire over as you work.

4 Start to form the dolphin's nose. I squashed the tip of the lower jaw with pliers to make a small point, shaped it slightly into a "happy" curve, then curved downward and trimmed the end of the wire to a length of approx. $^5/_8$in (16mm).

5 The upper jaw is slightly more bulbous and "bottle-nose" shaped. I have also started to form the eye using chain-nosed pliers to shape and squash the wire, especially at the corner of the eye.

6 Continue to shape the eye and curve the end of the wire following along the inside of the forehead.

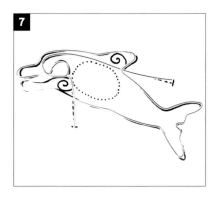

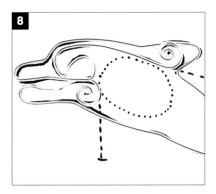

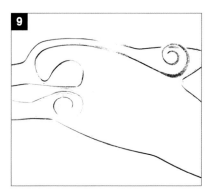

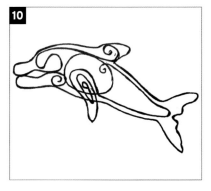

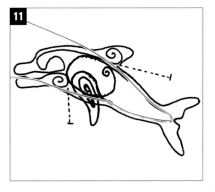

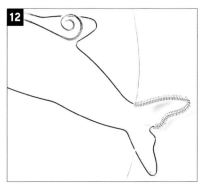

7 Cut the end of the wire to 1³/₁₆in (3cm) extending from the trailing edge of the dorsal fin. Use the template from Step 1 as a guide.

8 Make a little curl or spiral at each wire end of the main dolphin frame shape (see page 27). Press the spirals flat gently with flat-nosed pliers (so as not to mark the wire) and press the ends of the spiral flat so they don't make a scratchy end. Make sure they fit nicely into the spaces in the fin and jaw. The wire lengths given in Step 1 should give you the right length to make these curls; if the curls are too large, use little movements and squeezes of the spiral to make it smaller. If your dolphin is much larger or smaller and your wire lengths are longer or smaller, use the inward spiral technique (see page 28) to achieve a spiral shape that fits into the frame space.

9 Hammer the spirals using a small-faced hammer, if possible.

10 I have drawn onto the template from Step 1 an internal body frame, forming the lower fin and the outside frame for the cabochon. (Also see the template on page 291.)

11 Take another 12in (30cm) length of 18AWG (1mm) wire and start to form an internal body shape wire. Make a sharp-pointed angle in the center of the wire and make a V while shaping the sides of the V along the inside of the upper and lower tail section of the dolphin. Do not shape the wire further at this stage—do this after binding it to the main dolphin frame, when it is easier to get the wire frame pieces to fit together properly.

12 Take 80in (2m) of 26AWG (0.4mm) wire and wrap at the midsection of the 26AWG (0.4mm) wire around the top tail fin of the dolphin. Stop at two the points shown, ready to bind on the inner frame here.

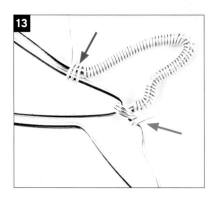

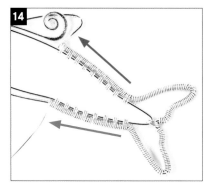

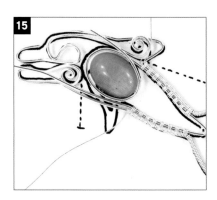

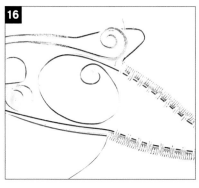

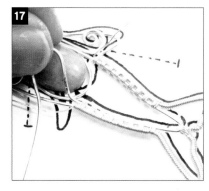

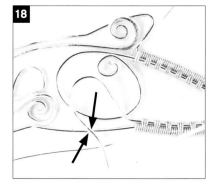

13 Bind the pointed tip of the internal body frame to the outer frame at the center of the tail with two to three wraps around both frames (depending upon what will fit without the wraps overlapping). Continue to tightly wrap the 26AWG (0.4mm) wire around the whole of the end of the tail (see green arrow in image). Bind three times around the back of the dolphin where it meets the tail and the internal frame where it touches against the outer frame at this point (see red arrow).

14 Using the ends of the 26AWG (0.4mm) wire, neatly wrap around both frame sections three times, keeping the wraps close together. Then wrap three times around the outer frame only. Repeat the pattern, working along the direction of the red arrow in the image, until you reach the base of the top fin.

Using the other end of the 26AWG (0.4mm) wrapping wire, wrap around the lower edge of the tail, then weave in the same way (three around outer only and three around both frames) following the direction of the green arrow in the image, up to the same level as on the top edge. Stop here for the moment.

Tip

Take care to press the wraps close together with your fingers or carefully with pliers (this has to be done carefully or you will break or damage the wire) and try not to overlap the wraps as this will look messy.

15 Place the dolphin over the template referred to in Step 10. Taking the upper of the internal body frame wires, shape a backing frame for the cabochon by curling the wire around the oval shape drawn,

overshooting it by ⁵⁄₈in (15mm) and cutting the wire end at this point. Check that the cabochon fits into the frame.

16 Curl the wire end from Step 15 into a little curl to start forming a backing setting for the cabochon.

17 Start to shape the lower/ventral fin, following the template from Step 10. Bend the lower inner frame wire end upward and kink upward so it will fit over the cabochon (it may help to have the cabochon in place while doing this).

18 Gradually shape the front edge of the fin with a little bend to mark where it crosses the cabochon frame (for future attachment; see arrows in image) to make the fin lie flat in its tip section.

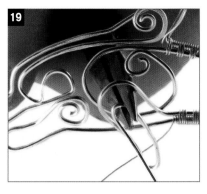

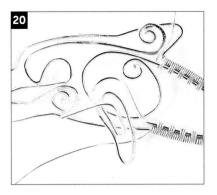

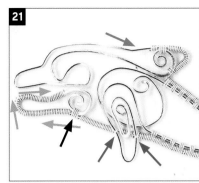

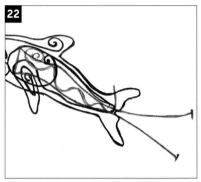

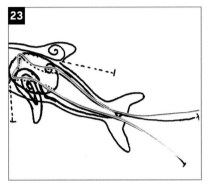

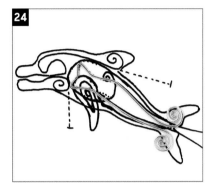

19 Form the fin tip, then gradually form the inner shape using the outer to inner spiral technique (see page 28), but with extra shaping with chain-nosed pliers to make the internal fin shapes.

20 Use the template from page 291 to help you form these shapes. Leave a ¹⁄₄in (6mm) wire tail.

21 Curl the tail to sit inside the fin shape. Wrap the 26AWG (0.4mm) wire from Step 14 (base of top fin) along the top fin binding across to the tail fin curl three times at the two points where it touches against the fin. Stop at the leading edge of the top fin (see green arrow in image). Trim and tuck in the 26AWG (0.4mm) wire end. Take the wire from Step 14 (back edge of the lower fin) and wrap along the lower fin binding to the trailing and leading edges (not the inner curls) of the

lower fin where it crosses the lower edge of the dolphin's abdomen (red arrows). Wrap along the lower jaw in the direction of the blue arrows in the image. Bind across to the lower jaw swirl as you pass it, at the level of the black arrow in the image, then along to the lower edge of the lower jaw and around it. Stop just before the two jaws would hinge together. Trim the 26AWG (0.4mm) wire.

22 Make a backing frame for the cabochon. I have drawn this on the template on page 291, referred to in Step 10 as a green line inside the circular line for the cabochon outline, extending along the tail and forming tail projections.

23 Make a wire shape from 18AWG (1mm) wire following the template.

24 This shape makes a backing frame for the cabochon and a tail panel frame. The wire ends should project 1³⁄₁₆in (3cm) from the end of the tail. Loosely curl the ends of the shape so the curls will fit inside either side of the tail flukes.

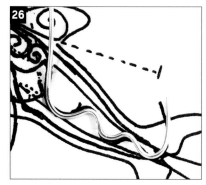

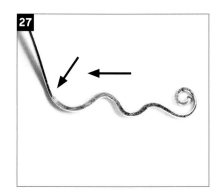

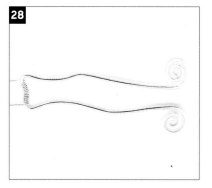

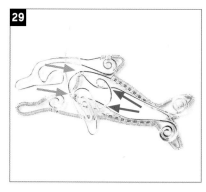

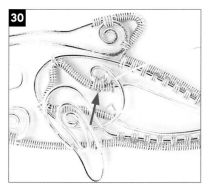

25 Hammer just the curled ends but not the rest of this shape.

26 Also in Step 22 I have drawn a wavy detail in red on the template to fit inside the tail panel. This panel will also form part of the cabochon covering. Take 6in (15cm) of 18AWG (1mm) wire and form the wavy detail following the template. Do not shape the curl over the cabochon yet; this will be done later.

27 Curl the end and hammer the whole of the length of the wavy shape, except the tail that will curl over the cabochon, up to the level of the arrow in the image.

28 Wrap 40in (1m) of 26AWG (0.4mm) wire around the top of the backing shape for the cabochon (at the midsection of the 26AWG/0.4mm wire). Stop just before you reach the corners of the shape.

29 Place the backing shape so that the top part backs against the back of the cabochon frame, the curly tails of the frame pass under the trailing edge of the cabochon frame (see red arrows in image), and the wire tails rest over the top surface of the tail. Bind the 26AWG (0.4mm) wires around the leading edge of the cabochon frame with two or three wraps at either corner (blue arrows), then continue to wrap along the cabochon backing frame.

30 Make sure the backing plate lies to the side of the first attachment (a little squeeze with pliers across the wrapping point can help to position the frames correctly). Reshape the frame a little and the internal curl of the cabochon so they don't cross over each other at this point. Wrap along the backing frame until you reach the other edge of the cabochon frame. Bind to the curl of the cabochon frame as well during this step (see red arrow in image).

31 Place the wavy frame inside the tail section of the backing frame and check that the gemstones you have chosen fit into the frame.

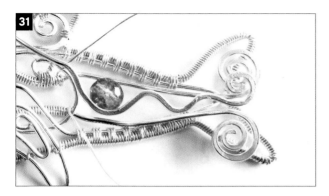

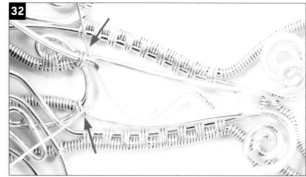

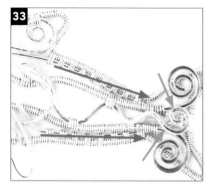

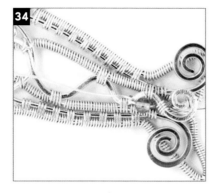

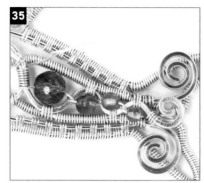

32 Bend the wire end of the wavy frame upward where it crosses the cabochon frame and the backing frame. Bind the 26AWG (0.4mm) wire around all these three pieces with two or three wraps. In the same step, bind the 26AWG (0.4mm) wire around both the lower backing frame wire where it crosses the cabochon frame with two or three wraps (see red arrows in image).

33 Wrap the 26AWG (0.4mm) wire along the lower and upper edges of the backing frame tail section, in the direction of the green arrows in the image, binding to the wavy section where it touches against the lower and upper backing frame wires. When you reach the end of the tail, wrap either side of the bare wires at the tip of the V-frame wrapped to the center of the tail (blue arrows). Bind to the sides of

the end of the wavy section. Cut and tuck in the 26AWG (0.4mm) wire ends after wrapping along the bare wires of the V-frame section. You may have to move the tail spirals a little to make sure you can wrap along the bare V wires. Press the spirals back into place.

34 Add gemstones into the tail section. Reshape the backing frame tail section and the wavy frame slightly to help the gemstones fit. Take 40in (1m) of 26AWG (0.4mm) wire and wrap one end near the end of the wavy tail section four times. Add a 2mm-diameter apatite bead onto the long end of the 26AWG (0.4mm) wire. Bind into the nearest wavy space, wrapping once around the other side of the space ready to add another bead into the next space. It is best to end up with the 26AWG (0.4mm) wire end uppermost.

35 Add beads in the same way to the other wavy spaces along the tail. Take time to select beads and gemstones that fit into the spaces nicely. I added another 2mm bead, then a 3–4mm bead, and finally a 6mm apatite. Wrap the largest bead to the cabochon frame. Do not cut the long 26AWG (0.4mm) wire end. Cut the short 26AWG (0.4mm) wire end, tucking it under the spiral lying over the midline of the tail. Wrap the 26AWG (0.4mm) wire along the cabochon frame and the wavy spiral wire end until you reach the point where it is already bound to the cabochon frame from Step 32.

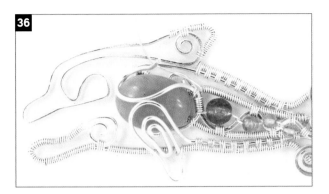

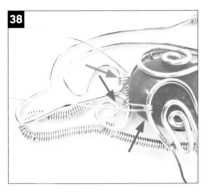

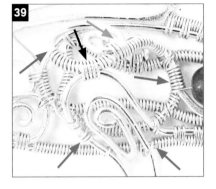

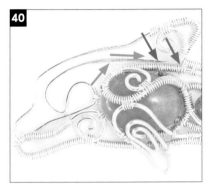

36 Place the cabochon onto the backing frame. Shape the top wire end from the wavy detail you made in Step 26 around and over the top of the cabochon, touching against the top of the fin to make a detailed enclosed cabochon setting. The cabochon will move around, so the shape of the top of the setting may require adjustment later. Just make sure there is a good entrapment of the stone, with no gaps around the setting that let the stone to fall out.

37 Take the stone out of the setting and curl the top wire end so it lies over the top side of the cabochon.

38 Add a fresh section of 26AWG (0.4mm) wire to the front of the cabochon setting. Wrap at the midsection of the 26AWG (0.4mm) wire two or three times (see blue arrow in image). Wrap across to the lower jaw curl with three binding wraps and to the back edge of the eye socket with one or two weaving wraps, adding a 2mm silver bead with each outward wrap in the direction of the red arrow in the image. Working with the stone in place, taking it out if you need to wrap around the fin then replacing it to check the fit every so often, weave from the cabochon frame setting up to the upper leading edge of the fin and wrap around here

three times. Pull fairly firmly (as firmly as you can without the stone slipping out of position) to bring the upper edge of the fin down against the stone (green arrow). Weave down to the cabochon setting again and wrap three times around the setting.

Tips

If the space is a little too large to bind across, add a bead into the traversing wrap. This will add detail to this area and help you cope with any problems fitting the frame together. In my case I was able to bind across without adding a bead, but it took a little tension and holding of the jaw in place as I did so.

Make sure at this stage the nose ends are lined up properly and that the top jaw is not overshooting the bottom jaw and vice versa.

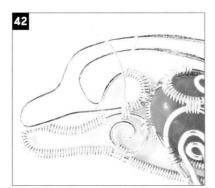

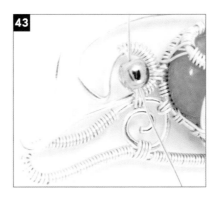

image, bind also to the little curl in the frame made in Step 16 (at the back; see red arrow in image). Wrap along the back inner frame rather than the cabochon setting for about ⅛in (3mm). Trim and tuck in the wire end when you reach the top back edge of the setting (green arrow).

41 Take a new 40in (1m) length of 26AWG (0.4mm) wire. Wrap around the base of the eye socket and the upper line of the lower jaw to bind them together with a 12in (30cm) length of wire leading toward the back of the eye and the longer length leading to the nose.

42 Wrap along the back of the eye, passing the 26AWG (0.4mm) wire under the attachment in Step 38. Stop at the top of the eye.

43 Find a bead to fit inside the eye socket to contrast with the body and tail color. I chose a 4mm-diameter silver-coated hematite, but lapis lazuli would also work. Choose a bead with a large drill hole that can fit two 26AWG (0.4mm) wires through it. Thread one 26AWG (0.4mm) wire from Step 42 through one side of the bead and the other wire end through the other side of the bead. Attach with a criss-cross bead wrap attachment, pulling the 26AWG (0.4mm) wires firmly to bring the bead into the eye socket.

39 Carry on weaving to and fro between the lower edge of the cabochon setting and the leading and trailing edge of the fin under the lower backing frame wire (see green arrows in image) until you reach the point of attachment of the gemstones from Step 35. Cut and tuck in the lower 26AWG (0.4mm) wire at the level of the red arrow in the image. This can be fiddly, as you have to pass the 26AWG (0.4mm) wire up and down through the fin as you weave along the cabochon setting only. As long as you weave down through the same space in the fin either side of the cabochon frame, you won't catch the wire on the fin frame.

At this stage, push the cabochon into the setting to make sure it fits into all the edges of the setting, then remove it and put to one side. Use the 26AWG (0.4mm) wire end left from attaching the gemstones to the tail section and wrap along the upper cabochon setting curl (created in Step 37). Bind first also to the inner curl of the upper spiral (blue arrow) and then to the upper edge of the fin three to four times (black arrow). Make sure the wraps lie side to side and don't overlap (a gentle crush of this binding wrap will help you achieve this). Wrap along the upper cabochon curl a few times, then cut and tuck in the wire at the level of the purple arrow in the image.

40 Replace the cabochon and start to wrap and bind along the upper edge of the cabochon setting, weaving and wrapping to the upper curl edge using basket weave with three wraps around each frame before each traverse (see page 24). As you work along the upper cabochon frame in the direction of the blue arrows in the

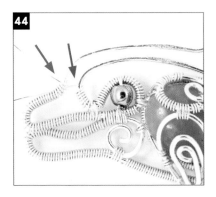

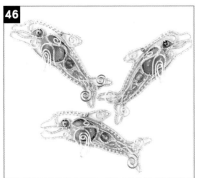

44 Wrap the 26AWG (0.4mm) wire (now the shorter length of wire) at the top of the eye socket along the top of the eye socket, finishing at the base of the forehead (see red arrow in image). Wrap the longer length of 26AWG (0.4mm) wire a few more times around the lower jaw and eye socket then along the upper jaw only, binding a couple of times to the leading edge of the eye socket then along and around the nose (green arrow).

45 Trim the shorter 26AWG (0.4mm) wire from Step 41. Using the longer 26AWG (0.4mm) wire from this step, perform a basket weave for ⁵/₁₆in (8mm) along the forehead (following the red arrow) and then a three-by-three weave (see page 26) until you reach the leading edge of the dorsal fin. Add in a 2mm hematite bead with a weaving wrap (green arrow). Wrap up to the edge of the wraps already in place on the leading edge of the dorsal fin, cut and tuck in the 26AWG (0.4mm) wire.

This dolphin can be used to make a brooch or a simple pendant, but in the following steps I describe how to make the larger feature necklace.

46 Repeat Steps 1–46 to make a second dolphin facing the same way as the first one you made. Then, using the template, flipped in mirror image, make another dolphin facing in the opposite direction.

47 I have drawn a plan for a clasp for you to use if you wish this (see image and page 291).

48 Take 8in (20cm) of 18AWG (1mm) wire and make a small spiral at one end.

49 Make a shepherd hook's shape by using bale-making pliers, looping round a mandrel, knitting needle, or pen, round-nosed pliers, or just using your fingers to shape the wire. Hammer the clasp only.

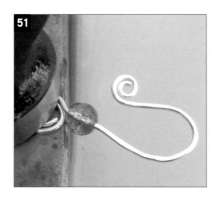

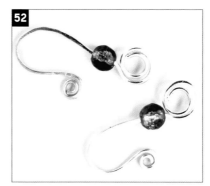

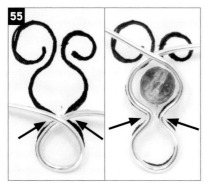

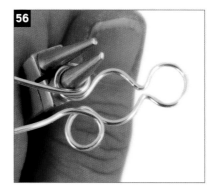

50 Thread on a 6mm bead to just beyond the hammered hook section. Leave a cut end of wire 1$^9/_{16}$in (4cm) long at the other side of the bead.

51 Curl the other end loosely.

52 Hammer the curl, taking care not to damage the bead by placing the curl only on the edge of the steel block.

53 Wrap a little 26AWG (0.4mm) wire around either side of the bead, trapping it in place. Wrap a little around the curl on the loop side and cut and tuck in the 26AWG (0.4mm) wire ends. Repeat to make another clasp exactly the same.

54 To make the necklace sides, make a necklace link like a little dolphin's eye. Draw around a 6mm gemstone.

55 Take 4$^3/_4$in (12cm) of 18AWG (1mm) wire. Following the template, form the first loop with the mid-segment of the wire with the wire ends crossing over each other. Use chain-nosed pliers to bend the 18AWG (1mm) wire at the waist section on either side (see black arrows in the images).

56 Make a semicircle shape either side of the waist section. Either use small movements of chain-nosed pliers, or use round-nosed pliers, a 5–6mm-diameter pen, or a Gizmo mandrel to form the circular shape. Follow the template and check the gemstone fits nicely within this space. Make a smaller loop at the top and a larger loop using round-nosed pliers.

57 The smaller loop can be made using a wrap of the wire three-quarters of the way along your round-nosed pliers. The larger loop can be wrapped around the base of one of the tips of your round-nosed pliers. The wire ends to the loops should be nearly closed with very little gap.

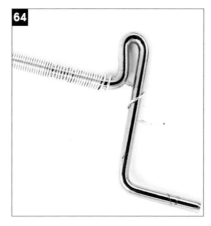

58 Hammer the shapes to flatten and work-harden them.

59 Take 12in (30cm) of 26AWG (0.4mm) wire. Wrap around the waist between the two large circular shapes at the midsection of the 26AWG (0.4mm) wire, bringing the 26AWG (0.4mm) wire ends up from behind into the middle circular space.

60 Thread a 6mm bead onto both 26AWG (0.4mm) wire ends and push it firmly into the middle circular space. Place one 26AWG (0.4mm) wire end in between the two end wire curls. Wrap along the upper smaller curl for 1/8in (3mm), then cut and tuck in the 026AWG (0.4mm) wire.

61 Wrap the other 26AWG (0.4mm) wire end twice around the lower loop and the middle circular space (see red arrow in image), then three times around the two end loops (green arrow).

62 Bind on a 2mm bead to the space between the two ends loops. Wrap the 26AWG (0.4mm) wire down along the larger loop for 1/8in (3mm), then cut and tuck in the 26AWG (0.4mm) wire neatly.

63 Attach a dangle to the larger loop using a ball headpin with a fancy bead and a 4mm silver bead with a wrapped loop. If you can, curl the end of the headpin over the silver bead to add detail. Make five right-handed links and five left-handed in mirror image.

64 Make 30 jumprings of 5.0 size ID and 7.0mm size ED with 18AWG (1mm) wire made on a 5mm-diameter Gizmo mandrel (see page 31). I cut these jumprings using flush cutter pliers so they fit together well when the rings are closed, but you can saw cut them instead.

NOTE: If you use 18AWG (1mm) wire, you will have to pair the rings up in each link so two rings are used to take the strain of holding the design together.

65 A little section to help the middle dolphins hang nicely is made from a little rounded U-shape of wire that will fit a 6mm bead inside with two equal looping spirals at either side; this is formed from two 1⁹/₁₆in (4cm) length wire ends.

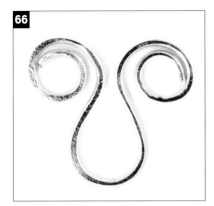

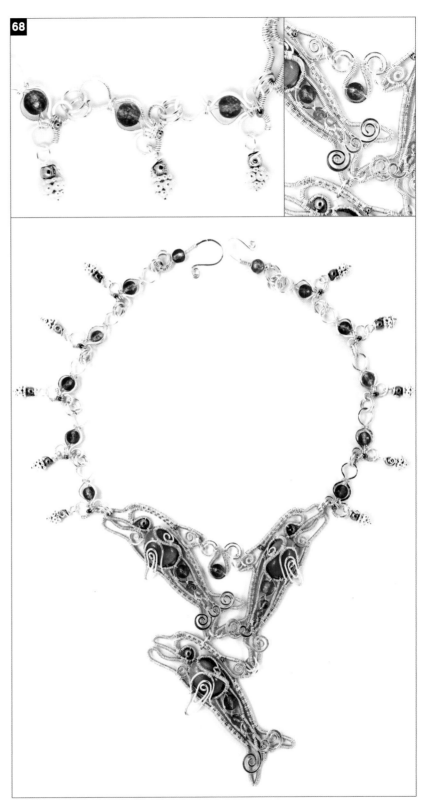

66 Hammer the little shape you make from spiral-curling the wire ends.

67 Take a section of 26AWG (0.4mm) wire and wrap on a 6mm bead into the loop. Wrap up each side for a short length, then trim and tuck in the 26AWG (0.4mm) wire ends.

68 Attach the sections together with chainmail double links at each point for strength. The dolphins may need some adjusting and balancing to make them hang correctly. Your beautiful leaping dolphins necklace is completed and ready to wear.

Seahorse pendant

Here is a little seahorse pendant, encrusted with gemstones including sodalite, lapis lazuli, apatite, hematite, and pearls in a design that could easily be adapted to make up as a brooch.

Templates
See page 295 for the template for this design.

Materials
18AWG (1mm-diameter) round silver or silver-colored copper wire
(20AWG/0.8mm-diameter wire can be used in some components instead of 18AWG/1mm wire)
26AWG (0.4mm-diameter) round silver or silver-colored copper wire
30AWG (0.25mm-diameter) round silver or silver-colored copper wire
(Copper, bare copper, or gold-plated wire will also work)
3mm and 4mm hematite round beads
3mm apatite round beads
1 x 6mm pearl
Puffy oval or rice apatite beads approx. 8 x 5mm
Beadsmith 8/0 3mm-diameter silver-plated copper beads
2mm-diameter silver color, silver-plated, or coated hematite or copper beads
1 x 25 x 18mm (could also be 20 x 15mm or 22 x 16mm, for example) oval-shaped gemstone or cabochon, no drill hole required
(I used lapis lazuli; amazonite would also work well)

Tools
General tools (see page 10) plus:
Gizmo tool with a 1mm-diameter mandrel (or you can hand-wind directly onto 18AWG/1mm wire)

Dimensions of finished piece
(These measurements are very approximate as the piece can vary considerably and end up at a different length): 3$\frac{1}{2}$–4$\frac{1}{4}$ x 2in (9–11 x 5cm)

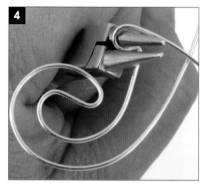

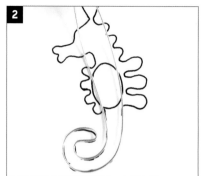

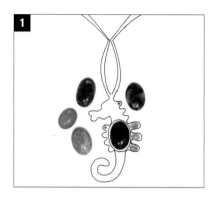

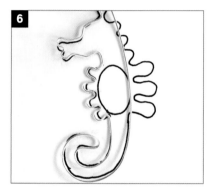

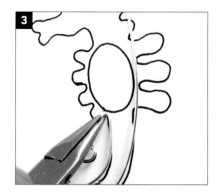

1 On page 295 there is a template to scale for you to shape the wire over. As can be seen in the image, above, I have drawn around the oval-shaped cabochon so you can see how a cabochon frame section will start to fit into the seahorse shape. I have placed gemstones inside the surface projections on the abdomen and back to check they fit inside the frame shapes. If your cabochon or the gemstones for embellishment in the projections around the seahorse are different, draw your own template using this one as a basis. Trace over difficult shapes like the head, tail, and body.

2 Take a 31in (78cm) length of 18AWG (1mm) wire and start to shape around the seahorse's tail, abdomen, back, and head. Start by shaping the tail and work along the front and back, repeatedly placing the wire frame on the template to check the shape.

3 Use your fingers and gentle plier shaping movements to form the curves along the back and neck, following the template. Chain-nosed pliers can be used to make sharp bends.

4 Round-nosed pliers can be used to make small round curves.

5 Fingers can be used to shape long gentle bends and to pull wire into shape before fine-tuning with pliers. Squeeze at the base of projections from side to side with chain-nosed pliers to tighten up the bends.

6 Shape the abdomen, lower jaw, mouth, and forehead on one side.

7 Shape the back and neck projections on the other side.

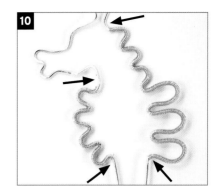

8 At the top of the head, make a bend upward and form a gentle curve to make a leaf-shaped bale frame on either side with a wire tail of 2in (5cm). I bound scrap wire onto the frame to hold the shape in place while photographing.

9 Gently hammer the seahorse frame on a rubber or steel block (to work-harden but not flatten the frame). Do not hammer the bale end wires; they require more shaping later.

10 Remove the scrap wire binding the frame. Use 40in (1m) of 30AWG (0.25mm) wire to wrap around the frame you have just made over the abdomen and 80in (2m) over the back. Stop at the levels marked by arrows in the image. Cut the 30AWG (0.25mm) wire ends and tuck them in, smoothing them around the frame.

11 Take 6–8in (15–20cm) of 18AWG (1mm) wire and make the inner bale frame using the template from Step 1 as a guide. Bend the wire in two at the center point of the wire. Use your fingers, then pliers to make a gentle curve in the wire to make a thinner leaf shape than the outer bale wires. Bend at the end of the bale shape, leaving wire tails 1¹³/₁₆in (4.5cm) long. The wire ends will not need to angle steeply outward as you want them to sit inside the larger main bale frame.

12 Start to weave the bale; you can use 30AWG (0.25mm), 28AWG (0.3mm), or 26AWG (0.4mm) wire. Using a scrap piece of 26AWG (0.4mm) wire, bind the top end wires of the bale loosely together so they don't overlap each other but lie side by side with the smaller leaf-shaped bale section ends lying inside the main bale. This temporary fixing will help keep the bale wires in place as you weave (see black arrow in image). Take 40–60in (1–1.5m) of 26AWG (0.4mm) wire. Wrap near one end of the 26AWG (0.4mm) wire a few times around one side of the base of the outer bale section. Wrap across to the other side of the main bale frame, wrapping around it several times (see red arrow). Wrap to, and around, both the opposite side of the small bale section and the same side of the base of the main bale frame a few times. Wrap to the other side bale wires and repeat the two wraps around them (see green arrow).

NOTE: Do not cut the short wire end; you will need it for wrapping along the bale end wires later.

   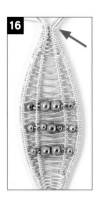 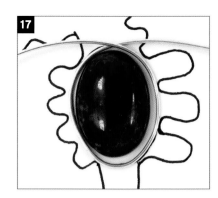

13 Repeat this weave a few times until there is space to weave between the two outer frame wires and the inner frame wires as well at about the level shown in the image. Start to form a basket weave up the bale using the long end of the 26AWG (0.4mm) wire. To do this, you need to wrap to the opposite face (front or back) of the adjacent bale wire, from the side you are wrapping from. Wrap exactly once around that wire then pass the wire along to the opposite face of the next wire.

NOTE: If the wire coming from the outer bale wire is from the front of the wire, pass the 26AWG (0.4mm) wire across the back of the adjacent inner bale wire. Wrap the 26AWG (0.4mm) wire around in a 180-degree loop with the wire passing from the back of the inner leaf frame wire and wrap across to the front of the other inner leaf bale frame wire.

14 Wrap once around and pass to the next frame wire in the same way until you get to the other side of the bale. Wrap three times around the outer bale frame wire, exiting at the front of the outer frame wire with the third wrap. Weave all the way back to the opposite side of the bale, weaving front to back with one wrap around each bale frame until you reach the side you started from, and three wraps around the outer side. Continue weaving in this way until you reach just over one-third of the way along the bale.

NOTE: When performing the basket weave back across to the other side of the leaf frame, instead of wrapping at the front on the first pass, on the return pass, the wrap will be around to the back. This creates the weave texture with alternating directions of wire adjacent to each other.

NOTE: Three wraps are used around the outer frame wires as the outer frame wires are a longer length/distance compared to the inner leaf frame wires. Also, the inner leaf frame wires are effectively wrapped across twice with each to-and-fro weave across. Thus, three wraps on either outer frame wire will help keep the weave balanced so that the outer wraps don't lag behind the inner weave wraps.

Tip

It can be difficult at first to keep the weave traverses close together in the small spaces at the tip of the leaf shape. A top-to-bottom press downward on the weave wires (gently so as not to distort the weaves) with chain-nosed pliers will help to compress the inner weaves more tightly together.

15 At this stage, you can add in a row of beads with 2mm beads in the outer spaces and two 3mm beads in the central space.

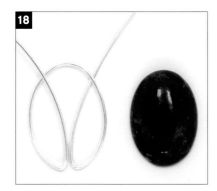

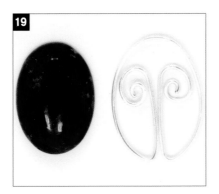

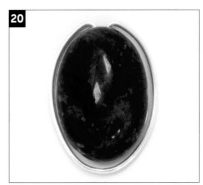

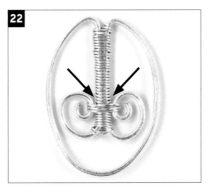

16 Choose your beads to fit into the gaps nicely. Continue basket weaving with another row of beads just beyond the widest point of the bale until you reach the end of the bale. As you weave along the last ³/₈in (10mm) of the bale, revert to the weave around both bale side wires used in Step 13 (see red arrow in image). You will also find it easier to remove the scrap wire at the end of the bale when performing the last weaves. Leave an end of 26AWG (0.4mm) wire about 6in (15cm) long to help secure the bale into shape later. Put this component to one side.

17 Make a backing frame for the cabochon. Take your cabochon, place it on a piece of plain paper and draw around it with a pen, leaving a ¹/₃₂in (1mm) gap around the cabochon. This gap allows for weaving and attachment of the backing plate to the rest of the frame later on. I have drawn this in Step 1; refer to this image to help you size it correctly. Take a 4³/₄in (12cm) length of 18AWG (1mm) wire and form it around the oval shape with the wires crossed at the top. Check the oval shape you have made against the template in Step 1.

18 Sharply bend the wires where they cross, using chain-nosed pliers so they bisect the circular shape. Trim the wire ends so they project ⁵/₈in (15mm) outside the edge of the circle.

19 Check the cabochon fits inside this shape with a ¹/₃₂in (1mm) gap around it. Curl the ends of the 18AWG (1mm) wire using round-nosed pliers so they loosely curl to fit inside the circular shape with the curl just touching the inner edge of the circle.

20 Check again that the cabochon fits inside this shape with a ¹/₃₂in (1mm) gap around it.

21 Gently hammer the shape using a flat jewelry hammer against a steel block to work-harden but not flatten it. Make sure the backing frame is nice and flat.

22 To strengthen the backing frame, take a length of 26AWG (0.4mm), or even 30–28AWG (0.25–0.3mm), wire and wrap along the midline wires of the shape. Bind to the inside edges of the loops to secure these in place (see arrows in image).

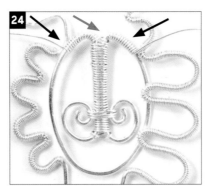

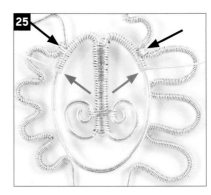

23 Make a little figure-of-eight (see page 24), weaving side to side at either end of the binding wraps made in Step 22. Cut the wire ends at either end, making sure the wire ends are uppermost so they will eventually be hidden as they face the back of the cabochon. Squash the binding wraps gently with pliers to flatten them to help keep the setting for the cabochon as flat as possible.

24 Take a 60in (1.5m) length of 26AWG (0.4mm) wire and attach it (at the midpoint of the 26AWG/0.4mm wire), see red arrow, across the top of the backing frame. Wrap along each side of the frame a short way until you reach a level where you could bind across to the main seahorse frame (see black arrows in image).

25 Bind around the backing frame and the seahorse frame at the points shown (see black arrows in image) three times. Wrap the 26AWG (0.4mm) wire along the backing frame until you reach a point midway along one of the projections from the front and back of the seahorse (red arrows).

26 For the front of the tummy, thread on a 4–5mm silver-coated hematite, agate, or metal bead. Pass the 26AWG (0.4mm) wire up and around the top edge of the projection and thread the wire end back through the 5mm silver bead in the opposite direction.

27 Carefully pull the excess 26AWG (0.4mm) wire into a loop with no tangles so it does not snag. Pull the 26AWG (0.4mm) wire end firmly so the bead is secured in place as the wire "bites" into the wire wraps already made along the projections in Step 11. Hold the bead in place with your fingers so it settles into the projection frame space nicely.

28 Use your pliers to help you pull the wire end if this helps.

NOTE: This action may strip coated wire if the bead hole is not quite large enough to allow two 26AWG (0.4mm) wires through it smoothly. You can reduce the wrapping wire to 30–28AWG (0.25–0.3mm) if this occurs, but this will lessen the strength of the attachment, so you may need to select lighter beads.

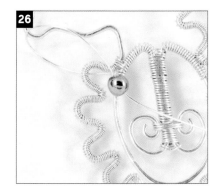

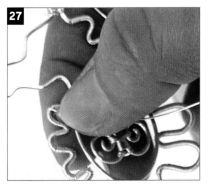

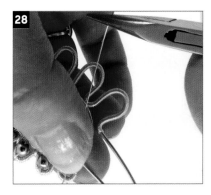

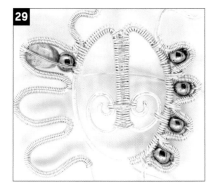

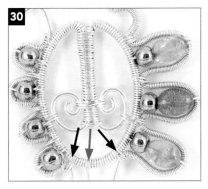

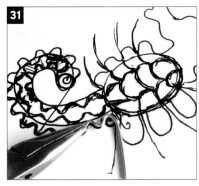

29 Wrap along the backing frame a little more until you reach the next attachment point for the projection. Wrap twice around this point and the backing frame, then wrap along the backing frame ready to attach the next silver bead. Complete the tummy and back in the same way as in Steps 26–29 except the three back projections can be filled with a bead and a teardrop, rice beads, small puffy ovals, rounds, etc. (anything that fills the spaces) threaded in the same way as in Step 27.

NOTE: There is an alternative option for bead attachment into the projections: The beads for the back projections are often more fiddly to thread through twice and if you have problems with this, you can make the return pass of 0.4mm (26AWG) wire *behind* the bead you threaded on the outward

pass of the wire. See Image 29, showing the *back* of the seahorse with the return pass of wrapping wire behind the beads. This method works better with opaque beads but can also help to stabilise puffy ovals in place so that they don't rotate in the setting. This can be a better attachment technique in this case, so I have used the alternative bead attachment method for the back projections.

Thus I have chosen in this case, to wrap the 0.4mm (26AWG) wire once around the end of the projection after threading on a 4–5mm bead and a 6–8mm x 4–5mm puffy oval and then passed the 0.4mm (26AWG) wire behind the gemstones back to the backing frame and continued wrapping.

30 When you reach an area where the backing frame curls touch against the sides of the backing frame, bind around these as well (see black arrows in image). This further strengthens the backing frame for the large cabochon. When you get to a level below the projections, wrap each 26AWG (0.4mm) wrapping wire along the base of the backing frame until they meet (at the level of the red arrow in the image), then cut them and tuck in the end around the backing frame. The image here shows the 26AWG (0.4mm) wire ends where they meet before cutting.

31 I have drawn two frame sections on the tail section for you to use as a template (see page 295). Take 12in (30cm) of 18AWG (1mm) wire and form the wiggly shape around the outside of the tail.

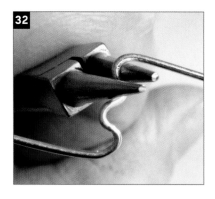

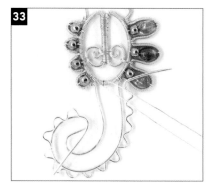

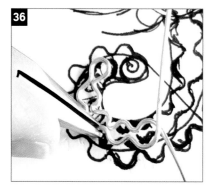

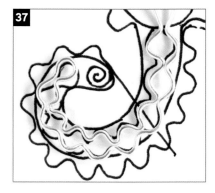

32 Use round-nosed pliers to form the little round wiggles.

33 Use chain-nosed pliers to form the sharper turns at the base of each projection. Squeeze the bases together side to side to bring them closer together. The wire ends need to be $^{13}/_{16}$in (20mm) at the top end and 1in (25mm) in length at the lower end. Use the diagram to help you form the shape, then hold over the seahorse frame that you have already made to check you have sized it correctly.

Tip
Form the wiggles at the same level on the round-nosed pliers to keep them looking evenly sized.

34 Take 31in (78cm) of 18AWG (1mm) wire and bend in the middle to form a small round circular shape with enough room to fit a 2mm bead inside.

35 Make a waist section and work up the tail making undulating shapes on each side, using the template as a guide.

36 The upper shapes in the tail need to be larger to fit 3mm beads inside. As the tail is curved, allow for a longer distance along the lower edge of the tail. The wire shapes need to be longer in between the circular shapes for the beads on the lower edge of the tail. This will need careful shaping and will take time. Practice using scrap wire to make the little shapes if necessary.

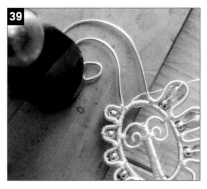

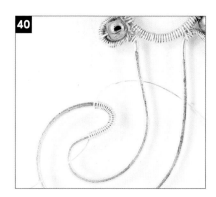

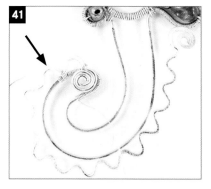

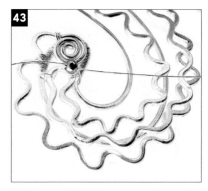

37 Tiny little shaping and reshaping movements with the tips of your chain-nosed pliers are required to make this little wiggly shape. Leave the wire ends for forming the body details and face details later. Check the fit against the diagram and also the seahorse frame at this stage.

Tip

You can select your own beads to fit inside the tail just as long as your internal tail frames are sized to fit them. If you feel the wire shape inside the tail is too advanced for you at the moment, you have an option to basket weave up the tail, adding in beads as you go as you did for the bail.

38 Now curl the wire ends for the shape made in Step 33 (see page 27).

39 Hammer onto a steel block, working on the back of the wavy tail shape, the seahorse tail, and the internal tail frame shape only.

40 Attach the tail in place. Use 26AWG (0.4mm) wire, but only if two 26AWG (0.4mm) wires can fit through the holes in the beads you are using (otherwise use 30AW/0.25mm wire). Take 80in (2m) of 30AWG (0.25mm) wire and wrap around the end of the tail, stopping at points where you can start to bind to the tail frames.

41 Take the outer tail frame and wrap at the point just behind the tail spiral three or four times (see arrow in image). Wrap along the inside and outside tail with either end of the 30AWG (0.25mm) wire until you are ready to bind to the inner tail frame.

42 Bind to the inner tail frame wrapping at the level shown, at the widest point of the end circular shape on the inner tail frame.

43 Thread a 2mm bead onto one 30AWG (0.25mm) wire end. Thread the other wire end through the other side of the bead and attach using a criss-cross attachment (see page 26).

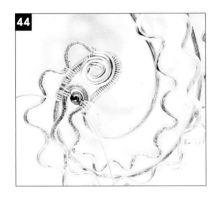

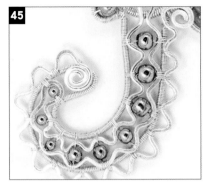

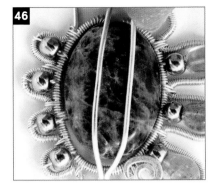

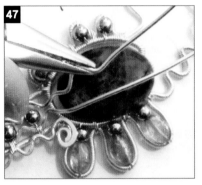

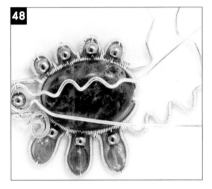

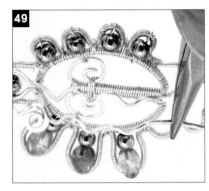

44 Pull the 2mm bead into place firmly into the circular space.

45 Wrap another time around the inner tail frame and the tail frame. Then wrap along the tail frame *only* on either side until you reach areas where the outer tail frame touches the main tail frame (bind them together). When you reach the outer bulges of each inner tail frame, attach 2, 3, 4, or 5mm beads into the spaces with a criss-cross bead attachment. As I have nine spaces, I had three 2mm beads, then three 3mm beads, and lastly three 4–5mm beads. Work along the whole tail in this fashion until you reach the top of the tail. Use your pliers to keep the wraps tightly packed and neat. Make sure the wiggly outer tail frame lies *next* to the main tail frame, not under

or above it. Make sure the inner "waisted" tail frame lies on top of the main tail frame. Work at the same level as you go, working on the same shape from top and bottom as you work along the tail. Adjust the little inner frame shapes a little as you go to make sure the two halves of each circular frame shape line up nicely. Cut and tuck in the two 30AWG (0.25mm) wire ends.

46 Make the rest of the cabochon setting and the body details for the abdomen to mimic the surface texture of a natural seahorse. I have drawn a body detail pattern onto the diagram from Step 12 (see also page 295) to use as a template. Place the cabochon into the setting. Start to bend the wires from the internal tail frame over the

cabochon. Don't press down too much over the top of the cabochon yet, but make the upward bend of the wire at the base of the cabochon setting.

47 Gently shape both wires into little wavy shapes with four dips along each wire to finish at the top of the cabochon.

48 The shapes should be fairly equally spaced with the halfway point exactly midway up the stone (two dips above and two below this point).

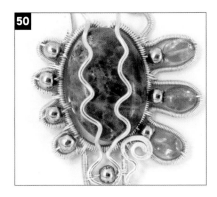
50

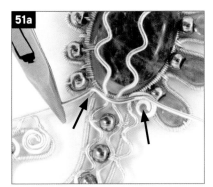
51a

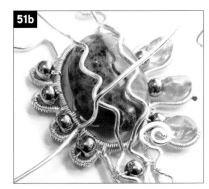
51b

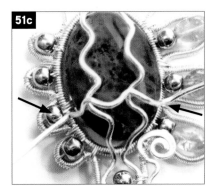
51c

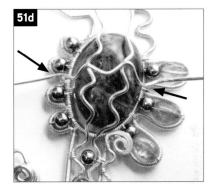
51d

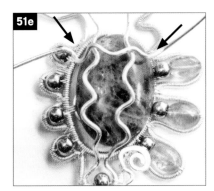
51e

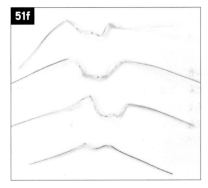
51f

49 It helps to keep the stone in place while shaping the wire. Work over a soft surface to prevent breakage of the stone if it falls off the setting. If it helps, remove the stone, shape the wire, and replace the stone to check the fit. Shape the wires toward the back over the top of the stone. Make a bend at the top edge of the setting so that the stone is encased vertically and the wires are ready to be shaped later to make the head, face, and mouth details.

50 Check the fit is good around the stone.

51a Make the horizontal abdomen details. Here I have drawn on the diagram from Step 32 (see also page 295) where these details should be placed. These horizontal frame wires should have a crenated appearance, with dips to lie in between the outer edges of the cabochon frame. The vertical wires running over the cabochon should have wire tails of 1in (25mm) at the front and 1³/₁₆in (3cm) at the back of the seahorse. Take 4in (10cm) of 18AWG (1mm) wire and make the little shapes. Each one will be different, as they run over different parts of the cabochon and link various points across the cabochon.

Look at the diagram to see the four little shapes you need to make and the points that they touch on the left and right side of the cabochon (see arrows on images). Make sure you shape them to lie over the cabochon carefully. Take time to get the fit right. This shows the lowest in place.

51b This image shows the second from lowest being formed.

51c This image shows it made.

51d This image shows the second from top shape after formation.

51e This image shows the top wire shape.

51f This image shows all the shapes that need to be made to cover the abdomen. Study the images carefully to get a better idea of the shapes you are trying to achieve.

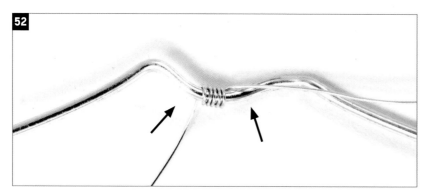

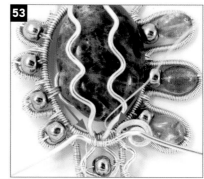

52 Start to attach the horizontal shapes, working with the bottom one first. Wrap with the midsection of a 31in (78cm) length of 30AWG (0.25mm) wire at the midsection of the shape for 1/4in (6mm) until you reach a level where you can bind to the vertical wires (see arrows in image).

53 Bind the shape to the vertical wires on either side of this wrap with three to four wraps, then wrap along the shape on either side (see arrows in image).

54 Wrap along either side to a level where the shape crosses the edge of the cabochon setting and bind here with three wraps (see red arrows in image). Wrap along the wire end for 5/16in (8mm) at the front and 1/2in (12mm) at the back.

55 Cut and tuck in the 30AWG (0.25mm) wire end smoothly. Repeat the methods in the previous steps to attach the next horizontal shape up. Start in the midsection as before and bind to the vertical wires at the points shown in the image (see red arrows in image).

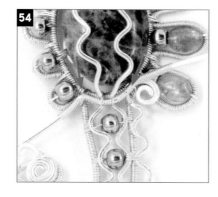

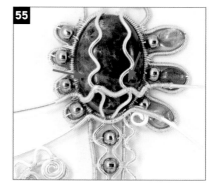

Tip

Make fine adjustments as you go to check the shapes fit. Press the wraps closely together. You can work with or without the stone in place. I found it useful to have the stone in place to check the fit and also to press the frame wires down onto the stone, to mold them into shape more easily.

56 Add in horizontal shape three and then four in the same way.

57 Cut the front wires to 13/16in (20mm) in length and the back wires to 1 3/16in (3cm). Curl the wires (see page 27). Use the tips of your pliers to make the little curl as tight as possible. The front curls have been shaped to lie as close to the front beads as possible. Turn the back curls inward and upward, and press down over the sides of the cabochon with pliers, then fingers, or the rubber ends of your pliers.

58 You should end up with the curls as in the image here.

NOTE: If you want to make a design variation, you can choose not to fold the curls over the cabochon. If you want more of the cabochon visible, feel free to arrange the curls this way.

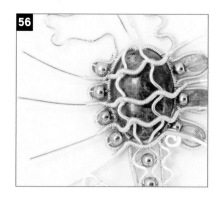

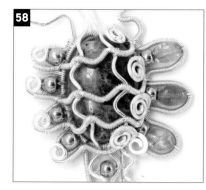

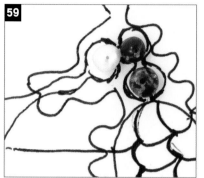

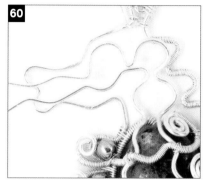

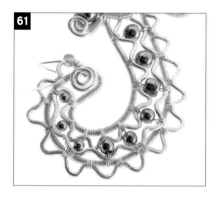

Tip

If your wire breaks at any stage, cut it back to just above the cabochon. Curl these cut ends to the side and make a face section with a new section of wire, binding it to the cabochon frame and working upward with the same methods as if it had not broken.

61 To further embellish the tail, take some 2mm rounds of apatite (or sky-blue quartz or turquoise beads) and thread them onto a 20in (50cm) length of 26AWG (0.4mm) wire bound onto the end of the tail projections. Wrap across to the other side of the tail projection and onto the next projection. Wrap once around one side of the base of the projection, adding a 2mm bead and wrapping with one binding wrap to the other side of the base of the projection.

62 Wrap your way up the tail in this fashion and cut and tuck in the 26AWG (0.4mm) wire end.

59 Plan the neck, eye, and mouth frame wires. Here I have drawn out a wire plan on the diagram on page 295, so refer back to this figure. Make sure the gemstones you want to use will fit inside the little shapes you make from the vertical wire tails from Step 59.

60 Form the wire shapes carefully following the template. The wire ends need to extend for ¹³/₁₆in (20mm) from the mouth.

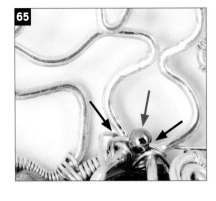

63 Now add some 3–4mm apatite gemstones into the spaces of the neck projections. Attach 31in (78cm) of 26AWG (0.4mm) wire at the base of the back of the neck and cut and tuck in this wire end. Thread a 4mm apatite bead onto the 26AWG (0.4mm) wire and wrap to the other side of the projection.

64 Wrap around the base in between the next projection and add another 3–4mm bead and a third to the top neck projection. Wrap along the bare wire at the back of the head and bind with three wraps to the inner frame wires (see arrow in image). Wrap back to the main frame at the base of the bale. Do not cut the 26AWG (0.4mm) wire at this point.

65 Take 40in (1m) of 30AWG (0.25mm), 28AWG (0.3mm), or 26AWG (0.4mm) wire after checking that two wires will fit through the drill holes of the beads you are using. I chose 26AWG

(0.4mm) wire as it will fit through my beads if doubled up and is also stronger than 30AWG (0.25mm) wire. Attach the 26AWG (0.4mm) wire at its mid-segment at the top of the cabochon where the two wire tails forming the face exit the top edge of the cabochon (see black arrows in image). Both wire ends should end up either side of the vertical wires at the top of the cabochon. Wrap on a 2mm silver bead at this point (red arrow) with one wire around both vertical wires with the 26AWG (0.4mm) wires, ending up where you started.

66 We are going to add beads into the head and neck frames to emulate the lovely surface texture of natural seahorses. I am suggesting bead sizes to fill the spaces in the following steps, but you may find different bead sizes to fit the spaces you have made. Add a 3mm silver bead to the 26AWG (0.4mm) wire leading to the back of the neck (see green

arrow in image). Wrap around the notch between the lower and middle back neck projections three times, binding also to the lowest inner neck frame spaces at the same time, leaving the 26AWG (0.4mm) wire at the midsection of one side of this space (red arrow).

67 Thread a 3mm silver bead onto the 26AWG (0.4mm) wire end leading to the front of the neck. Bind to the front of the neck (see red arrow in image). Weave up the front of the neck in a basket weave across the front main frame wire and the leading face detail frame wire, in the direction of the black arrow in the image, adding in a 2mm silver bead to the other side of the lowest inner neck frame. Wrap back, under the 2mm bead that you just added, to the front of the neck. Wrap up a little further and bind twice around the widest point of the lowest inner neck frame space, adding in another 2mm silver bead as you do this (green arrow).

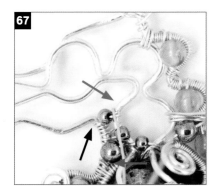

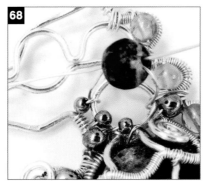

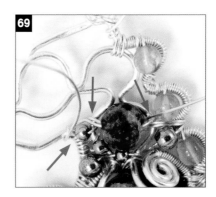

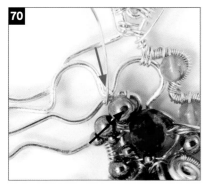

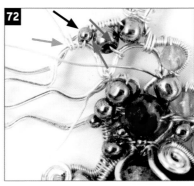

68 Thread a 6mm lapis lazuli round gemstone into the lowest neck space with both 26AWG (0.4mm) wire ends, using a criss-cross bead attachment.

69 Pull tightly to position the gemstone into place. Wrap the 26AWG (0.4mm) wire ends once back around the internal frame sides (see red arrows in image). The front wire needs to be wrapped to the front of the neck again (green arrow).

70 Thread on a 2mm, then a 3mm, then a 4mm silver bead onto the front neck wire and perform a binding wrap to the upper neck/head frame space in the direction of the black arrow in the image. Wrap this wire along the lower

front edge of the upper neck head frame space and bind once at the back of the eye frame space (see red arrow). Leave this wire here for the moment.

71 Take the 26AWG (0.4mm) wire from Step 69 at the back of the lower neck space and add in a 4mm silver bead (see red arrow in image). Make a binding wrap for this bead to the lower edge of the upper neck frame space. Using the 26AWG (0.4mm) wire tail left at the back edge of the base of the bale from Step 66, wrap across to the other side of the base of the bale, adding in a 4mm bead in the direction of the green arrow in the image. Wrap along the top of the head for ⅛in (3mm) (see black arrow).

72 Add another 4mm bead and wrap to the upper edge of the upper neck frame space, in the direction of the red arrow in the image. Wrap back to the top of the head, passing the 26AWG (0.4mm) wire under the bead you have just added in the direction of the green arrow in the image. Wrap a little further along the top of the head. Add a 2mm silver bead (see black arrow) and wrap along to the top of the eye frame. Pass the 26AWG (0.4mm) wire back up to the top of the head, wrap along the head a little further, and wrap twice around the top of the eye and the top of the head frame to attach them together at this point (see blue arrow).

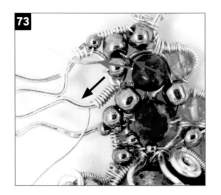

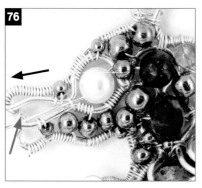

73 Take the 26AWG (0.4mm) wire from the back of the neck/upper neck space (see red arrow in Step 73). Thread on a 5mm lapis lazuli, binding across to the front of the upper neck space in the direction of the red arrow in the image. Thread on a 3mm silver bead to the same wire and wrap across to the back of the eye space. Leave this wire for the moment (green arrow). Wrap the 26AWG (0.4mm) wire (from the direction of the red arrow in Step 73 at the lower edge of the eye space until halfway along the eye socket in the direction of the black arrow in the image.

74 Thread on a 3mm silver bead. Wrap to and along the lower jaw until you are ready to add another 3mm silver bead, then wrap to the lower front edge of the eye space. Wrap along to the front lower eye corner in the direction of the red arrow in the image. With the 26AWG (0.4mm) wire at the top of the head from the blue arrow in Step 73 wrap more times around the top of the eye frame binding it to the top of the head. Wrap a couple of times only around the top of the nose following the direction of the green arrow in the image. Thread on an 8mm pearl to the 26AWG (0.4mm) wire from the direction of the green arrow in Step 73. Lay it across the eye socket in the direction of the black arrow in the image, but do not bind it to the frame yet.

75 Take the 26AWG (0.4mm) wire from the lower corner of the eye and wrap it around the corner of the space and the 26AWG (0.4mm) wire with the pearl on it, trapping the pearl into the eye socket space (see red arrow in image). Thread on another 3mm silver bead and wrap down to the lower jaw (green arrow). Wrap along the lower jaw for a short distance. Add on a 2mm bead, wrapping up to the midline of the nose and back down to the lower edge of the jaw. Wrap along the lower edge of the jaw and stop at the end of the nose. Work along the lower jaw in the direction of the black arrow in the image. Cut and tuck in the 26AWG (0.4mm) wire end.

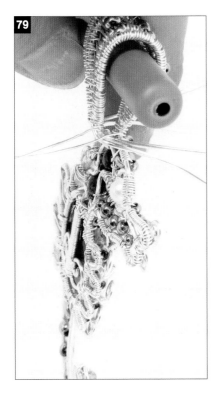

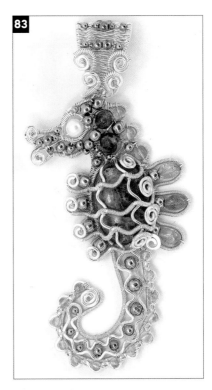

76 Use the 26AWG (0.4mm) wire from the top jaw (see green arrow in Step 75). Work along in the direction of the black arrow in the image, and add on a 2mm bead in a binding wrap to the midline of the nose. Wrap back up to the top of the nose. Wrap along the top of the nose frame, binding around the top neck detail wire, wrap two more times between the two mid-nose frame wires, and cut and tuck in the 26AWG (0.4mm) wire end at the level of the red arrow in the image.

77 Thread a 2mm, then a 3mm, then a 2mm bead onto the 26AWG (0.4mm) wire leading from the eye and the pearl (see red arrow in image). Wrap around the mouth end of the frame, down around the lower neck detail wire, and down around the lower jaw (black arrow).

Cut and tuck in the 26AWG (0.4mm) wire end at the level of the green arrow in the image.

78 Curl the mouth wires and press them into position over either side of the mouth.

79 Take a pen-sized mandrel and bend the bale into shape around the mandrel.

80 Use any 26AWG (0.4mm) wires left over from wrapping the bale to bind the base of the bale together with tight wraps around the front and back wires at the bale base on either side. Try to keep these binding wraps as hidden as possible.

81 You will have four bare wire tails at the base of the bale. Trim the lower bale wires to a length

of 1³/₁₆in (3cm) and the upper bale wires to 1⁹/₁₆in (4cm) on either side. Wrap along each bale wire with 26AWG (0.4mm) wire, leaving ⁵/₈in (15mm) of bare wire end. Use any spare 26AWG (0.4mm) wire tails left over from the bale wrap and binding, or add in new wire to the base of the bale.

82 Curl the bale wires and press into place.

83 Your beautiful seahorse pendant is finished.

NOTE: To create a brooch, just cut the bale wire ends very short at the top of the head and curl them to add detail to the top of the head. Make a brooch pin (see pages 32–33). Attach at various points to the back of the seahorse using 26AWG (0.4mm wire).

Tumbling leaves necklace

Celebrate the beauty of falling leaves by learning how to make this attractive and seasonal leaf necklace. If the leaves are made individually, this design can be adapted to make a pendant or wired over the front of a cabochon. The leaves can be made in copper, gold, or silver-colored wires and are light enough to work on hairpieces or brooches.

Templates
See page 297 for the templates for this design.

Materials
18AWG (1mm-diameter) antique bronze round wire
26AWG (0.4mm-diameter) antique bronze round wire
9 x 4mm-diameter faceted round peridot through-drilled beads
1 x strand of 2–3mm round peridot beads with drill hole
   (although any berrylike beads will work)

Tools
General tools (see page 10) plus:
Gizmo tool with 3.2mm-diameter mandrel

Dimensions of finished piece
Necklace length approx. 18in (45cm)
Each large leaf 3 x 1$^9/_{16}$in (7.5 x 4cm)
Each small leaf 1$^9/_{16}$ x 1in (4 x 2.5cm)

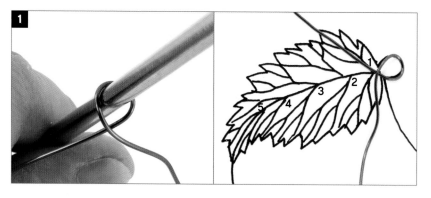

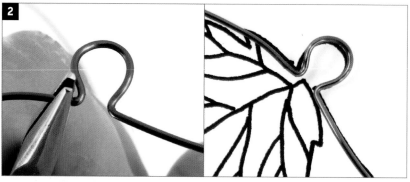

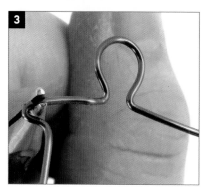

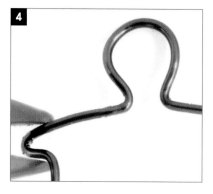

2 Shape the bends at the ends of the loop with chain-nosed pliers, using the template as a guide.

Tip

Avoid too much reshaping of the wire at tight bends as the wire may break. Practice with scrap wire first.

3 Shape the long end of the 18AWG (1mm) wire around the outside of the leaf template using chain-nosed pliers, making small movements to shape the wire with little points.

4 Clamp your chain-nosed pliers either side of each little bend in the leaf, as close to the bend as possible, to make the bend sharp and defined. Squeeze either side of bends to sharpen them up as well.

5 It does not matter if there are slight variations in the leaves you make, as this reflects nature, as long as the main outline shape of each is as similar as possible.

6 Make a gentle bend in the wire to mark where you want to bend it, then check against the template. Reshape if necessary, then make the final bend. It is useful to shape the wire over the template, over a hard surface. The leaf frame should be approximately $2^3/_4$in (7cm) long (including the loop but not the end wires for the spirals); the maximum width should be about $1^1/_2$in (3.8cm).

1 Draw a leaf shape template on a piece of paper to help you get the shape right. The template on page 297 can be used to help you make multiple leaf shapes of approximately the same size and shape. I have drawn an outer solid line for the main leaf frame and thinner lines for the leaf veins. The wire tails at the top and bottom of the leaf need to be about $1^3/_8$in (3.5cm) long. I have numbered the leaf vein pairs; this will help you in Steps 12–39. Cut a 32in (80cm)

length of 18AWG (1mm) wire. Using small and gentle movements of chain-nosed pliers and your fingers, make a leaf frame shape using the template to shape the wire. The loop at the top of the leaf (about $1/_4$in/6mm in diameter) should be shaped first at a point 2in (5cm) from the end of the 18AWG (1mm) frame wire. It can be made by wrapping the wire around a marker pen or mandrel to help you achieve a circular shape.

MASTERING WIREWORK JEWELRY

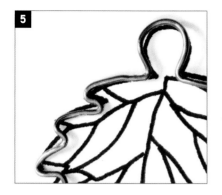

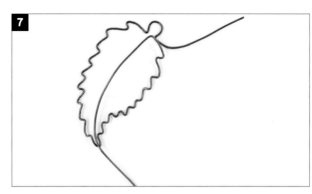

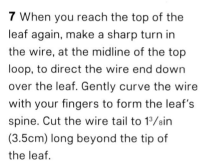

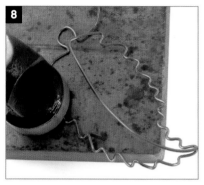

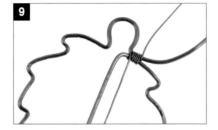

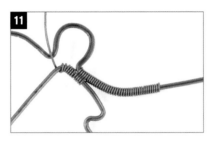

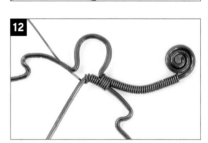

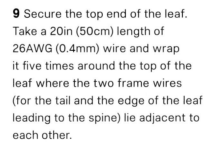

7 When you reach the top of the leaf again, make a sharp turn in the wire, at the midline of the top loop, to direct the wire end down over the leaf. Gently curve the wire with your fingers to form the leaf's spine. Cut the wire tail to 1³/₈in (3.5cm) long beyond the tip of the leaf.

8 If your wire is soft, you will need to gently hammer the frame to work-harden but not flatten it. Hammer the loop end a little more to flatten it and create a reflective surface. Do not hammer the wire end tails as they still need shaping. Do not hammer where the wires cross over each other at the leaf tip or you risk weakening and breaking the wires.

9 Secure the top end of the leaf. Take a 20in (50cm) length of 26AWG (0.4mm) wire and wrap it five times around the top of the leaf where the two frame wires (for the tail and the edge of the leaf leading to the spine) lie adjacent to each other.

10 Wrap along either side of this attachment until you reach the central spine on the left, and wrap for ⁵/₈in (15mm) along the tail on the right. Cut the 26AWG (0.4mm) wire leading along the tail as close to the 18AWG (1mm) wire as possible. Tuck this in neatly with smoothing movements around the wire in the direction of the wrap using chain-nosed pliers.

11 Do not cut the 26AWG (0.4mm) wire end near the leaf spine.

12 Curl the wire end you have just wrapped (see page 27) in a tight spiral until you reach the wrapped section.

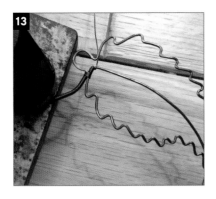

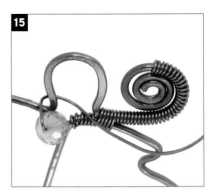

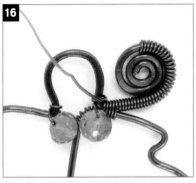

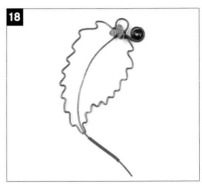

13 Hammer the curl, avoiding the wrapped section in case you damage it. A small-faced hammer will be useful.

14 Curl the rest of the curl with your fingers so the wrapped part of the wire forms the outer part of the spiral.

15 Take a few 4mm beads (I used faceted peridot; any 4mm bead in your choice of color will work). Thread one onto the 26AWG (0.4mm) wire end. Wrap across from the spine to the base of the loop opposite the wire curl and back again to the spine.

16 Wrap the 26AWG (0.4mm) wire around the spine once. Add on another 4mm bead to the area at the base of the loop. Add a third in between and above the first two, wrapping to the opposite side of the base of the loop until you achieve a "cluster of berries" effect here.

17 Bring the 26AWG (0.4mm) wire end up from the last bead wrap to the top to the leaf spine under the berry cluster. Wrap the end around the spine for two to three wraps (to a point above the top set of leaf veins) and cut and tuck in the wire end (see arrow in image).

18 Secure the base of the leaf. Take 12in (30cm) of 26AWG (0.4mm) wire and hand-wrap along the base of the leaf spine for 7/8in (22mm). Cut the wire ends and tuck them in.

19 Push the coil along the leaf spine so it sits 1/2in (12mm) up inside the leaf and touches against the bottom pair of leaf veins (see arrow in image).

20 Take a 12in (30cm) length of 26AWG (0.4mm) wire and wrap around the tip of the leaf and across the spine wire a few times to secure it into place (see red arrow in image). Wrap up either side of the tip for 5/16in (8mm) on the left and 5/16in (8mm) on the right until you reach where the bottom leaf veins on the template would wrap onto the outer leaf frame (blue arrows). Cut and tuck in the 26AWG (0.4mm) wires.

21 Curl the wire tail at the tip of the leaf as in Step 12, with the spiral following the curve direction of the leaf spine, as shown.

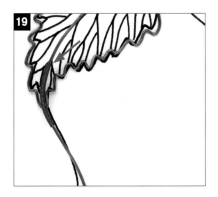

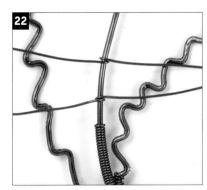

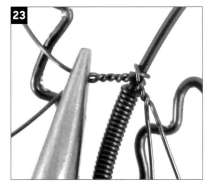

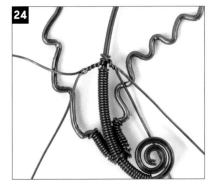

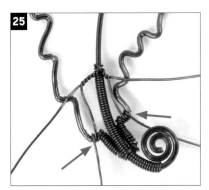

22 Please refer to the template on page 297. There are five pairs of leaf veins. The vein pairs have been numbered so you can work up the leaf from pair 5 at the bottom to pair 1 at the top. Start with the bottom leaf vein bundle, pair 5. Take two lengths of 26AWG (0.4mm) wire about 16in (40cm) long. Attach each wire length, one above the other, with a single 180-degree wrap around the central spine wire, with the wire ends at the top of the wrap (not the back of the spine). You have two wires emerging from each twisted wire section: these individual strands need to be wrapped toward the main leaf frame.

NOTE: I have given distances and lengths but your leaf may be sized differently. If you have drawn your own template, refer to this for distances and vein positioning.

23 Push these wires down close to the edge of the wrapping along the spine from Step 20 (red arrow) and start to twist the wires. Use your fingers or gentle grips with pliers to do this. Chain-nosed pliers allow you to control the location of the twist better than your fingers can.

NOTE: Don't twist too much or the wires might snap. If this happens, wrap in another length of 26AWG (0.4mm) wire around the spine at a level where you can twist the wires around the vein with the snapped wire and add it into the twists along the vein formation.

24 Twist the wires on the right side of the spine for about $^1/_8$in (3mm) and on the left side for about $^3/_{16}$in (4mm).

25 Push the 26AWG (0.4mm) wire pairs firmly down against the top of the wrapped spine. Take the bottom veins first pulling them firmly downward toward the leaf frame toward the top edge of the wire wraps from Step 20 (see red arrows). Wrap the 26AWG (0.4mm) wires around the leaf frame on either side, then wrap up the leaf frame to the level where the upper wires will connect to the leaf frame.

NOTE: The veins run downward and outward from the spine, not directly horizontally across, to achieve a more natural look.

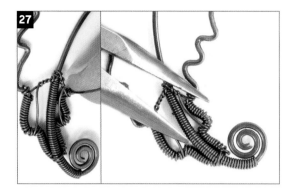
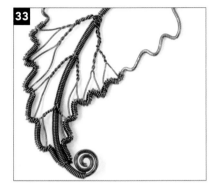

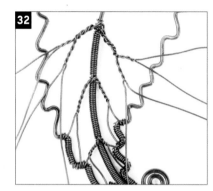

Tip

With this first bind, make sure the spine section stays where you planned it to be and does not get pulled toward the side you are binding toward. Hold the spine and frame section firmly with one hand while wrapping around the frame to ensure the spine stays balanced and the frame does not distort. When you wrap the opposite upper leaf vein segment, this is a chance to pull the spine and bale into line to correct any distortion from the midline.

26 Continue to wrap the lower leaf vein wires up to a level where the upper leaf veins will need to be attached to the leaf frame. Cut and tuck in these 26AWG (0.4mm) wire ends around the frame at the level

of the red arrows in the image. Wrap the upper two 26AWG (0.4mm) vein wires onto the leaf frame and wrap up the frame sides to the level where the lower wires from leaf vein bundle pair 4 will attach.

27 Use firm pressure from your fingers, and the wrapping wire pulled tightly over the fingers as you wrap, to help you place the wraps as closely together as you can. You will only need to wrap two or three times (as the lower wires from group 4 will attach close to these wire attachments), then cut and tuck in the 26AWG (0.4mm) wire ends. Use your pliers to gently squash the wraps together to keep them neat and close together.

28 You will end with the pair 5 leaf veins looking like the image.

29 Now make leaf vein bundle pair 4. Take a new section of 26AWG (0.4mm) wire. Wrap up along the leaf spine from the top of the pair 5 spinal attachment for $^{11}/_{16}$in (17mm) (or up to the attachment point for pair 3). Cut and tuck in the 26AWG (0.4mm) wire ends (see arrows in image).

30 Attach two 20in (50cm) lengths of 26AWG (0.4mm) wire to the central spine in the same way as in Step 22. Twist both left-hand wires for $^3/_8$in (10mm) and the right-hand wires for $^1/_4$in (7mm). Repeat methods from Steps 22–28, wrapping the lower wires first to the leaf frame and then the upper wires.

31 Make leaf vein bundle pair 3. Take a new section of 26AWG (0.4mm) wire. Wrap up along the leaf spine from the top of the pair 4 spinal attachment for $^1/_2$in (12mm) (or up to the attachment point for pair 2). Cut and tuck in the 26AWG (0.4mm) wire ends (see arrows in image). Attach four 20in (50cm) lengths of 26AWG (0.4mm) wire to the central spine. Twist all four left-hand wires for $^5/_{16}$in (8mm) and the right-hand wires for $^5/_{16}$in (8mm). Divide the left-hand wires into pairs of two; do the same for the right-hand wires.

32 Twist the lower left-hand wires for $^5/_{16}$in (8mm) and the upper left-hand wires for $^3/_{16}$in (4mm). Twist the lower right-hand wires for $^3/_{16}$in (5mm) and the upper right-hand wires for $^1/_4$in (7mm).

33 Repeat methods from Steps 22–28, wrapping the lower wires first to the leaf frame following the template, then the middle wires, then the upper wires.

34 Make leaf vein bundle pair 2. Take a new section of 26AWG (0.4mm) wire. Wrap up along the leaf spine from the top of the pair 4 spinal attachment for $^3/_8$in (10mm) (or up to the attachment point for pair 1). Cut and tuck in the 26AWG (0.4mm) wire ends (see arrows in image). Attach four 20in (50cm) lengths of 26AWG (0.4mm) wire to the central spine. Twist all four left-hand wires for $^1/_4$in (7mm) and the right-hand wires for $^5/_{16}$in (8mm). Divide the left-hand wires into pairs of two; do the same for the right-hand wires.

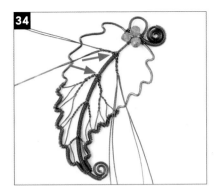

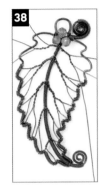

35 Twist the lower left-hand wires for $^1/_4$in (6mm) and the upper left-hand wires for $^3/_{16}$in (5mm). Twist the lower right-hand wires for $^1/_4$in (6mm) and the upper right-hand wires for $^3/_{16}$in (5mm).

36 Repeat methods from Steps 22–28, wrapping the lower wires first to the leaf frame following the template, then the middle wires, then the upper wires.

37 Make leaf vein bundle pair 1. Take a new section of 26AWG (0.4mm) wire. Wrap up along the leaf spine from the top of the pair four spinal attachment for $^1/_4$in (6mm) (or up to $^1/_{16}$in/1.5mm) beneath the wrapping down the spine from the bead attachment in Steps 15–17. Cut and tuck in the 26AWG (0.4mm) wire ends (see arrows in image). Attach three 20in (50cm) lengths of 26AWG (0.4mm)

wire to the central spine. Twist all three left-hand wires for $^3/_{16}$in (5mm) and the right-hand wires for $^1/_4$in (6mm). Divide the left-hand wires into a lower pair of two and one upper single wire; do the same for the right-hand wires.

38 Twist the lower left-hand wires for $^3/_{16}$in (5mm) and the lower right-hand wires for $^1/_4$in (6mm).

39 Repeat methods from Steps 22–28 wrapping the lower wires first to the leaf frame following the template, then the middle wires, then the upper wires. Your leaf component is finished.

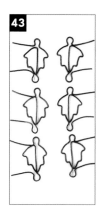

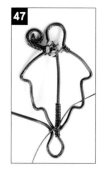

40 To make this necklace design, make two further leaves in the same way, with one in mirror image to the other two. Use the flipped image in the templates on page 297 to help you assemble these leaves. Arrange all three leaves in the pattern shown to create the effect of tumbling leaves. Link with jumprings at the four points shown with red arrows. This may take some adjustment until the leaves hang in balance. The leaves are joined together with doubled-up 7mm-diameter jumprings made on a 5mm-diameter mandrel with 18AWG (1mm) wire.

NOTE: If you use 18AWG (1mm) wire to make the jumprings, you will have to pair the rings up in each link, so two rings are used to take the strain. I flush cut these jumprings so they fit together well when the rings are closed (see page 31). However, if you have the

equipment to saw cut them, you will gain a flush-cut edge and clean closure of the rings.

41 You can make up the necklace sides with Viking knit, kumihimo, chain, or a rosary link chain of beads. Here I continued the design by making little leaf links and leaf clasp components. These are just smaller versions of the larger leaves and are made in a very similar way. Leaf templates for the clasp components and links are shown here (see also template on page 297). The leaves are 1in (25mm) wide and 1⁹/₁₆in (4cm) long. The clasps are a little longer. The wire tails at each end of the leaf are ¹³/₁₆in (20mm) long.

42 Make the frame for a necklace component using the techniques from Steps 1–9.

43 Make six necklace components. Three will eventually make left-handed leaves for one side of the necklace and three right-handed leaves. At this stage they are all made identical over the same template.

44 Use the techniques from Steps 9–35 to make up the smaller leaves. Attach 26AWG (0.4mm) wire to the top of the leaf as in Step 9 and follow through the subsequent steps, in smaller scale. Bind the frame together, winding ³/₁₆in (5mm) along the top wire tail.

45 Curl the wire as shown.

46 Hammer the little curl before curling the wrapped section manually. Bind on several 2mm peridot beads in a cluster at the top of the leaf.

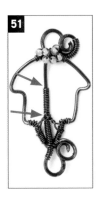

spine on either side and binding to the leaf frame. Repeat Steps 44–53 for the other five leaf components.

47 Wind 26AWG (0.4mm) wire around the base of the leaf spine as in Steps 18–19, from the tip to the level of the first vein attachment.

48 Attach 26AWG (0.4mm) wire to the base of the leaf component using methods from Step 20.

49 Curl the wire tail using methods from Step 21. Hammer the curl, then press the little curl over the loop at the tip of the leaf. Make three right-handed versions for one necklace side and three left-handed for the other. From here, form the first set of leaf veins from the leaf tip, following the techniques in Steps 22–28.

50 Bind on two 6in (15cm) lengths of 26AWG (0.4mm) wire around the spine and twist either side for ¹/₈in (3mm). Anchor the vein wires by binding to the leaf frame on either

side at the levels shown in the image. Bind on the lower pair first, cut those wire ends, then bind on the upper pair for a few wraps and cut those ends.

51 Wrap ¹/₄in (6mm) of 26AWG (0.4mm) wire along the leaf spine (see arrows in image), then cut the little wire ends.

52 Form the second set of leaf veins using the methods in Steps 22–28, twisting from the double 26AWG (0.4mm) wire attachment to the spine on either side and binding to the leaf frame.

53 Wrap on ³/₁₆in (5mm) of 26AWG (0.4mm) wire along the leaf spine (see arrows in image), then cut the wire ends. Form the third set of leaf veins using the same methods, twisting from the double 26AWG (0.4mm) wire attachment to the

54 Make the leaf clasp components. Use the frame template on page 297 and shown in image 41. Make the frames in the same way as in Step 44, but add a longer loop and a ¹³/₁₆in (20mm) tail at the tip to make the loop and hook sections.

55 Coil the wire tails and hammer the loops and coils but not the body of the leaf.

56 Repeat Steps 44–53 to make up the clasps. Do not bind the hook end of the clasp to the leaf tip but bind the loop end near the coil, to close the loop end (see arrow in image).

57 Attach the sections together with the chainmail double jumpring links at each point for strength. Your beautiful necklace is completed and ready to wear.

Gecko brooch

These endearing lizards were considered by the Ancient Greeks to be symbols of good fortune and intelligence. This little jewel-encrusted gecko brooch features natural stone cabochons within the structure.

Templates
See page 297 or the templates for this design.

Materials
18AWG (1mm-diameter) round antique bronze copper wire
(20AWG/0.8mm-diameter wire can be used in some components instead of 18AWG/1mm wire)
26AWG (0.4mm-diameter) round antique bronze copper wire
30AWG (0.25mm-diameter) round antique bronze copper wire
(Copper, bare copper, silver, or gold-plated wire will also work)
2mm antique bronze round beads
4mm antique bronze round beads
3mm-diameter lapis lazuli round beads
4mm lapis lazuli round beads
1 x 20 x 15mm pear/teardrop-shaped gemstone or cabochon, no drill hole required (I used turquoise)
1 x 20 x 15mm oval gemstone or cabochon, no drill hole required (I used turquoise. Make sure the teardrop and oval cabochons are the same dimensions as each other if you use smaller or larger gemstones)
3 x 8mm-diameter round cabochons (two must be color-matched as they will form the gecko's eyes). I used turquoise

Tools
General tools (see page 10)
4mm mandrel

Dimensions of finished piece
Approx. 3³/₈ x 2¹/₂in (8.5 x 6cm)

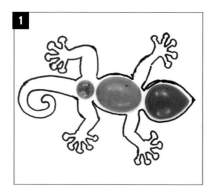

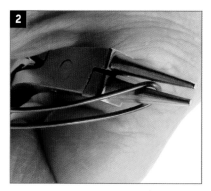

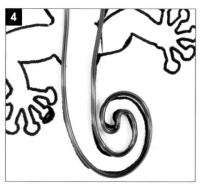

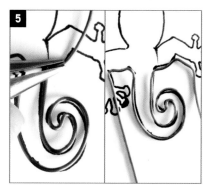

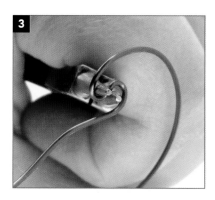

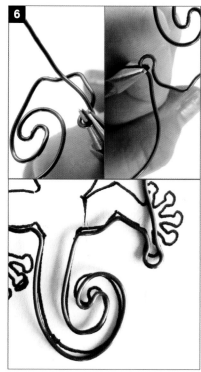

1 To start, I have drawn around the pear, oval, and round gemstones in a line and drawn legs and a tail to form an outline for the gecko brooch. You can use the template on page 297, or this diagram as a basis for your design.

2 Take a 60in (1.5m) length of 18AWG (1mm) wire. Start to shape the tail using round-nosed pliers.

3 This image shows the shaping of the tail around both ends of chain-nosed pliers.

4 Use the template from Step 1, or on page 297, to shape the curve of each side of the tail.

5 At the base of the tail, use chain-nosed pliers to make a little bend outward on either side to form the lower leg. Use little shaping movements and repeated checks on the template and form the base of the lower leg and inside edge of the foot on each side. Make a gentle bend first, then check on the template before making a sharp bend (repeated reshaping of sharp wire bends will weaken and damage the wire). Make sure the thigh has a little curve to it. Sharpen up bends in the wire by repeatedly clamping both sides of the bend.

6 Make the little toes using chain-nosed pliers: work near the tips of the pliers to make the lengths of the toes and round-nosed pliers to make the ends of the toes. The toe sides are about $1/8$in (3mm) long below the toe tip round. The round toe ends need to be large enough to fit a 2mm round bead inside. Wrap the 18AWG (1mm) wire around the round-nosed pliers, forming almost a complete circle. Bend the wire with chain-nosed plier tips to make the other straight side of the toe. If making a smaller gecko, you won't be able to fit beads inside each toe.

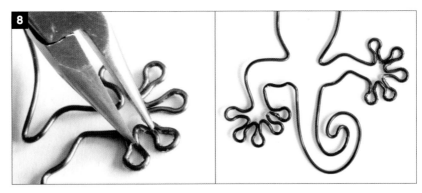

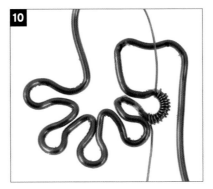

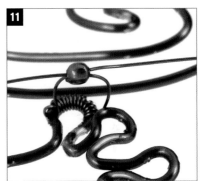

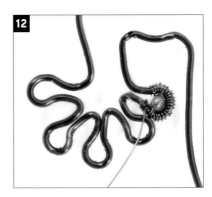

7 Use your chain-nosed pliers to make the bend at the other side of the toe tip and the other side of the toe. Clamp either side of the straight sections of the toes below the circular tip to bring the parallel straight sections closer together.

8 Clamp either side of this bend to tighten up the bends at the base of the toes. Make the bend outwards for the next toe along. Make sure the toes are of equal length and the round tips are the same size. Make five toes for a larger gecko and it is easier to form just three toes for a smaller gecko. This will take a lot of careful shaping work and I recommend practicing forming the toes with small pieces of scrap wire first. Form the upper surface of the lower leg and bend upward to start to form the sides of the abdomen. Make the other lower foot in the same way.

9 Hammer the tail and lower legs only, but not the body.

10 Before forming the upper limbs, work on the tail and lower legs: then, if this work distorts the frame in any way, there has not been too much shaping of the abdomen, upper limbs, and face. First work on the toes. Take 8in (20cm) of 30AWG (0.25mm) wire and wrap around the ends of one of the toes until you reach halfway up each side.

11 Thread on a 2mm antique bronze bead using a criss-cross bead attachment (see page 26) with one 30AWG (0.25mm) wire through one side of the bead and the other end through the other side of the bead.

12 Position the bead into place by pulling on both wire ends and wrap the 30AWG (0.25mm) wire up to the top of the toe circle. Cut the short end of the 30AWG (0.25mm) wire, leaving the longer end for the next step.

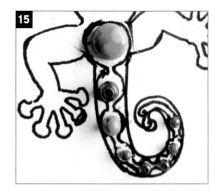

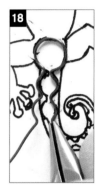

13 Weave up the little toe with a figure-of-eight basket weave (see page 24), then cut the 30AWG (0.25mm) wire at the base of the toe.

14 Repeat Steps 10–13 for all the other toes for the lower legs.

15 Make a frame for the circular 8mm stone and the tail section.

16 I have drawn onto the template from Step 1 to help you achieve this frame shape (see the template on page 297). This will be used to attach gemstones into the tail with waist sections between them, making sure the oval cabochon still fits into the abdomen frame space.

17 Take 6in (15cm) of 20AWG (0.8mm) wire. Form a circular shape using a 9mm-diameter mandrel at the midpoint of the wire large enough to fit around the 8mm cabochon with a ¹⁄₃₂in (1mm) gap around it.

18 Bend the 20AWG (0.8mm) wire ends out from the circle where they cross and start to form a wavy shape along the tail following the template.

19 Here I have shaped about two-thirds of the tail frame; during attachment to the tail, the end portion may be need to be reshaped due to the curliness of the tail.

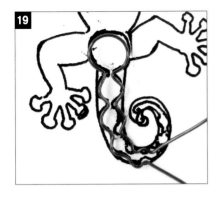

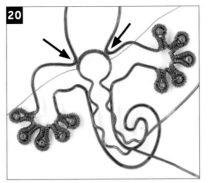

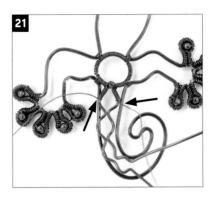

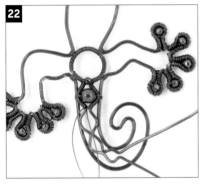

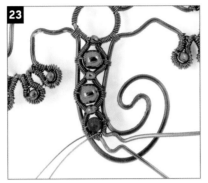

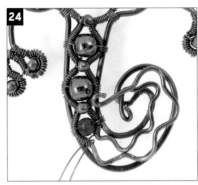

20 Take 80in (2m) of 30AWG (0.25mm) wire. Wrap at the midpoint of the 30AWG (0.25mm) wire around the tail detail shape made in the previous step along from the 10 to 2 o'clock positions (see arrows in image). Attach to the upper corner of the base of each lower leg with three wraps around both frames. Continue wrapping along the circular segment of the tail frame.

21 When you reach the 7 and 5 o'clock positions, pull the tail frame toward the circular frame section. Bind here to the base of the tail, then wrap down to the first waist section. Now add in a 2mm antique bronze bead with a criss-cross bead attachment (see page 26). Wrap down to the widest point of the next circular space with the 30AWG (0.25mm) wire ends on both sides (see arrows in image).

22 Add in a 4mm antique bronze bead with a criss-cross bead attachment (see page 26). Wrap around the tail detail and the tail frame a few times on both sides. Then wrap down to the next waist in the tail detail frame.

23 Continue in the same fashion, adding in 2mm beads to the waists, then another 4mm antique bronze bead, 2mm to the next waist, then a 3mm lapis round to the next space.

24 Shape the rest of the tail detail frame with three more spaces and a $^3/_8$in (10mm) long frame tail. Make sure the curves are larger on the outside of the tail compared to the inner curve.

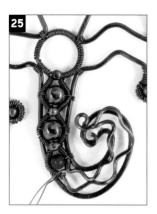

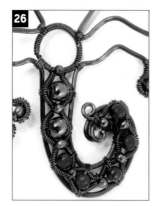

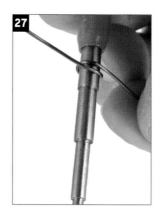

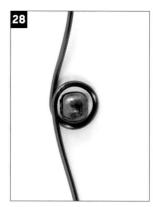

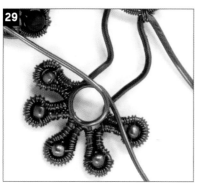

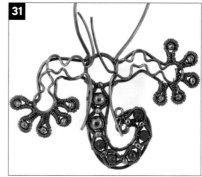

25 Curl the ³/₈in (10mm) tails using the tips of round-nosed pliers. Cut the curl end a little to a nice circular shape, then curl again with round-nosed pliers.

26 Carry on adding beads to the tail, repeating Steps 21–23. Finish by binding the 30AWG (0.25mm) wire ends to both the tail curls and the tip of the tail. Cut and tuck in the 30AWG (0.25mm) wire ends.

27 Make the leg details frame and "palms" for the hind legs. Take 6in (15cm) of 20AWG (0.8mm) wire and wrap at the midsection around a 4mm-diameter rod or mandrel.

28 Check the fit of this circle against a 4mm bead.

29 Also check it against the palm of your gecko.

30 Bend the wire where the wires cross up in the direction of the leg making little circular spaces, about three along the leg, in the same way as in the tail, to fit 3 and 4mm beads. Leave a ⁵/₈in (15mm) tail at either end of the shape.

31 Make a similar shape in mirror image for the other lower leg, with adjustments for leg positioning.

32 Take some 30AWG (0.25mm) wire and start to wrap around one of the little "foot" circles for ¹/₈in (3mm). Bind to the base of the middle toe with two wraps. Continue to wrap around the foot circle, also wrapping to each toe.

33 When you reach the midpoint of the foot circle, as in image 30, add in a 4mm antique bronze round bead with a criss-cross abead ttachment and wrap up to the top of the foot circle.

34 Work your way up along the leg using the techniques in Steps 20–24 for the tail. Add in two further 3mm lapis rounds and a 4mm antique bronze bead into the spaces and 2mm antique bronze beads at the waist sections. You may need to reshape the detail frame wires as you go if you find they don't fit properly. Use small movements to adjust the angles for each bead space to get them to sit correctly along the limb. Do not cut the 30AWG (0.25mm) wires. Do not attach the leg detail frame to the circle frame between the two hind legs; this will be done later. Bend

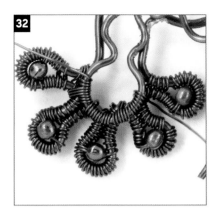

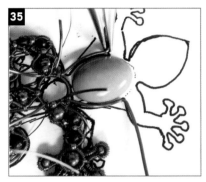

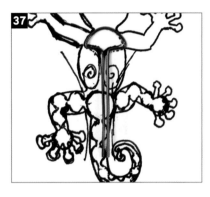

the wire tails upward so they are out of the way for the next stage. Take the other leg frame piece for the other lower leg and attach it into place using the techniques from Steps 20–24.

NOTE: This step can be fiddly. Try raising the leg detail frame a little in the unattached section so you can pass each wire wrap along the wires. Remember to press them back down into place as you attach them.

35 Shape the body and upper limbs, checking that your oval cabochon will fit into the body space. Use the techniques from Steps 2–8 to shape the body and upper limbs and following the template from page 297. See also image 36.

36 Make a little bend at the neck. Start to form the head with a gentle inward curve on either side (checking against the template and the pear-shaped cabochon). Leave a 2in (5cm) wire tail at each side of the nose to use to form nostrils later. Hammer the abdominal sides, arms, and side of head, but not too near the nose tip yet. Reshape to fit the template again as hammering can splay the wire shapes out of shape.

37 Make a backing frame for the oval cabochon. This will also help you when making up the cabochon setting for the front of the cabochon, as it will provide a continuous frame setting for weaving and attachment. Using the template on page 297, make a curved shape from 8in (20cm) of 18AWG (1mm) wire. Bend toward the midline and then downward, leaving 1¹/₂in (3.8cm) wire tails.

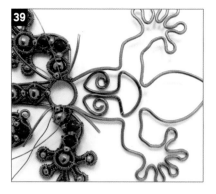

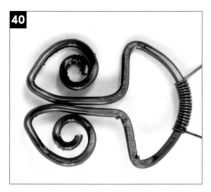

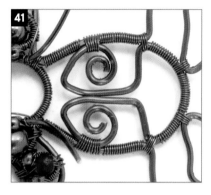

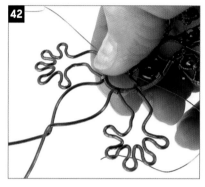

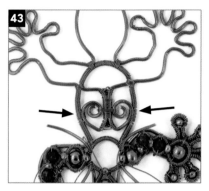

38 Curl the wire tails to fit nicely inside the cabochon shape on the template (see page 297). Hammer this little shape.

39 Reshape and check against the gecko's main frame and cabochon to make sure everything fits properly.

40 Take 40in (1m) of 30AWG (0.25mm) wire and wrap along the top of the curve of the backing plate shape to the levels shown in the image. Bind to the base of the neck/top of the shoulders, taking care to get the spacing right so that the arms are in the correct place and the cabochon still fits nicely into the setting.

41 Wrap along the backing frame and bind with the 30AWG (0.25mm) wire across to the underside of the forearms. Wrap along the abdomen. Cut the 30AWG (0.25mm) wrapping wire when you meet the top of the circular setting.

42 Press the binding wraps flat with your fingers (pliers may damage the 30AWG/0.25mm wire, but a gentle crush will be okay) to make the wraps as flat as possible so they fit nicely against the back of the stone later.

43 Bind the midline of the oval backing frame to further strengthen this section. Using 20in (50cm) of 30AWG (0.25mm) wire, make a figure-of-eight wrap at one end of the midline wires. Then wrap along and around the midline, also wrapping to the edges of the curls where they touch the midline (see arrows in image). Perform another figure-of-eight wrap at the other end. Cut and tuck in the 30AWG (0.25mm) wire so the cut end will sit against the stone later. Press the wrapping flat with your fingers to make a flat backing section.

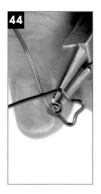

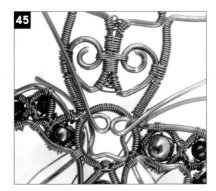

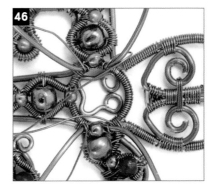

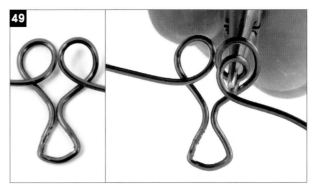

44 Make the backing section for the circular setting. Take a 1⁹/₁₆in (4cm) length of 20AWG (0.8mm) wire and make a little shape as shown. Use chain-nosed pliers to make a zigzag bend to form a crinkly square and the tips of the round-nosed pliers to form the circles.

45 Make sure the backing fits inside the circular frame by placing it over the back of the gecko.

46 Cut the excess wire from the circles and gently hammer the shape to strengthen it.

47 Take 20in (50cm) of 30AWG (0.25mm) wire and wrap along the lower part of the backing plate until just before the lower two corners. Then bind to the circular setting.

48 Carry on wrapping the 30AWG (0.25mm) wire along the side of the settings. Bind at the top two corners and across to the midline curls. Bind here and cut and tuck in the 30AWG (0.25mm) wire. Leave the 30AWG (0.25mm) wire ends at the front; they will be hidden against the stone when it is set later.

49 Make the backing section for the head setting. Take 6in (15cm) of 20AWG (0.8mm) wire and make the shape to fit inside the gecko's head with a triangular shape at the bottom and then two outwardly spiralling loops (see left hand image). Then work inside the two loops making spirals of wire, using round-nosed pliers and the outer to inner spiral technique from page 28. The base of the triangular shape has a slight curve. The shape is not symmetrical as the gecko's head is designed at a slight angle to the body.

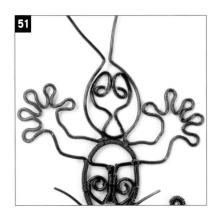

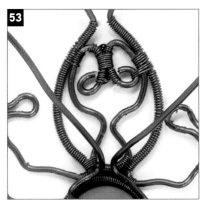

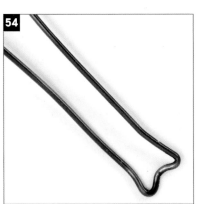

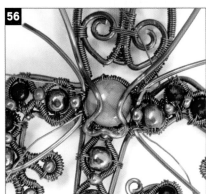

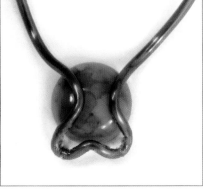

50 Check the fit against the frame and the cabochon after hammering the backing frame.

51 Reshape any wire shape splay due to hammering.

52 Wrap across the midline of the backing shape in a similar way to Step 45 for the oval cabochon backing plate. Attach the backing frame using 30AWG (0.25mm) wire, pressing the wraps flat with your fingers as you place them (see arrows in image).

53 Cut the 30AWG (0.25mm) wires at the tip of the nose and bend the nose wires upward a little.

54 Make the frontal setting for the cabochons. Take 16in (40cm) of 18AWG (1mm) or 20AWG (0.8mm) wire. Make a shallow "W" shape to fit at the bottom of the circular setting.

55 Place the little round cabochon on a rubber bead mat so you don't break it by pressing on it. Form the wires running from the "W" so they lie over the little round stone and then run upward ready to be formed over the oval cabochon. Use chain and round-nosed pliers to shape the curve and check it frequently over the cabochon on the mat as you place it. This will take careful formation, so practice may be required.

NOTE: The "W" needs to fit over the little 2mm bead attached at the top of the tail.

56 Take some 30AWG (0.25mm) wire, wrap along the "W" and attach to the bottom of the setting.

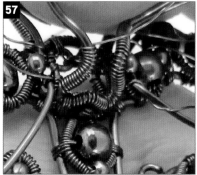

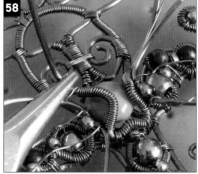

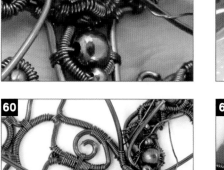

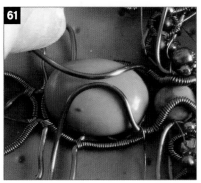

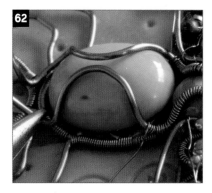

NOTE: The image for Step 53 was taken from a later stage of the gecko (hence you can see wires from the cabochon setting lying over the head section). This is because no image had been taken of the finished point of Step 56 at the time.

57 Wrap along the W-frame (lifting up the setting as you wrap if this makes it easier) until you reach the top of the setting.

58 Insert the 8mm round cabochon into the setting. Bend the wires a little using pliers to adjust the fit.

59 Push the round cabochon firmly into the setting with the rubber end of your plier handles so as not to damage the stone.

60 Wrap the W-frame wires to the lower side edge of the oval setting with several binding wraps for each wire (see arrow in image). Wrap for a few wraps along the W-frame wires, then stop.

61 Make the front setting for the oval cabochon. Place the oval stone onto the setting placed on a rubber bead mat to protect the stone from too much pressure when shaping the wire. Bend the 18AWG (1mm) wires on each side around and over the oval stone so they touch in the middle and bend downward to the base of the upper limbs.

62 Curve the wires around flat so they follow the upper edge curve of the oval setting,

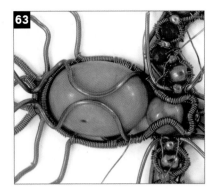

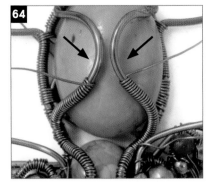

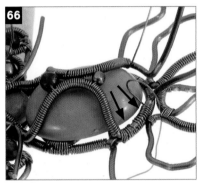

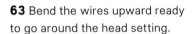

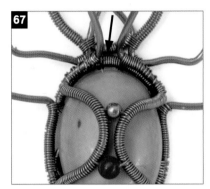

63 Bend the wires upward ready to go around the head setting.

Tip

Use the warmth of your hands to warm the wire to make it easier to shape.

64 With the stone in place, wrap the 30AWG (0.25mm) wire along each front wire until just before the wires come together (see arrows in image).

65 Add in a 3mm lapis lazuli bead with a criss-cross bead attachment and carry on wrapping along the front wires on each side (see red arrows in image). Wrap along the front setting as in the previous step, adding in another 2mm antique bronze bead where the two front wires start to move away from each other (see green arrows).

66 Wrap along the front wires and bind the front wires to the top edge of the oval setting to lock the oval stone into its setting (see arrows in image and the next step).

67 Cut the 26AWG (0.4mm) wires at the levels of the arrow in the image.

68 Work on the 18AWG (1mm) wire ends from Step 30 at the base of the legs. Bend the bottom two wire ends over the base of the tail. Bend the top wire ends up toward the base of the oval section.

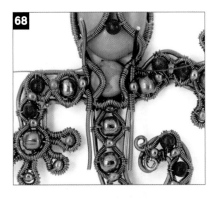

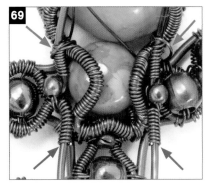

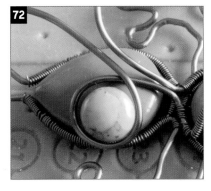

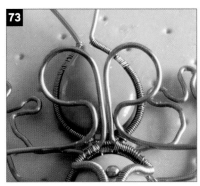

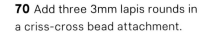

69 Wrap the 30AWG (0.25mm) wire ends you have attached to these wires along each wire for $1/4$in (6mm). Cut the 30AWG (0.25mm) wires at the lower two wire ends (see red arrows in image). Wrap the upper 30AWG (0.25mm) wire around the front wires at the top of the round setting a few times (see green arrows—this is fiddly to thread through; use chain-nosed pliers to help you grab ends).

70 Add three 3mm lapis rounds in a criss-cross bead attachment.

71 Wrap along the top wires for $1/16$in (2mm), cut the 30AWG (0.25mm) wire ends, and smooth the end around the 18AWG (1mm) wire. Curl the wire ends, pressing them into place with your fingers or the rubber-coated ends of your pliers.

72 Work on the head. This is a little complicated, but we are going to mount two little cabochons as eyes on top of the head cabochon. Take the 18AWG (1mm) wire ends from Step 63 and shape them around the cabochons, leaving a $1/32$in (1mm) gap. Make sure these round frames sit at the widest part of the teardrop shape.

73 Bend the wire at the point where it has curved round to the midline again so it runs laterally. Trim to $13/16$in (20mm) on each side.

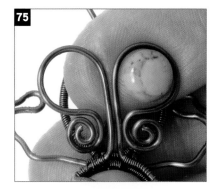

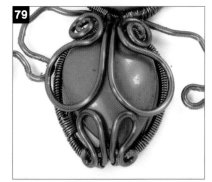

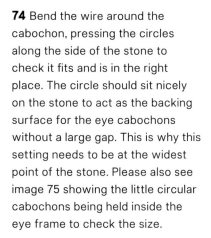

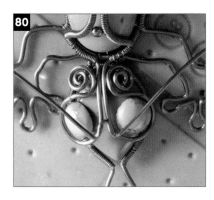

74 Bend the wire around the cabochon, pressing the circles along the side of the stone to check it fits and is in the right place. The circle should sit nicely on the stone to act as the backing surface for the eye cabochons without a large gap. This is why this setting needs to be at the widest point of the stone. Please also see image 75 showing the little circular cabochons being held inside the eye frame to check the size.

75 Spiral the tail of wire coming from the end of the eye socket on each side.

76 Shape the nose/nostril section of the gecko. Bend the two end wires up at the tip of the nose and trim to $^{13}/_{16}$in (20mm).

77 Make a wiggly shape with the wire, looping it about $^{3}/_{8}$in (10mm) from the nose tip.

78 Make a little curl outward at the tip of the wire end using the tips of your round-nosed pliers.

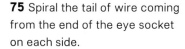

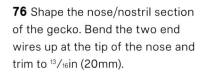

79 Manipulate the nostril shape, bending it either side with your chain-nosed pliers until it forms a shape fitting over the stone, touching the leading edge of the eye socket.

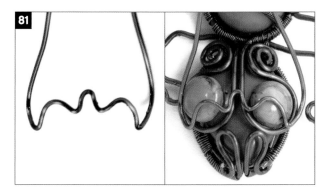

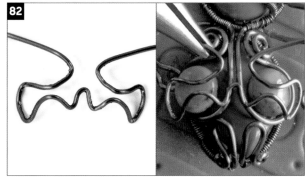

80 The front casing for the eye stones need to be made to mimic the pupil of a gecko's eye. Take 4in (10cm) of 20AWG (0.8mm) wire. Make a $^1/_8$in (3mm) deep V-shape in the midsection of the wire that fits between the eye frames.

81 Make tiny semicircles fitting over the round eye stones with a bend in the wire, shaping around the side of the eye socket for one-quarter of the circle.

82 This is a complex fitting; several tries may be required to get this right. Make sure the wire fits nicely over the stone and does not allow it to slip out of the setting. The semicircle needs to be smaller than the diameter of the setting. Shape the wire back now over the eye stones in another little semicircle in mirror image to the first ones you made. Bend outward again where the wire touches the midline with a $^5/_8$in (15mm) tail on either side.

83 Curl the eye wire ends loosely to allow for reshaping if required. Again, this setting is very fiddly: don't worry if you get it wrong first time.

84 Connect the face together. With the pear cabochon in place, take an 8in (20cm) length of 30AWG (0.25mm) wire and bind the nostril section together at the tip of the nose.

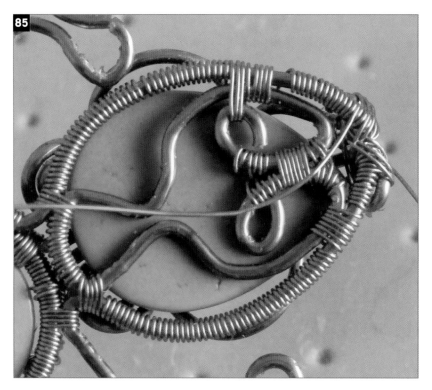

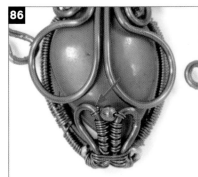

85 Use a figure-of-eight weave (see page 24) along the nostrils, tucking in one end under the jaw.

86 Weave up to the top of the nostrils, adding in a 2mm antique bronze bead. Cut and tuck in the wire end, hiding it away (see red arrow in image).

87 Bind the eyes and rest of the head together. Take 20in (50cm) of 30AWG (0.25mm) wire. Bind at the base of the head around the midline, near one end of the 30AWG (0.25mm) wire, wrapping around the midline a few times with each 30AWG (0.25mm) wire. Cut and tuck in the shorter end. Do not cut the other 30AWG (0.25mm) wire end. Also bind on a 2mm bead at this point.

88 Perform a figure-of-eight basket weave (see page 24) along the midline of the head with the 30AWG (0.25mm) wire, also binding to the eye spiral you made in Step 75, until you reach a point where you can bind to the eye covering frame (see arrow in image).

NOTE: The basket weave you are performing in this step is one where you are wrapping around two frame wires on one side before making the weave pass to wrap around two frame wires on the other side. Please study the image carefully.

89 Wrap a length of 30AWG (0.25mm) wire around the V-point of the little front eye frame made in Step 80 ready for use to bind onto the head. Use the 30AWG (0.25mm) wire in the previous step to bind the eye and head frame together, wrapping on a 2mm antique bronze bead at the same time (see black arrow in image).

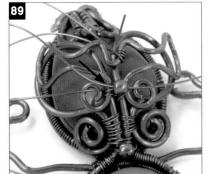

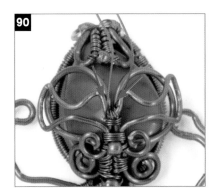

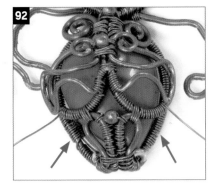

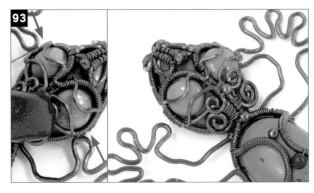

90 Pass the 30AWG (0.25mm) wire a couple of times through the bead, binding to the head frame at the same time. Wrap along up the midline and also to the front eye frame curls for three to four more binding wraps. Wrap up to the point of the "V" of the front eye frame and cut and tuck in the 30AWG (0.25mm) wire. You now have two 30AWG (0.25mm) wire ends added to the point of the V-frame. Wrap each end around both eye settings (see red arrows in this image and previous step) for $1/16$in (2mm), then wrap along the leading edge of the eye socket. Attaching the V section to the eye frame section is fiddly but will stay in place more easily the more you bind it into position.

91 You will be able to wrap around the leading edge of the eye socket, as the eye sockets are not fully bound in place yet, but it is fiddly. Bend the little 30AWG (0.25mm) wire end to help you hook it through small spaces and use the tips of chain-nosed pliers to grab the end of the wire.

92 Slide the eye cabochons into place and press the frontal frames over the stones to make sure they fit. Bind along the side of three frames (eye frontal, socket, and head) to bind them all together and fix the eye cabochons into place (see red arrows here and in next step). Use pliers to help thread through tricky spots. Cut the end off the wire if it gets too ragged and it will thread through small spaces more easily. Cut the wire at the end of this side frame and tuck in the ends. The eyes should now be securely wired in place.

93 Press the curls at the base of the eye against the eye stones using the rubber ends of your pliers to give them even more stability.

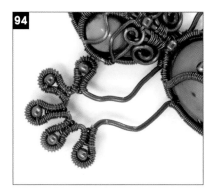

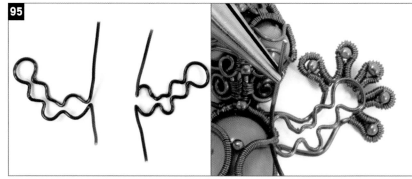

94 Weave the toes of the upper limb as in Steps 10–14.

95 Make upper limb detail frames as in Steps 27–31.

96 Attach and add beads as in Steps 32–34, wrapping the 26AWG (0.4mm) wire along up the top wires of the arm detail frames for ³/₁₆in (4mm). Cut and tuck in the 30AWG (0.25mm) wire ends.

97 Curl the wire ends up over the gecko with the top wires over the top of the oval setting and the lower wires over the side of the oval setting. The main gecko component is now finished.

98 Make a brooch pin (see page 32) to fit the gecko from midway along the head to the base of the tail.

99 To attach the brooch pin to the gecko, wrap 30AWG (0.25mm) wire along the back of the brooch pin until you reach a point where you can also bind to the gecko frame.

100 More than two attachment points are ideal, and the more the better for a secure pin attachment. Make sure the attachment points are hidden in the design. If you find an attachment point is too obvious, add a bead into the design to hide it. I found good points to attach under the backing frame for the oval and pear cabochons and at

MASTERING WIREWORK JEWELRY

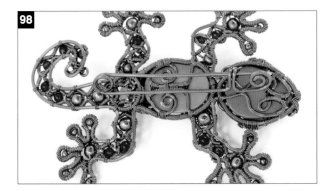

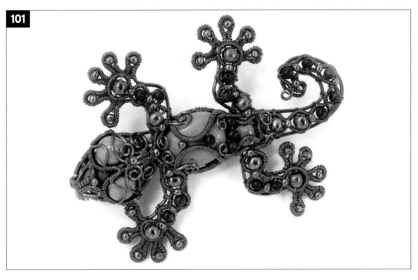

the base of the neck and tail (see arrows in this image and Step 99). Make sure attachments are placed either side of the brooch catch, as this will stop the pin sliding up and down on its attachments and weakening them. I bent the tail curls up a little temporarily to make the attachment and pressed them back into place afterward.

Wrap three times at least around any single attachment point and use your pliers to grab end to help thread them through. When you reach the clip for the brooch, you can wrap a little 2mm antique bronze around it to add detail (see red arrow). Wrap along the base of the brooch pin after making the attachments and cut and tuck in the wire ends.

101 Your beautiful gecko brooch is finished. Loops can be added into the design for making into a pendant or necklace component. Make sure you add them into the main frame design in your version of Step 1, or template on page 297.

Silver angel pendant

This silver angel pendant, combining wirework with the natural beauty of blue opal and silver hematite, is something to be treasured for generations. This design would also look lovely in gold-plated or colored wire.

Templates
See page 295 for the templates for this design.

Materials
18AWG (1mm-diameter) silver round wire
20AWG (0.8mm-diameter) silver round wire
26AWG (0.4mm-diameter) silver round wire
28–30AWG (0.3–0.25mm-diameter) silver round wire
1 x 30 x 18mm amethyst pear/teardrop-shaped cabochon (25 x 15 or 18mm will also work, but you may need to draw your own diagram using mine as a basis from which to work. I used blue opal, but clear quartz, moonstone, fluorite, amethyst, or amazonite would also look nice. Make sure the cabochon is flat-faced and not too domed as you want it to sit like a panel on the angel. If the stone is bow-fronted, it will unbalance the angel so it may not hang nicely. A flat panel of abalone or shell may be suitable.)
1 x 6mm-diameter feature silver bead
3–4mm-diameter silver-coated agate/hematite or metal plain round beads
4–5mm-diameter silver-coated agate/hematite or metal plain round beads
2mm-diameter silver-coated agate or hematite or metal plain round beads
7–8mm-diameter silver-coated agate or hematite or silver metal star-shaped beads or charms
Ball-end silver headpins

Tools
General tools (see page 10)

Dimensions of finished piece
3¹/₂–3³/₄ x 3in (9–9.5 x 7.25cm)

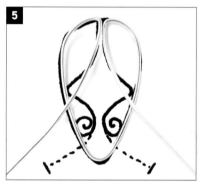

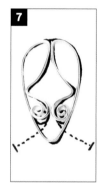
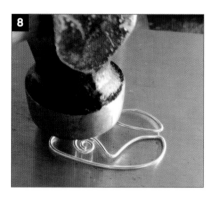

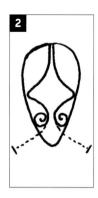
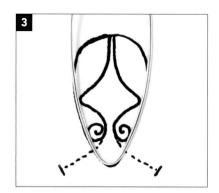
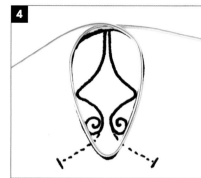

1 Start by making the central teardrop cabochon setting. Take your pear/teardrop cabochon, place it on a piece of plain paper, and draw around it, leaving a ¹/₃₂in (1mm) gap to allow for weaving and attachment of the prong setting around the cabochon later.

2 Draw lines from the top of the pear, bisecting the shape and projecting for ¹/₂in (12mm) from the edge of the cabochon. These will form the backing frame for the cabochon.

3 Take an 8¹/₂in (22cm) length of 18AWG (1mm) round wire and form a V-shape at the center of the wire using chain-nosed pliers.

4 Use the natural curve of the wire to help you, making sure the curve is on the inside of the "V". Check the shape you have made against the template from Step 1. Shape the wires so that the wire ends cross at the top of the pear shape.

5 Using chain-nosed pliers, sharply bend the wires where they cross to bisect the pear shape. Clamp the pliers along the midline wires and also at the top of the bend to shape them. Check all wire ends are symmetrical.

6 Shape the wires over the diagram to form a backing support frame for the cabochon. Trim the wire ends to project ¹/₂–⁵/₈in (12–15mm) outside the edge of the circle.

7 Curl the ends of the 18AWG (1mm) wire using round-nosed pliers so that they loosely curl to fit inside the circular shape with the curl just touching the inner edge of the frame. This will form a backing plate for the cabochon to sit on.

8 Gently hammer the shape using a flat jewelry hammer against a steel block to work-harden but not flatten the wire.

9 Take a 12in (30cm) length of 28AWG (0.3mm) wire and bind together the midline wires of the backing plate. Use a two-by-two basket weave (see page 24). Cut and tuck in the 28AWG (0.3mm) wires on the side that will face the cabochon so that it does not catch against the skin. Put this section aside.

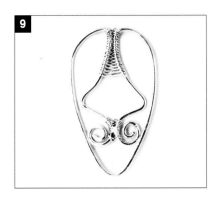

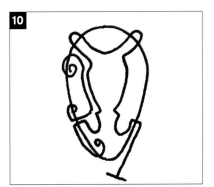

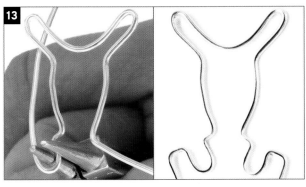

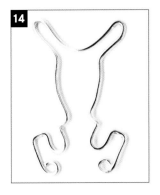

10 Trace the backing plate and plan the angel's arms sections; these will fit over the cabochon. Make the tracing using the impression method (see page 39). I have drawn two line shapes over the outline of the backing frame to act as arm detail and arm frames. The arm frame lies outside the edge of the cabochon frame to allow for the greater distance over curvature of the stone compared to the flat 2D shape drawn around the stone. This will be different for stones of different curvature. The arms need to be wide enough to hold the stone in place and have attachment points around the side that also stop the stone slipping out of the side. The wire tails for the arms are ⁵/₈in (15mm) on each side for the arm shape.

11 Take 8in (20cm) of 18AWG (1mm) wire and shape the arm frame, starting with the curved midsection.

12 Form the sides of the arms following the template. Make the bend sharp at the edge of the sleeve using plier-clamping techniques (see page 24).

13 About ¹/₁₆in (2mm) from this first bend, make a loop with round-nosed pliers for the hand. Use chain-nosed pliers to bend the bottom edge of the hand and then the sleeve about ¹/₈in (3mm) from the bottom corner of the hand. Cut the wire tail ⁵/₈in (15mm) from the lower sleeve corner on both sides.

NOTE: This is a complex little shape. Take your time to get the shape right and practise with scrap wire until you feel you can make the formation easily.

14 Curl the wire tail ends to make cuff details for the sleeves, as shown in the image.

15 If you have a small-faced hammer, hammer the cuff end curls, hands, and neckline curve, but not the rest of the shape.

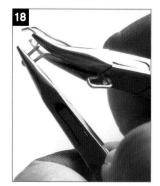

16 Make the inner sleeve detail on either side using Step 10 as a template. Use 2³⁄₄in (7cm) of 18AWG (1mm) wire for each side.

17 Shape one side and then another using the same diagram, flipping the shape over get a mirror image. Check the inside outer arm shape made in Step 11. Leave wire tails ¹⁄₂in (12mm) long and then curl them. Hammer just the curls of the shapes with a small-faced hammer.

18 Mold the outer and inner frame shapes so they fit over the stone. Mold the outer frame first. Use finger pressure to mold over the stone (over a soft surface like a bead mat so as not to fracture the stone) and then use chain-nosed pliers to angle and shape the wire.

Tip

I used two sets of pliers: one to hold the top table of the inner frame setting flat in one plane, and the other to gently move the "prong" section of the setting downward to fit over the side curve of the stone. Use this technique for the hand section as well.

19 The side wires need to be flat to the table surface so they will fit onto the backing frame nicely. The midsection needs to curve inward and over the top of the stone, and the cuff curls need to fold against the side of the pear tip.

20 The inner arm detail shape needs to be molded carefully over the top of the stone, with gentler angles over the top so that it will fit around and against the stone and the outer arm setting in later steps.

21 Join the arm shapes together. Using 12in (30cm) of 28AWG (0.3mm) wire, bind the top section together with two points of five wraps around both frames (see red arrows in image) interspersed with wraps around just the arm frame. Wrap along the sleeve binding with three wraps across both frames (blue arrow), stopping ¹⁄₁₆in (2mm) from the base of the setting. Bind once with four wraps across both frames to the top edge of the upper curl (green arrow). Wrap along the prong, stopping ¹⁄₁₆–¹⁄₈in (2–3mm) from the base of the setting.

22 Repeat for the other side of the setting. Check the fit over the stone.

220

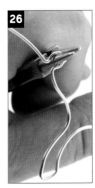

23 Attach a jumpring to the hands with some wraps around the ring and hands with a short length of 28AWG (0.3mm) wire. Each stone is different; you may need to make a specific sized jumpring to fit the space. In my case, I used 18AWG (1mm) wire on a 6mm-diameter mandrel to make a 7mm jumpring (see page 31). Put this section a side for the moment.

Tip

If you have a 6–7mm-diameter closed jumpring in your stash, you can use this. You will have less trouble wrapping over the join in the jumpring with an open jumpring.

NOTE: A closed jumpring is soldered shut and has no cut join that can be opened and closed with pliers.

24 Place the backing plate on some paper and start to plan the framework to go around it. I sketched out a potential angel shape—this template is on page 295. We need to use this template to make a structural outline frame upon which we will build up the angel. I have drawn a thicker black line on the drawing; this is the first frame shape you are going to make. I have sized it on the page to be the same size as the angel you are going to make. If you print this template out, make sure it is to scale—then you can use it as a template over which to shape your wire shapes. If your beads or cabochon are a different size or you want to make a larger angel for a Christmas decoration, or smaller for a little pendant, you might need to scale the template up or down when printing.

25 Take 43in (110cm) of 18AWG (1mm) wire and start forming the halo frame shape at the midpoint of the wire. Using the natural curve of the wire, shape it around the curve of the halo using your fingers, holding the wire onto the paper with one hand and pulling it around the head with the other. Use chain-nosed pliers to shape the bends of the neck at the side of the halo. Place the wire repeatedly over the template on page 295 to check the shape.

Tip

When bending and shaping such a long length of wire, the last thing you want is wire breakage. Avoid too much reshaping, especially at a sharp bend. Use a gentle bend to mark where you want to place a bend, then check over the template to avoid having to reshape a sharp bend (and potentially weakening the wire, with risk of breakage) if you have put a bend in the wrong place.

26 From the curve of the shoulder, make a bend upward to start shaping the top of the angel's wing and the round loop at the top end of the wing. Use the template to help you form the shapes.

NOTE: This loop is here so you can attach chain for your necklace. If making a tree decoration, you can attach cord or ribbon to the loops.

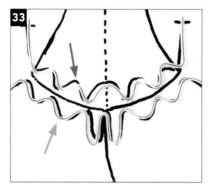

27 Pinch the base of the loop with your pliers to bring the base of the loop together.

28 Start to form the side of the wing, then the tip of the first feather. Use chain-nosed pliers to make the bend for the wing tip. A gentle bend at first and a check on the template will help you size the wing correctly. Make the bend more sharply once you are sure it is in the right place. Then shape the bend in between the first and second feathers.

Tip
To help you form this bend, clamp either side of it with your pliers and squeeze the wires together.

29 Form the rest of the feathers. You can shape five or six, each gradually reducing in length as you move inward along the wing. Check against the template in Step 24 to help shape the feathers.

30 Make a sharp bend at the base of the last feather and start forming the side of the skirt. Make a bend at the base of the angel's skirt and another in the midline of the skirt. The wire end projecting downward from the midline/base of the skirt can be trimmed to 1^3/$_{16}$in (3cm). I bound the base of the angel with a little scrap wire to help hold it in place for photography. This temporary attachment also helps when you are making the hem details.

31 Use the template on page 295 to shape the other half of the angel. Curl the wire ends projecting from the base of the skirt upward and outward. Use round-nosed pliers to start the curl and fingers and pliers to finish the curl using techniques from page 27.

32 Hammer the loops and spirals with a small-faced hammer. Hammer the rest of the angel gently to work-harden but not flatten it. We will hammer the wing tips later after decorating them.

Tip
Hammer the back of the shape so that any marks are more likely to be made on the back of the frame.

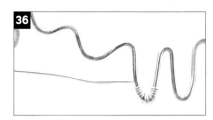

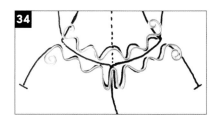

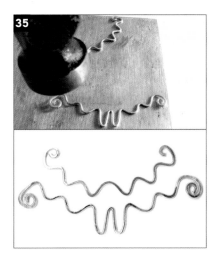

37 Start to weave along the little pointed foot section using the long end of 28AWG (0.3mm) wire. Use a standard figure-of-eight weave with two wraps of the 28AWG (0.3mm) wire around each frame side before each traverse to the opposite frame side wire (see page 24). You will end up with a woven foot shape. Repeat this step for the other foot. Stop weaving at the tip of the foot shapes.

38 Wrap 24in (60cm) of 28AWG (0.3mm) wire around the base of the angel frame at the midsection of the 28AWG (0.3mm) wire. You can bind a 2mm bead on at this stage if you want. Try to make two passes of the 28AWG (0.3mm) wire through the bead to strengthen this attachment. Note which is the front side of the piece so hammer marks are made to the back. At this stage the frame is not very securely attached together; make sure the bottom of the skirt is lined up nicely, with repeated readjustment, until later steps make this area more secure. Wrap the 28AWG (0.3mm) wire along either side of the attachment at the midline of the angel for six to seven wraps.

33 I have drawn a wavy hemline (see blue arrow on image) and a wavy skirt detail (red arrow) onto the template on page 295. It is more or less to scale so you can use it as a template over which to shape your wire, or draw the same shape onto your own template. The middle two projections are the angel's feet pointed downward. Take 8in (20cm) of 18AWG (1mm) wire and shape the hemline and feet with a curve of wire either end, 1in (2.5cm) long, following the template. Make the wavy skirt detail using a 6in (15cm) length of 18AWG (1mm) wire. Each end of the skirt detail is a curve of wire about ⁵/₈in (15mm) length.

34 Curl the ends of the shapes made in Step 33 using the techniques from Step 18. Check the fit of the shapes against the main angel frame.

35 Hammer the shapes to flatten and work-harden them. You may need to reshape the wavy shapes to fit the angel frame if the hammering process has splayed them. Achieve this with squeezes either side of the bends with chain-nosed pliers.

36 Take 10in (25cm) of 28AWG (0.3mm) wire (you can also use 30AWG/0.25mm wire for this section if you prefer) and wrap, near one end of the 28AWG (0.3mm) wire, around the tip of one of the toes. Make four to five wraps either side of the tip then stop. Cut and tuck in the short end of the 28AWG (0.3mm) wire, leaving the longer end for weaving in the next step.

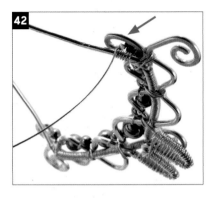

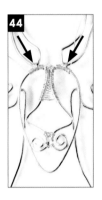

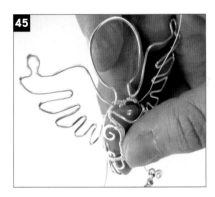

39 Hold the wavy skirt shape and skirt detail in place against the bottom of the angel's skirt with one hand (this is fiddly until the first wraps are in place). Wrap the 28AWG (0.3mm) wire twice around the points where these two shapes touch against the main skirt frame on either side (see red arrows in image). Make sure the feet are centered nicely. Wrap the 28AWG (0.3mm) wire around the base of the main skirt frame only. Make sure that you hold the wavy frames above and below the main frame so they don't overlap the main frame but lie to the side of it. Continue to wrap along the base of the main angel skirt frame, attaching the wavy hem shape and the wavy skirt details to the main angel frame where they touch (see black arrows) with two binding wraps around all the frames. Continue

along the main angel frame until you reach the next attachment point. When you reach either side of the skirt base, wrap two to three times around the frame and the upward curl of the wavy skirt detail (red arrows). One of the 28AWG (0.3mm) wires will be used to attach beads in the next stages; the other can be cut away. I cut away the left-hand 28AWG (0.3mm) wire, leaving the one on the right, which was longer.

40 Use the 28AWG (0.3mm) wire ends from the previous step that are at the base of the angel's skirt to wrap on some beads to the hem to add detail. Thread a 2mm bead onto the other 28AWG (0.3mm) wire at the right side of the angel's hemline and wrap across to the nearest side of the wavy loop with one binding wrap around the loop.

41 Thread on a 3–4mm bead and wrap across to the other side of the loop with one binding wrap. Continue along the hemline, alternately adding 2mm beads to the V-shaped spaces between the larger loops and 3–4mm beads into the larger loop spaces. Finish with a 2mm bead at the other side of the skirt.

42 Wrap the 28AWG (0.3mm) wire around the side of the skirt a few times, concealing the wraps under the curl of the skirt detail (see red arrow in image). Cut and tuck in the 28AWG (0.3mm) wire end.

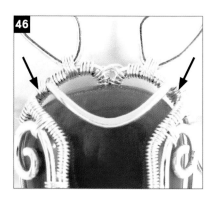

43 Now attach the arms, cabochon, and backing plate to the rest of the angel. Take 40in (1m) of 28AWG (0.3mm) wire and attach at the midline top of the backing frame. Wrap around the backing frame at the top on either side until you reach a level where you can bind on to the top edge of the upper arm.

Tip

Make sure the rough-cut 28AWG (0.3mm) wire ends on the backing plate are placed against the back of the cabochon.

44 Place the backing plate against the angel frame. Bind the plate to the shoulders with wraps of 30AWG (0.25mm) wire around both frames until you reach a level where you can bind to the arm frame setting (see arrows in image).

45 I found it easier to make the prong attachment with the stone inside the setting. This prevented the setting slipping around and made the binding process easier.

46 Bind to the arm prongs (see arrows in image). Wrap along to the lower edge of the arms and the arm curl where they cross the backing frame ready to bind to this point.

47 Work your way around the stone binding along the side of the angel frame and the cabochon backing frame to the back of the setting (see blue arrow in image).

48 Bind to the sleeve curl and the angel frame. As you bind to the sleeve curl, pass the wire around all three frames. You may need to use chain-nosed pliers to move the backing plate and frame closer together as you bind along the frame.

49 Stop binding just beyond this point for the moment. Make sure the angel frame lies behind the backing plate and does not slip in front of it as you bind along it.

NOTE: When binding to the sleeve curl, press the stone and setting together with your fingers and then manually pull the 28AWG (0.3mm) wire to cinch it into place. If you let the wire do all the work of pulling the components together, the wire can break.

Tip

If the wire tip gets ragged, cut it to get a fresh end. This is easier to thread through small spaces. Press the stone away slightly from the edge where you are threading through, to help you make a small space to pass the wrapping wire.

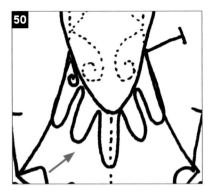

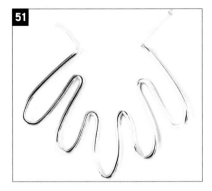

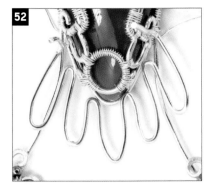

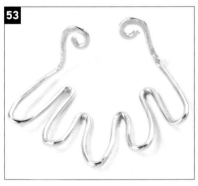

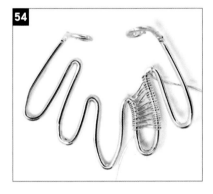

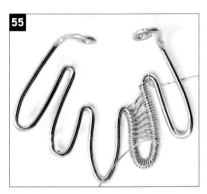

50 Plan the details for the skirt on the template from page 295. I have drawn a frilly layer for the skirt on the template from Step 24 (see red arrow in image).

51 Take 8in (20cm) of 18AWG (1mm) wire and shape it over the template with ⁵⁄₈in (15mm) wire tails on either side, as shown.

52 Bend the wire tails directly upward at 90 degrees to the frilly section. Check the fit against the angel frame.

53 Curl the wire ends loosely. Hammer the curl only with a small-faced hammer.

54 Weave each frill with a basket weave using 28AWG (0.3mm) wire (as for the feet in Step 37). The weave ratio is three wraps around the outer edge compared to two for the inner edge as the distance to weave along is longer on the outside edge of each frill. It helps to splay the shape while weaving, then press the frills closely together again afterward. Stop the basket weave about ¹⁄₄in (6mm) from the tip of the frill.

55 Wrap around the tip.

56 Add in a 3–4mm round bead with a final wrap and tuck in the 28AWG (0.3mm) wire.

57 Attach this section to the rest of the angel frame. Using the 28AWG (0.3mm) wire ends from binding the cabochon frame to the angel frame in Step 44, bind around the top side ends of the frilly skirt shape, binding on a 2mm silver-coated hematite bead with the wraps (see red arrows in image). Then wrap along the side of the angel skirt frame under the frilly frame for a few wraps and stop for the moment (see blue arrows).

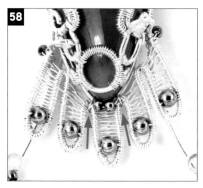

58 Take a new 24in (60cm) length of 28AWG (0.3mm) wire. Bind at the top of the middle frill, adding in two 2mm beads. Bind around the top side of the frill to the cabochon frame on either side for three wraps (see arrows in image).

59 Push the frilly frame close up toward the cabochon frame for a good fit. Bring the 28AWG (0.3mm) wires up between the frills ready to bind on more beads. Continue on either side, adding in 2mm beads to the top of each frond until you reach the side. Wrap around the side frame and cut and tuck in the wire end.

60 Press the curls at the side of the frilly frame over the frills at the side. Use fingers or the rubber tips of round-nosed pliers.

61 Bind along the angel frame and to the tips of the side fronds with the 28AWG (0.3mm) wire ends from Steps 44 and 57 (see blue arrows in image).

62 Now plan the lower skirt detail. I have traced a line inside the angel frame to get a better idea of the space to fill.

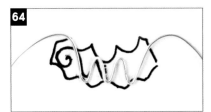

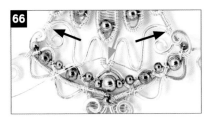

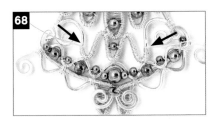

63 I have drawn on the diagram a shape for the frame for this section (see also template on page 295).

64 Make this section with 4in (10cm) of 18AWG (1mm) wire. Make a "V" in the midsection of the wire. Shape the wire on one side over the template. Turn the shape over. Form the other side over the same shape to get a mirror image.

65 Loosely curl the wire on either side using the outer to inner spiral technique (see page 28). Check the fit inside the angel frame. Hammer the shape and adjust to fit if splayed.

66 Attach the wavy shape at three points. First, bind the shape to the top point of the skirt detail with the midpoint of a 40in (1m) length of 28AWG (0.3mm) wire (see blue arrow in image). Then bind at each side of the skirt with the wrapping side frame using 28AWG (0.3mm) wire ends left from Step 57 (see the black arrows).

NOTE: Place the curls from the wavy shape *over* the skirt detail shape.

67 Wrap along the skirt detail at either side of the midline, adding in a 2mm bead with a criss-cross bead attachment (see page 26).

68 Carry on wrapping along the middle "V" on either side, also binding to the middle point of the frilly skirt shape. Then wrap along the skirt detail, binding to the wavy skirt shape at points shown by arrows. When you get to the point at the level of the arrows in the previous step, use a different weave technique. Add in a 2mm bead and wrap across to the adjacent wire curl on either side.

69 On the right of the angel I have wrapped twice around the curl, then woven back to the outside curl of the spiral, wrapping around six times. Continue around the spiral with this six to two weave ratio, adding in beads on each outer to inner weave pass. Make sure you also bind to the tip of skirt frill (see arrows in image).

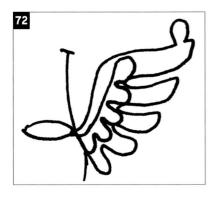

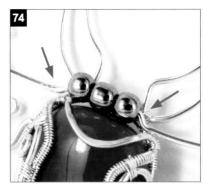

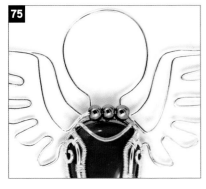

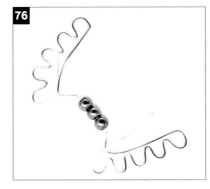

70 Cut and tuck in the wire when you reach the inner spiral and can add no more beads (see blue arrows in image).

71 Take a new 8–12in (20–30cm) length of 28AWG (0.3mm) or 26AWG (0.4mm) wire. Wrap twice either side of the wraps already in place at the center point of the wavy section (see arrows in previous step image). Add in a 3mm bead to either side, wrapping across the skirt detail and adding in 2mm beads to the next space. Bind on a 3mm bead to the last space (see blue arrows in image). Find a space to wrap then cut and tuck in the wire end.

72 Make a wing detail structure that serves to add strength to the wing and areas to attach and bind beads to. Please use the template on page 295 as a guide.

73 Take 16in (40cm) of 18AWG (1mm) wire and make a bend at the midsection into a slight concave curve to form a neck detail. Thread on three 5mm silver beads. Kink the 18AWG (1mm) wire slightly at the side of the row of beads so the wire can attach to the shoulder frame.

74 The beads act as a necklace detail for the angel. They are a little proud of the frame due to the 5mm bead diameter, which is why the kink in the wire is required. If using 4mm beads the kink will not be as large. Curve the wire downward so it runs around the shoulder of the angel (see red arrows in image) for about 1/4in (6mm) (this length will vary according to the width of your wing).

75 Make a curve in the wire on each side to follow the curve in the wing.

76 After checking this curve fits along the length of your angel's wing, make five little loops in the wire separated by bends. Each loop should correspond to a feather for the wing and fit into or over the base of each feather. Leave a 13/16in (20mm) tail at the base of the innermost first loop. Bend the wire tail upward out of the plane of the wing detail. Do this for both sides.

77 Check the fit over the angel frame. Curl the wire tails and hammer just the tails with a small-faced hammer.

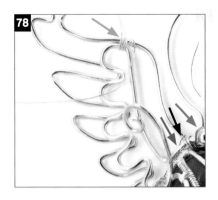
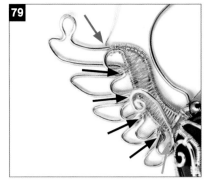
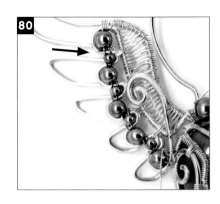

78 Attach the wing detail to the angel frame. Take a 40in (1m) length of 28AWG (0.3mm) wire. Using the midsection of the 28AWG (0.3mm) wire, bind the top and side of the shoulder to the shoulder section (just to the side of the waist section between the wing detail loops and the shoulder; see black arrow in image). One 28AWG (0.3mm) wire end needs to be brought up into the top space in the wing ready to make a two-by-two basket weave (see page 24) along the top edge of the wing later (red arrow). The other end of the 28AWG (0.3mm) wire needs to be along the neck (green arrow). Do this for both sides to fix the neck in place. I have also attached the end of another 40in (1m) length of 28AWG (0.3mm) wire to the other end of the wing detail loop section (blue arrow). This binding wrap will stabilize and strengthen the wing structure.

79 Bring the 28AWG (0.3mm) wire end inside the top end of the outer fifth wing space, ready to add beads later (see red arrow in image). Start a basket along the upper wing space section of the wing with one end of the 28AWG (0.3mm) wire attached at the blue arrow in the image. Weave between the top of the wing frame and the top of the wing detail frame to add strength, detail, and structure to the wing. Vary the weave ratio if one side is travelling up faster than the other, adding an extra wrap on the longer side until the weave is equal again. The black arrows indicate the spots where you need to bind around the inter-loop bends of the wing detail as you weave. You also need to bind to the base of the wing detail curl (blue arrow). Cut and tuck in the 28AWG (0.3mm) wire ends at this end.

80 Using the 28AWG (0.3mm) wire end from the level of the red arrow in the previous step, thread one 3mm bead onto the 28AWG (0.3mm) wire. Wrap across to the other side of the base of the largest feather to add this beaded detail. Wrap three times around both the base at the junction between the fourth and fifth feather and the bottom of the fourth loop space (see arrow in image). Bring the 28AWG (0.3mm) wire into the fourth feather base ready to attach another 2mm bead. Add another 2mm bead into the space at the base of the fourth feather frame, wrapping across to the other side of the feather frame, then up and around the intersection of the third/fourth feathers and the base of the fourth feather detail loop. Add beads in the same way to the rest of the wing and wrap at the lower edge of the base of the wing.

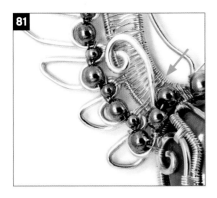

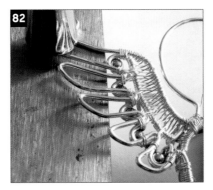

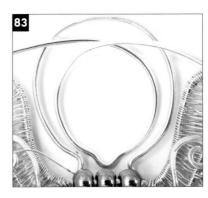

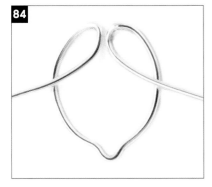

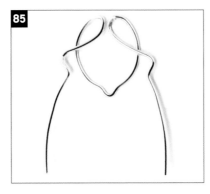

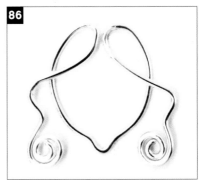

81 Using fingers or rubber plier handle ends, gently press the wing curl detail down over the upper wing frame weave. Use the wire end from the previous step to add in two 3mm beads along the base of the wing in the direction of the blue arrow in the image to hide any messy wirework. Wrap at the top of the shoulder and cut and tuck in the wire end.

82 Repeat Steps 79–81 for the other wing. You can either fill the rest of the wing tip with more beads or make a basket weave along the shaft of the feather. I chose simply to hammer the *back* of the wing tips with a small-faced hammer. Hammer carefully so as not to damage the weaving and binding wires.

83 Now make a face and hairline shape. Use the template from Step 24 if you like. Take 5in (12.5cm) of 18AWG (1mm) wire and gently bend halfway along around round-nosed pliers to start forming the chin. Bend the wire ends outward then curve upward to form the jawline and cheeks. Form an oval shape by crossing the wire ends over at the top of the oval.

84 Check this shape fits into the halo and neck frame portion of the angel; reshape if necessary. Bend the wire ends downward and outward where they were crossing over each other to form a midline hair parting.

85 Shape the wire ends to form a hairstyle with a gentle wavy shape and a straight wire end of about 1in (25mm). Trim to size. Keep both sides as mirror-image symmetrical as possible so the hairstyle frames the face nicely.

86 Curl the wire ends (see page 27).

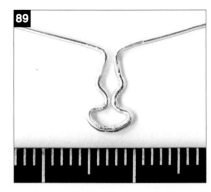

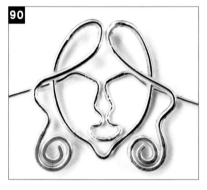

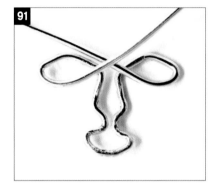

87 Hammer the hair curls. Check this shape fits into the halo and neck frame portion of the angel; reshape if necessary.

88 Make a little face shape. Use the template on page 295 if you like. Make a mouth shape with 6in (15cm) of 20AWG (0.8mm) wire. At the midsection of the wire, make a shape like a tiny sailing boat with both wire ends traveling upward from the top lip on either side of the midline, as shown.

89 This shape needs to be formed with the tips of chain-nosed pliers to make the small bends. Squash the top and lower lips together a little. Practice with scrap wire; it may take a few trial runs to get this face shape to work. Start to form a nose shape from the midline wires on each side. Bend the wire ends away from the nose out to the side to start forming the eyes.

90 Arch the wire ends upward, outward away from the nose circle. Make a little shallow pyramid shape to form the top of the eye to start forming the upper eye frames. Check this shape fits into the halo and neck frame portion of the angel; reshape if necessary. Notice where the eye frame crosses the angel's face; this is where the corner of the eye can be formed.

91 Bend the wire to form the corner of the eye with the wire end curving inward and upward over the bridge of the nose. This area can be shaped with chain-nosed plier tips.

92 Take your time to make the eyes symmetrical. Cut the wire ends with flush cutter pliers where they touch against the nose/inner corner of the eyes.

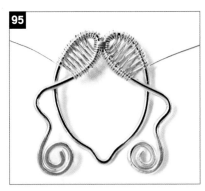

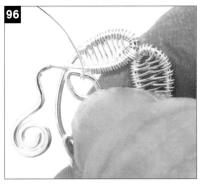

93 Check this shape fits into the face frame portion of the angel and reshape if necessary. Gently hammer the face shape and reshape any splaying caused by hammering.

94 Take the face and hair wire shape from Step 87. Bind a 31in (78cm) length of 28AWG (0.3mm) wire (at its central point) around the midline/hairline of the angel's face four or five times to join the head frame together. Carry on wrapping along the hairline for about six wraps on either side.

95 Using basket-weaving techniques (see page 24), perform a two-by-two figure-of-eight basket weave along the hairline on either side until you are about two-thirds down the hairline, ready to attach the eye/nose section.

96 Place the eye/nose section under the hairline. Bind to the face section with wraps to the upper eye wire and hairline to bind them together on either side. Hold the pieces in place with one hand while binding with the other.

97 Continue binding the 28AWG (0.3mm) wire around the eye socket and the hairline on either side. When you reach the corner of the eye, wrap along the bottom of the eye until halfway across for each eye, as shown.

98 Thread on a 2mm bead and bind across to the bridge of the nose on each side to act as the iris for the eyes. Wrap the 28AWG (0.3mm) wire toward the bridge of the nose, where you can stop wrapping. Cut and tuck in the 28AWG (0.3mm) wires on either side.

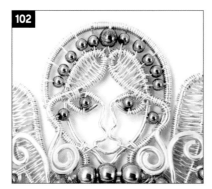

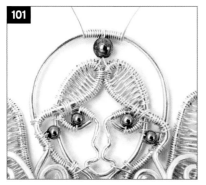

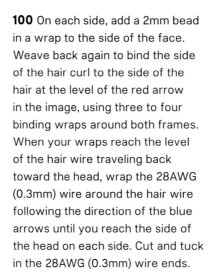

99 Place the face and hair section into the halo space in the main angel frame. Wrap up with the 28AWG (0.3mm) wire end left from binding on the wing detail in Step 78. Bind near one end at one side of the chin to the top of the neck section on the angel frame about three to four times, then wrap either side of this attachment around the angel frame. Wrap across to the mouth to secure it in place onto the face at each side of the mouth (see black arrows in image).

NOTES: Make sure the long end of 28AWG (0.3mm) wire lies above this attachment ready to wrap upward and around the halo section.

At this stage, the face can slip to one side more than the other. You need to pull the face back into a central position and keep it there so the attachments for the halo are symmetrical and balanced.

100 On each side, add a 2mm bead in a wrap to the side of the face. Weave back again to bind the side of the hair curl to the side of the hair at the level of the red arrow in the image, using three to four binding wraps around both frames. When your wraps reach the level of the hair wire traveling back toward the head, wrap the 28AWG (0.3mm) wire around the hair wire following the direction of the blue arrows until you reach the side of the head on each side. Cut and tuck in the 28AWG (0.3mm) wire ends.

101 Bind 40in (1m) of 28AWG (0.3mm) wire to the center parting of the top of the angel's head, passing both wires upward. Thread a 3mm bead onto both wires, then wrap along the halo frame on either side with each wire for nine wraps.

102 Add two 2mm beads and wrap across into the woven hairline, threading through the weave already there. Wrap around the head frame once and return up to the halo frame. Repeat this weave all the way around the halo, using a weave wrap ratio of nine wraps around the halo before each weave pass across to the woven hairline. Add a 2mm bead before each return traverse and wrapping nine times around the halo frame again. Do this until you reach the side curls that are already wrapped on either side. Cut and tuck in the 28AWG (0.3mm) wire on either side.

Tip

Try to keep the weave as mirror image as possible, with the same number of 2mm beads added on each side of the head.

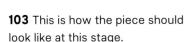

103 This is how the piece should look like at this stage.

104 Add some star charms onto the angel's hemline and wings using jumprings made with 18AWG (1mm) wire wound around a 3mm-diameter mandrel.

105 Make a little votive or lamp to hang from the angel's hands. I have used a detailed 6mm silver barrel bead; you could use a 6mm hematite round instead. Thread the 6mm bead onto a ball headpin with a 3–4mm hematite round next and make a wrapped loop at the other end of the headpin.

106 Loosen the edge of the jumpring over the cabochon. Thread a jumpring made with 20AWG (0.8mm) wire on a 3mm-diameter mandrel through it to attach the headpin bead component you have just made.

107 Close the jumpring. The lamp/votive should dangle nicely.

108 For the necklace, make 5mm and 7mm external diameter jumprings from 18AWG (1mm) silver wire using 3.2mm and 5mm Gizmo mandrels (see pages 29 and 31). Make the necklace by linking together alternating pairs of 5mm and 7mm jump rings finished with a clasp (see pages 22–23). Your beautiful angel necklace is now finished and ready to wear!

Butterfly cabochon pendant

This butterfly motif is designed to sit over the front of a plain cabochon as artwork over the stone. This design can easily be adapted to use smaller or larger cabochons in a variety of shapes and sizes. The butterfly can be placed at any angle as long as it fits into the space over the stone.

Templates
See page 293 for the templates for this design.

Materials
18AWG (1mm-diameter) round copper wire
(20AWG/0.8mm-diameter wire can be used in some components instead of 18AWG/1mm wire)
26AWG (0.4mm-diameter) round copper wire
30AWG (0.25mm-diameter) round colored copper wire
(Silver, bare copper, or gold-plated wire will also work)
2mm or 3mm copper beads
1 x 40 x 30mm pear/teardrop-shaped gemstone or cabochon, no drill hole required (I used purple agate. The flatter the face of the gemstone the better. If your cabochon is quite domed you will need to mold the butterfly to fit over the domed face of the gemstone and you may require an extra row of frame-setting wire to form the cabochon setting)

Tools
General tools (see page 10)
6mm mandrel, penor knitting needle

Dimensions of finished piece
2⁹/₁₆ x 1³/₈in (6.5 x 3.5cm)

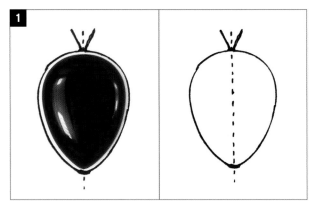

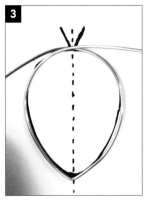

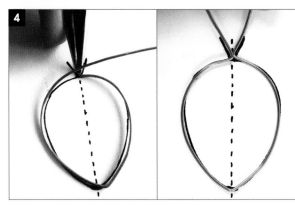

1 Take your cabochon, place it on a piece of plain paper, and draw around it with a pen, leaving a $1/32$in (1mm) gap to allow for weaving and attachment of wirework components later. Draw a line along the midline using a ruler; this will help you form the bale symmetrically. See also template on page 293.

2 Take a 16in (40cm) length of 18AWG (1mm) wire. Starting at the midpoint of the wire, bend it to a point to fit the tip of the cabochon.

3 Squash either side of the point with chain-nosed pliers a few times to sharpen it a little. Form it into a teardrop/pear shape (or the shape of your cabochon) using the drawing as a template. Use your fingers and pliers and the natural curve of the wire from the reel to help you shape the wire.

4 Bend the end wires upward using chain-nosed pliers. Make the first bend a gentle one. Check against the template and reshape if required. Too sharp a bend in the wrong place means the wire will need reshaping, which will weaken it.

5 Straighten the wire by stroking along it firmly a few times with thumb and forefinger. Each bale end wire should be 6in (15cm) long. Check the fit against the cabochon shape and the template.

6 Hammer the wire gently against a steel block to work-harden but not flatten it.

7 Draw a line $1/32$in (1mm) inside the first cabochon shape.

8 Take another 16in (40cm) of 18AWG (1mm) wire and shape it around the second inner template, again starting at the midsection of the 18AWG (1mm) wire.

9 Don't shape too sharply at the top of the teardrop shape; you will probably need to adjust this shape after weaving. Don't hammer this shape as you will need to reshape the top later.

MASTERING WIREWORK JEWELRY

10 Draw a third shape ¹/₃₂in (1mm) inside the second line drawn in Step 7.

11 Make another wire shape in the same way as in Step 8 using 16–20in (40–50cm) of 18AWG (1mm) wire.

NOTE: I chose a flat cabochon as fewer wires are needed to form the frame. If your cabochon is deep, you might need to make another inner frame layer to hold the cabochon in place. You will have to decide what to do with the extra end wires near the bale—maybe make another curl or two.

12 Take 80–100in (2–2.5m) of 26AWG (0.4mm) wire and wrap six times around the base of the largest wire frame from Step 2, using the midpoint of the 26AWG (0.4mm) wire.

13 Take the second smallest wire frame and hold it inside the first frame with a ¹/₁₆in (2mm) space between them. Wrap the 26AWG (0.4mm) wire from one end across to the inner frame, using a figure-of-eight movement (i.e., if the wire is coming from the front of the outer frame wire, pass to the back of the inner frame wire and wrap around three times). Don't pull the traversing weave wire too tight. You need to maintain a space between the wires, as you will use these to weave backing wire onto. Hold the frame wires apart with the fingers of one hand while weaving with the other hand to help achieve this spacing. It will get easier with more attachment weaves. Do the same with the other end of the 26AWG (0.4mm) wire. You will now have secured the frames together at two points.

14 Take the third and smallest frame and wrap across using both sides of the wire to bind this one onto the frame section using a figure-of-eight traverse across the space (see page 24) and three wraps around the frame.

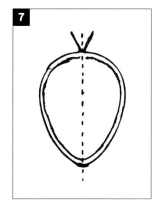

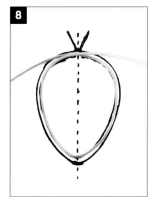

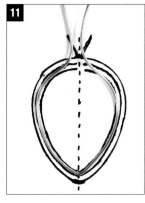

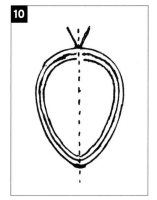

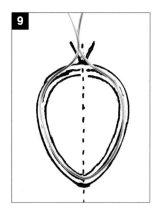

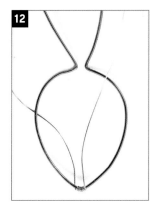

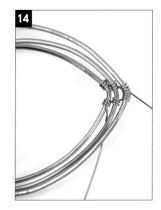

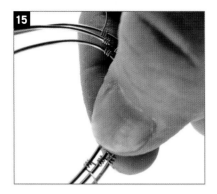

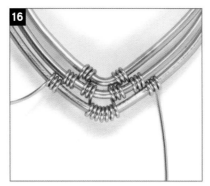

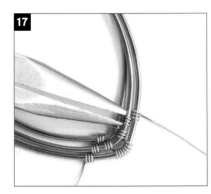

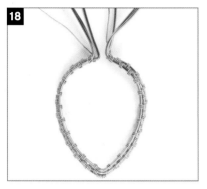

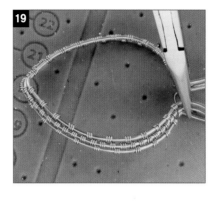

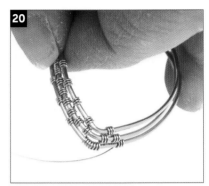

15 Keep the spacing even with thumb and forefingers; you will need these gaps as attachment spaces later. This is fiddly at the start, but as you secure more weaves the frames start to hold themselves in place more easily. This is a great weave to use for attachments of other wire components, as there are plenty of little spaces to bind wires into.

16 Weave and wrap down to the middle frame wire and then the outer frame wire in the same way until you make a zigzag pattern in the weaves.

17 Use chain-nosed pliers to neaten the weaves by gently squeezing the groups of three wraps from side to side.

18 Continue this weave along both sides and all around the frame until you reach the top. End at the top of the outer frame shape, ready to make the first binding wrap at the back of the setting.

19 You may need to gently reshape the two upper/inner frames as you go with pliers, checking the fit against the stone, especially as you approach the top.

NOTE: The outer frame (the first frame made) should not be reshaped as it has been work-hardened and specifically made to fit the gemstone.

20 Using your fingers, shape the frames to make them slope slightly with the outer frame at the bottom of the slope, as shown.

21 Check the fit against the cabochon. Press the inner frame upward to make it fit upward and around the cabochon nicely. Make final adjustments to the top wires to ensure they all fit well at the top. Press the top of the frame firmly against the cabochon. You might want to use a rubber mat for this step, placing the cabochon on top of the mat so that pressure from pressing the frame against the cabochon is less likely to break the stone.

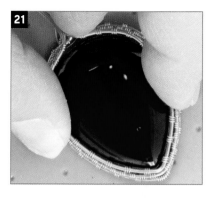

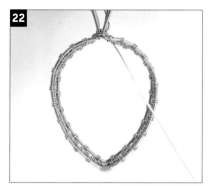

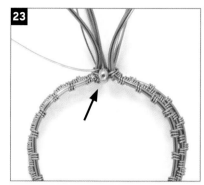

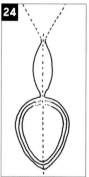

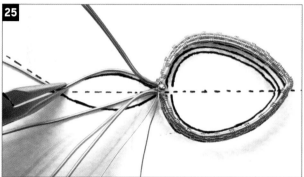

22 Bind the outer frame wires at the base of the bale with a few figure-of-eight wraps across the gap using one of the 26AWG (0.4mm) wire ends and bringing the sides of the back of the top of the setting tightly together. Bring the other of the two wires either side of the base of the bale to wrap once around the middle and inner/front frame wire. Pull the frames tightly together at the top with this bead attachment.

23 Here I bound a 3mm bead across the gap at the top of the inner/front cabochon frame to help join this section together and to help it fit over the stone properly (see arrow in image). Do not cut the 26AWG (0.4mm) wire ends.

NOTE: Step 22 shows the back and 23 the front.

24 Here I have drawn a bale shape on the drawing from Step 1. I have sized it to fit the cabochon I used so you can use it as a template if you wish (see page 293).

25 Shape the bale wires using the template as a guide.

26 Splay the outer two wires on either side slightly (from inner and middle frames) to move them out of the way for the moment. The central two wires from the outer frame at the back form an elongated leaf shape and the ends bend outward. I made the bale wires about 1⁹/₁₆in (4cm) long with a maximum width of ¹/₂in (12mm) to allow a chunky braid through it.

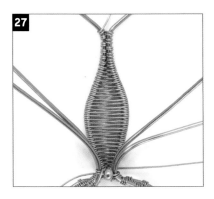

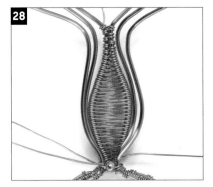

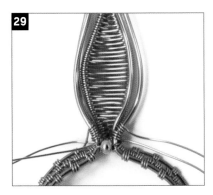

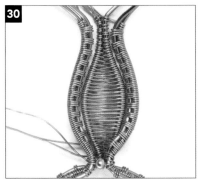

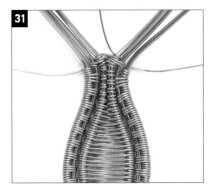

27 Take 120in (3m) of 26AWG (0.4mm) wire. Attach 40in (1m) from one end to the base of the bale and start a two-by-two cross weave up the bale with the 80in (2m) end. Use a standard figure-of-eight weave with two wraps of the 26AWG (0.4mm) wire around each bale side before each traverse to the opposite side bale wire (see page 24). Stop at the top of the leaf section of the bale. Do not cut the 26AWG (0.4mm) weaving wire ends, they will be used in later stages.

28 Now shape the outer bale wires. Take the middle frame wire first and shape it around the side of the inner bale wires woven in Step 27. Bend the wire at the same level as for the inner bale. Then shape the top (originally inner) frame wires

to lie outside the middle wire. The image shows all the wires shaped with pairs of wires on either side of the bale ready for the next weave wraps. Do not cut the 26AWG (0.4mm) wire ends; they will be useful later.

29 Take 120in (3m) of 26AWG (0.4mm) wire. Join at the midsection of the 26AWG (0.4mm) wire to the base of the bale, passing the middle of the 26AWG (0.4mm) wire along the back of the middle section of the bale so it is hidden. Wrap one 26AWG (0.4mm) wire end around one side of the paired bale wires three times, then three times around the outside bale wire only. Do the same on the other side of the bale with the other 26AWG (0.4mm) wire end.

30 Weave on up the bale on either side with a three-by-three weave (three across both and three across on the outside bale wire) until you reach the kink in the wires before the tail wires. Stop at the end of the bale woven section and don't weave along the bale end wires yet. Don't cut the 26AWG (0.4mm) wire. Keep the bales wires evenly spaced as you weave. You can push the weave together as you go with your fingers or carefully (so as not to damage the wires) with the tips of chain-nosed pliers. Make sure you end up with three wraps around the outer wires only.

31 Bind across the bale wires with the weaving wire end of the 26AWG (0.4mm) wires from Step 28 (central leaf-shaped section) to bind the bale frame wires together.

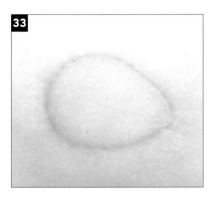

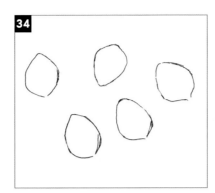

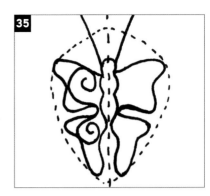

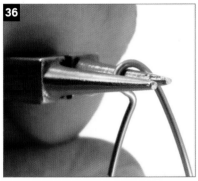

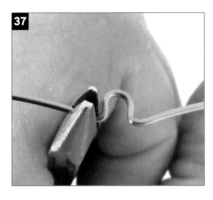

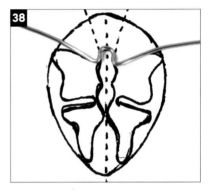

32 Turn the bale over and press the frame gently onto a sheet of plain paper, as shown.

33 Work over a rubber bead mat to get an impression of the inner frame size.

34 Draw over the impression line. This will allow you to plan your wire design later as you will know what space you need to fill. Draw a few versions so you don't have to worry about making a mistake when planning.

35 Take the drawing from Step 32 and start to plan the design. I have drawn a butterfly design that you can use as a template for the same size and type of cabochon that I used (see page 293). Make sure when you place your cabochon frame over this drawing that it fits nicely inside the frame space. If it is larger or smaller you may need to resize the drawing by scanning it and printing it out on a different size setting.

36 Take 31in (78cm) of 18AWG (1mm) wire (or, if you find it easier, 20AWG/0.8mm wire). Begin to form the main butterfly frame, starting with a round head loop section shaped around round-nosed pliers, leaving enough space to fit a 2–3mm bead inside this circular shape.

37 Now using chain-nosed pliers, make a bend in the wire on either side of the base of the head to direct the wire upward and outward to shape over the top edges of the top wings on either side. The bend angle needs to be fairly sharp. Use chain-nosed plier tips to help you achieve this.

38 Use the drawing as a template to guide you.

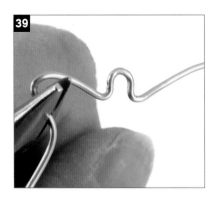

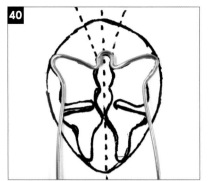

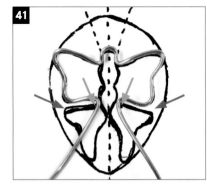

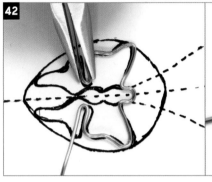

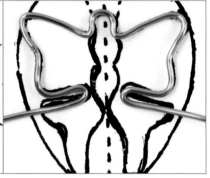

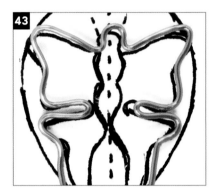

39 Shape the tips of the upper wings with a sharp bend downward and slightly inward to start forming the outer edge of the top wings with a little bend in the side of the wing.

40 Use the drawing as a template to help you keep the wings symmetrical.

41 Make a bend at the outer base of the upper wing inward toward the midline and form the base of the top wing (see red arrows in image). Make a sharp bend on either side at the junction between upper and lower wings where they will touch the body of the butterfly that you will form later (blue arrows).

42 Use the diagram to help you make sure these bends are in the right place and that the lower edges of the wings are symmetrical. Little squashes with chain-nosed pliers on both sides of these tight curves in the wire will help to make those angles more acute.

Tip
Practice with scrap wire until you are happy with the shape.

43 The wires from the tight bend will project outward, and you can start to form the upper edge of the lower wing. Make a bend downward to form the upper corner of the lower wing following the template. Form the side edges of the lower wing with a gentle bend in this edge to form a notch in the wing.

MASTERING WIREWORK JEWELRY

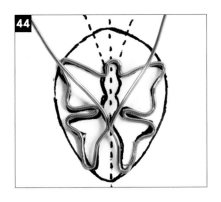

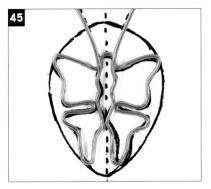

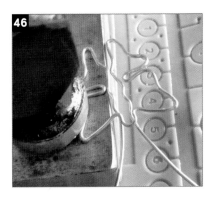

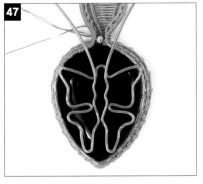

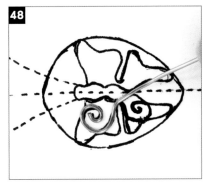

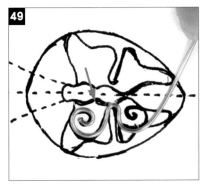

44 At the bottom corner of the lower wing, bend the frame wires sharply inward and upward. Shape both wire ends either side of the midline as shown, just touching the inner edge of the bend between both wings on either side.

45 Make sure the wire ends lie at the side of the head loop and project either side of the head for 1³/₁₆in (3cm). These wire ends will form antennae later.

46 Hammer the head loop and wings but not the body section or antennae yet. Do not hammer where wires cross; lift the antennae out of the way to hammer the head loop to avoid this.

47 Check that the shape fits over the front of the cabochon and the frame. Reshape after hammering if necessary as hammering may splay the shape a little.

48 Make wing detail curls. Use 3¹/₄in (8cm) of 18AWG (1mm) wire (or 20AWG/0.8mm wire, if you are using this gauge to make your butterfly). Following the template, make the larger upper spiral using the inner to outer spiral formation technique (see page 28). Curl and shape the bale wire ends using round-nosed pliers to start the curl at the end of the wire and fingers and flat/chain-nosed pliers to finish the curl. Make sure the spiral is loose rather than tight. Place the curl over the template to help you ensure the shape is correct.

49 Make two bends in the wire to form the wing intersection (see red arrow in image).

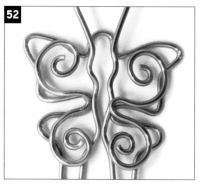

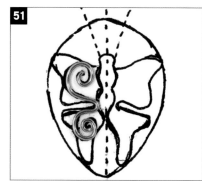

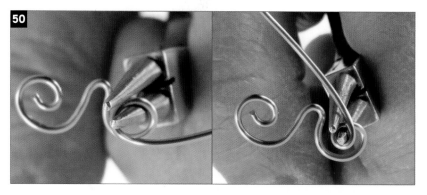

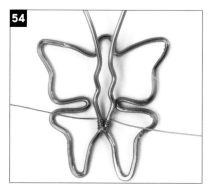

50 Form the lower spiral using the outer to inner spiral formation technique using round-nosed pliers (see page 28).

51 You should end up with a shape resembling the image here.

52 Make the second wing detail shape in mirror image using the same template (you can turn the shape over to make it mirror image). Check the details fit against the wings as shown and make any adjustments required.

53 Hammer the shapes and reshape if they have splayed.

54 Bind the head and body together, adding beads. Start at the tail end with 32in (80cm) of 30AWG (0.25mm) wire (26AWG/0.4mm wire can be used for larger butterflies). Wrap three times at the tail of the abdomen, leaving equal lengths of 30AWG (0.25mm) wire to wrap up either side of the body.

55 Wrap up either side of the body until you reach the widest part of the abdomen section.

56 Add a 3mm bead with a criss-cross bead attachment of the bead (see page 26). Pass one 30AWG (0.25mm) wire end through one side of the bead and the other wire through the other side of the bead.

57 Pull firmly to attach the bead in to place. At the same time, wrap around the wing intersection with three wraps. If you can, pass the 30AWG (0.25mm) wire through the bead again as you do this to strengthen the bead attachment, passing the 30AWG (0.25mm) wires behind the bead as well.

MASTERING WIREWORK JEWELRY

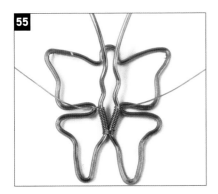

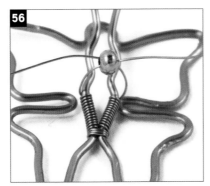

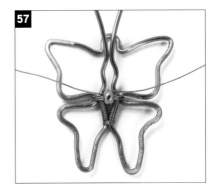

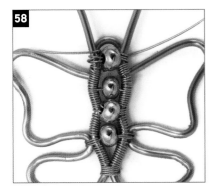

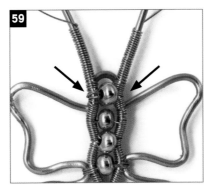

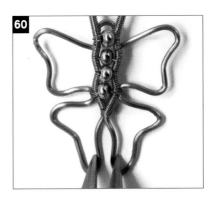

58 Continue wrapping the 30AWG (0.25mm) wire up the abdomen, binding around the waist section between the abdomen and thorax and adding in another 3mm bead with a criss-cross bead attachment. Another bead can be added in the thorax section. Wrap up to the head section binding the antennae to the head section.

59 The antennae can be bound to the head loop section on either side, adding in one more 3mm or even a 4mm bead to the head section as you go with a criss-cross bead attachment. The arrows in the image show the point of attachment of antennae to the head loop. Wrap a few times more above the head bead on each side, binding the antennae to the head section.

60 It often happens that the bottom wing tips splay out of shape after all the wire wrapping. A gentle squeeze of chain-nosed pliers at the wing tips can reshape this section, as shown in image. The bottom wing tips will fit more attractively into the pear-shaped cabochon frame if you do this.

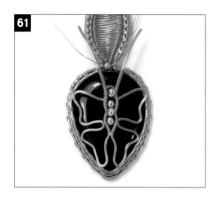

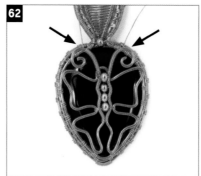

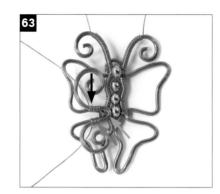

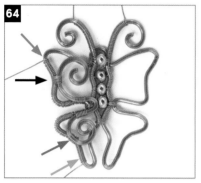

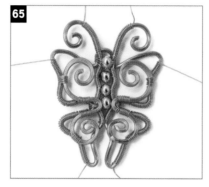

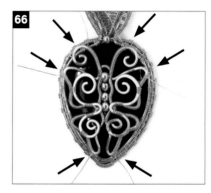

61 Place the butterfly over the setting to plan the size of antennae curl you need to make.

62 Curl the antennae loosely. Curl and shape the wire ends using round-nosed pliers to start the curl and fingers and pliers to finish the curl, using the inner to outer spiral curl technique (see page 27). Using a small-faced hammer and steel block, hammer the spirals so they have a flat surface. Check the butterfly fits inside the frame and the antennae touch against the setting at future potential attachment points. Use the 26AWG (0.4mm) wire ends to wrap along up both antennae. Stop at a point near the top ready to attach to the cabochon setting (see arrows in image). Do not cut the 26AWG (0.4mm) wire tails.

63 Attach wing details to the wings with 40in (1m) of 30AWG (0.25mm) wire (26AWG/0.4mm if making a larger butterfly) on either side. Place one wing detail over the main butterfly frame. Make sure the bend in the wing detail lies close to the bead in the center of the abdomen. You will have to lift the bend in the wing detail so it sits on top of the side of the abdomen, hiding the wraps in Step 57 that attached the abdomen bead (see blue arrow in image). Start by binding at the bend in the wing detail (black arrow) to the lower edge of upper wing with six to seven wraps. Wrap along where the wing detail shapes touch the wing edges until they start to separate from each other slightly. Stop for the moment. Pass the other end of the 26AWG (0.4mm)

wire down to the upper edge of the lower wing. Bind the wing detail to this section of the main butterfly frame at the level of the green arrow in the image. Wrap along where the wing detail shapes touch the wing edges until they start to separate from each other slightly and stop for the moment.

 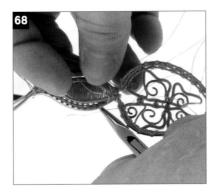 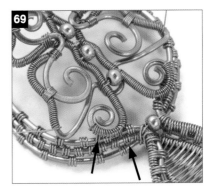

64 Continue with the top wing wrap along the lower edge of the wings (on either side) up the side edge of the upper wing, binding also to the side of the wing detail upper spiral four times where it touches the wing edge (see black arrow in image). Continue wrapping along the outer edge of the wing on both sides until you reach just before the top outer wing tip (green arrow). Stop here for the moment and do not cut the 30AWG (0.25mm) wire. Returning to the lower wing, wrap the 30AWG (0.25mm) wire along the upper edge of the lower wing and around the corner. Then wrap with four binding wraps around both the side of the lower wing detail curl and the outer edge of the lower wing (purple arrow). Wrap the 30AWG (0.25mm) wire down to the lower wing tip and stop here (blue arrow).

65 Repeat Steps 63–64 for the other side of the butterfly in mirror image. Now you are ready to attach the butterfly to the setting. You should have six points for attachment:
• two for each antennae
• two for upper wing tips
• two for lower wing tips
The image shows the attachment wires running away from the butterfly outline.

66 Check the fit of the butterfly shape inside the cabochon frame by placing the stone into the setting and placing the butterfly shape on top within the frame. You can also plan attachment points for the 6in (15cm) tails of 30AWG (0.25mm) wrapping wire exiting from the six points of the butterfly shape (see arrows in image).

Tip

If you take a photo at this stage, you can refer back to it when you are attaching the shapes as an aid to remembering sites for attachment.

67 Bind the butterfly frame and the cabochon setting at the six points shown in the previous image, wrapping 30AWG (0.25mm) wire around the butterfly frame and the cabochon setting frame three or four times. You need to pass the 30AWG (0.25mm) wire in the spaces between the inner (front frame wire) and the middle frame wire to attach to the cabochon frame by wrapping only around the inner/front frame wire (see arrow in image).

68 If it helps, turn the setting over and thread the wires through from the back. Also use your pliers to help you grab the wire if the space is too small for your fingers to grab the wire ends.

69 In the case of the antennae attachments, continue wrapping along the antennae for a $1/16$in (2mm), then cut and tuck in the 30AWG (0.25mm) wire end at the back of the antennae. If you can, wrap at a second point to the cabochon frame to further bind these pieces together (see arrows in image).

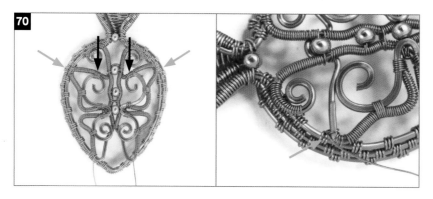

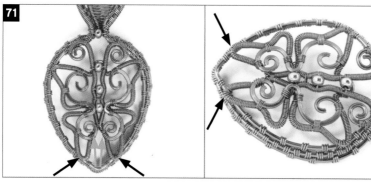

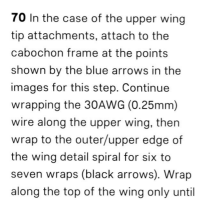

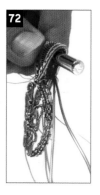

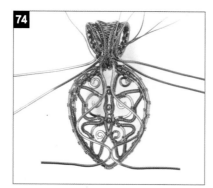

Also bind to the inner edge of the lower wing spiral at two points (blue arrows). Wrap along just the inner edge of the base of the lower wing, then cut and tuck in the 30AWG (0.25mm) wire at the base of the body. Your butterfly is now attached to the cabochon.

72 Take a 6mm-diameter mandrel, pen, or Gizmo rod (a knitting needle will also work) and bend and gently curl the bale into shape using your fingers around the mandrel. Take care to bend the outer bale wires and the leaf shape evenly. Use slow movements to shape the bale. Make sure you form at different points along the bale to make a nice shape.

73 Use a couple of the 26AWG (0.4mm) wire ends to bind the base of the bale together with a few wraps around either side and front to back of the bale. Try to hide these wraps as best as you can at the base of the bale. Do not cut the 26AWG (0.4mm) wires; you will use them to wrap along the bales wires later.

74 You should have six 18AWG (1mm) bale end wires and six 26AWG (0.4mm) wrapping wire ends. Bend the outer four bale wires sideward and slightly upward. Bend the 18AWG (1mm) bale wires from the middle leaf section of the bale along the back of the pendant and shape them symmetrically using fingers and pliers. They will form the backing frame for the pendant. Trim the 18AWG (1mm) wire ends of this backing frame so they project 1³/₁₆in (3cm) beyond the frame.

70 In the case of the upper wing tip attachments, attach to the cabochon frame at the points shown by the blue arrows in the images for this step. Continue wrapping the 30AWG (0.25mm) wire along the upper wing, then wrap to the outer/upper edge of the wing detail spiral for six to seven wraps (black arrows). Wrap along the top of the wing only until

you reach the body. Cut and tuck in the 30AWG (0.25mm) wire at the back of the butterfly, where it will be hidden against the cabochon.

71 In the case of the lower wing tip attachments, bind them to the cabochon frame at the points shown by the black arrows in the images. Continue wrapping along the inner lower wing frame edge.

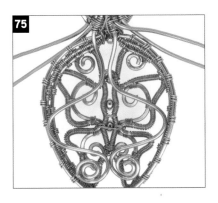

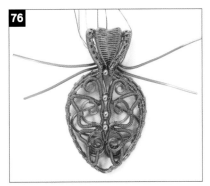

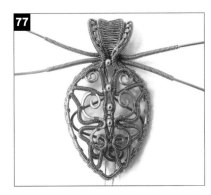

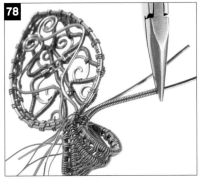

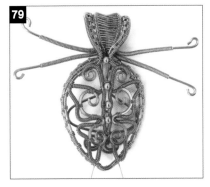

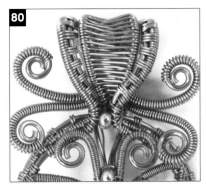

75 Curl the wire ends from the backing wires shaped in the previous step into place using the inner to outer spiral-making technique (see page 27). Feed the longest 26AWG (0.4mm) wires through so they are ready to wrap along these backing wires for the cabochon. Wrap them a couple of times around the backing wires so you can remember which wire is which. Thus you have chosen those to act as future backing wire wraps, for which you need long 26AWG (0.4mm) wire lengths.

76 Trim the remaining 18AWG (1mm) bale wires to 1⁹/₁₆in (4cm).

77 Take each 26AWG (0.4mm) wire tail at the base of the bale and wrap one each along the four bale wires projecting to the side of the bale. Cut the 26AWG (0.4mm) wire, leaving ⁵/₈in (15mm) of bare wire at the tip.

78 Cut the 26AWG (0.4mm) wire ends that you have used to wrap along these bale wires with flush cutter pliers. Stroke along the wire end with chain-nosed pliers with a rotational movement around the 18AWG (1mm) wire in the direction of the coil of the 26AWG (0.4mm) wrap to tuck this wire end in neatly so it does not catch.

79 The four bale wires you have wrapped along are ready for shaping. The top wires will have an upward curl; the bottom two wires will have a downward curl.

80 Curl and shape the bale wire ends using round-nosed pliers to start the curl and fingers and pliers to finish the curl.

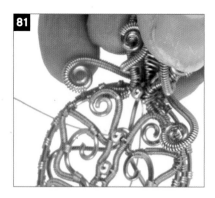

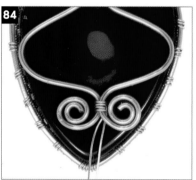

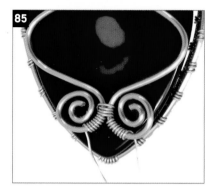

81 Do not use pliers to make the curls or you risk damaging the delicate 26AWG (0.4mm) wraps around the bale wires. Even nylon-jawed pliers may crush the wraps. Instead use your fingers to form the curls. Press the bale curled ends into place with your fingers.

82 Adjust them so the curled ends are balanced and symmetrical. You will need to twist the top two bale end curls.

83 Insert the cabochon into the setting. Press the setting around the cabochon using a rubber bead mat to help protect the stone from too much pressure that might cause it to break.

84 Start to attach the backing frame wires. Attach 20in (50cm) of 26AWG (0.4mm) wire to the middle of the bottom spirals attaching them together, bringing the upper wire down behind this joining wrap to hide it.

85 Wrap both wires along the lower edge of the bottom spirals until you reach a level where you can wrap across to the back of the cabochon frame in the gap between the backing frame and the middle frame wire.

86 Wrap the 26AWG (0.4mm) wire to the spaces at the tip of the cabochon frame and back again.

Tip
If the wire is difficult to thread through spaces, use the tips of chain-nosed pliers.

87 Pull this wrap firmly to bring the backing frame and cabochon frame tightly together as much as possible to pull the backing wires over the back of the stone.

88 Continue to wrap along the backing frame attaching a couple more times, then wrap around the backing frame only. If it helps, bend the spiral up a bit and then press back down flat again after wrapping. Cut the 26AWG (0.4mm) wires and tuck in.

Tip
Trim the tip of the 26AWG (0.4mm) wire if it looks ragged; this will make it thread through gaps more easily.

MASTERING WIREWORK JEWELRY

89 Wrap the 26AWG (0.4mm) wires along either side of the backing frame wires, wrapping across to the back of the outer frame at a few points. Criss-cross the 26AWG (0.4mm) wires at the back of the pendant in the middle of the back frame between the two backing wires a few times to add strength to the backing frame (a bit like lacing a corset).

90 Continue to wrap along the backing wires on each side with occasional weaves across to the cabochon frame, especially where the frames lie closest to each other (see arrows in image). Cut and tuck in the wires when you near the binding wrap between the lower spirals.

91 Your beautiful pendant is now finished. You can thread the pendant on a pearl necklace, a kumihimo braid in silver metallic thread, or mesh. You could also use a multiple-chain necklace or Gizmo coils.

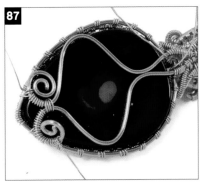

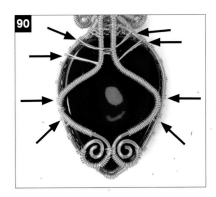

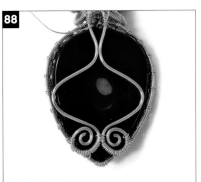

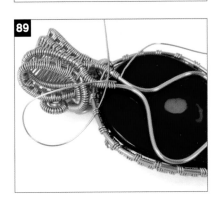

DESIGN ALTERNATIVE

These designs can easily be adapted to use smaller or larger cabochons in a variety of shapes and sizes. They can also be converted with loops or clasps to make necklace components and brooches. The butterfly could be placed at any angle over the stone as long as it fits into the space over the stone, as in the image here.

Little fish pendant

This lovely fish design featuring a natural stone cabochon has a Mediterranean feel to it. This design can easily be adapted to use smaller or larger cabochons in a variety of shapes and sizes.

Materials
18AWG (1mm-diameter) round wire
26AWG (0.4mm-diameter) round wire
30AWG (0.25mm-diameter) round wire
2mm-, 3mm-, and 4mm-diameter round ball beads, through-hole
1 x large oval flat-backed cabochon (use a larger or smaller one depending upon the size of pendant you want. Choose as a flat cabochon if possible as fewer wires are needed to form the frame)

FOR THE NECKLACE SIDES
Wire mesh kumihimo braid and clasps, or chain, or Viking knit

Tools
General tools (see page 10)

Dimensions of finished piece
2³/₄ x 2³/₄in (7 x 7cm) (but can be made any size)

MASTERING WIREWORK JEWELRY

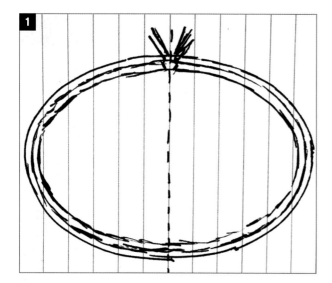

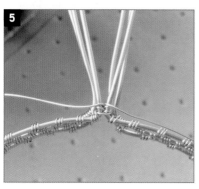

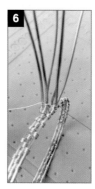

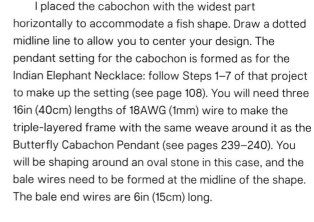

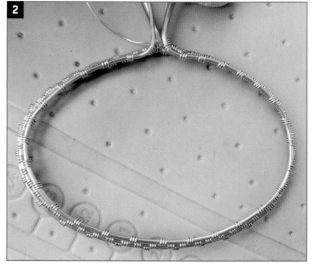

1 Take your cabochon, place it on a piece of plain paper, and draw around it with a pen, leaving a $^1/_{32}$in (1mm) gap to allow weaving and attachment of wirework components later in the assembly.

I placed the cabochon with the widest part horizontally to accommodate a fish shape. Draw a dotted midline line to allow you to center your design. The pendant setting for the cabochon is formed as for the Indian Elephant Necklace: follow Steps 1–7 of that project to make up the setting (see page 108). You will need three 16in (40cm) lengths of 18AWG (1mm) wire to make the triple-layered frame with the same weave around it as the Butterfly Cabachon Pendant (see pages 239–240). You will be shaping around an oval stone in this case, and the bale wires need to be formed at the midline of the shape. The bale end wires are 6in (15cm) long.

NOTE: I chose a flat cabochon as fewer wires are needed to form the frame. If your cabochon is deep, you might need to make another inner frame to hold the cabochon in place.

2 Use the same weave as in the Butterfly Cabochon Pendant (see pages 239–240) around the frame with 80in (2m) of 26AWG (0.4mm) wire, starting at the midline base of the frame. Continue this weave along both sides and all around the frame until you reach the top. You may need to gently reshape the two inner frames as you go, especially as you approach the top. Try to make sure you end up at the top of the outer frame shape.

3 Start to shape the frames with your fingers, making the frames slope slightly with the outer frame at the bottom of the slope.

4 Check the fit against the cabochon. You need to press the inner frame upward to make it fit upward and around the cabochon nicely. Make final adjustments to the top wires to ensure they all fit well at the top. Press the top of the frame firmly against the cabochon. It is important to have the fit as good as possible around the stone. You will have extra support for the stone from the fish design at the front and the backing wires at the back, but you don't want the stone to be moving around in its setting.

Tip

I used a rubber mat for this, placing the cabochon on top of the mat, so that pressure from pressing the frame against the cabochon is less likely to break the stone.

5 Bind the outer frame wires at the base of the bale with a couple of figure-of-eight wraps across the gap using the 26AWG (0.4mm) wire ends and bringing the ends tightly together.

6 Bring the two wires from the back of the frame either side of the base of the bale to wrap once around the middle and inner frame/bale wire.

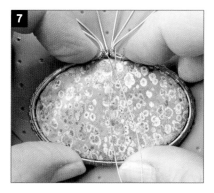

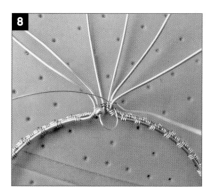

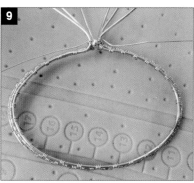

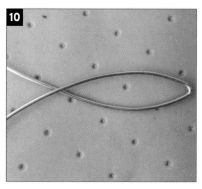

7 This image shows the wires coming from the front of the pendant ready for the next step. Check the fit of the frame against the cabochon over a rubber mat to absorb pressure. You need to press the inner frame upward to make it fit upward and around the cabochon nicely. Make final adjustments to the top wires to ensure they all fit well at the top. Press the top of the frame firmly against the cabochon.

8 Using one of the 26AWG (0.4mm) wires projecting from the front of the bale, bind a 3mm bead across the gap at the top of the inner/front cabochon frame to help bind this section together and help it fit over the stone properly. The image shows the addition of the 3mm bead and where to thread the 26AWG (0.4mm) wire.

9 This image shows the bead pulled tightly into place. Check the fit of the cabochon again after wrapping the front of the cabochon frame with the 3mm bead.

10 Take 12in (30cm) of 18AWG (1mm) wire and make an acute angular bend in the midsection of the wire to form a small leaf shape with the end wires crossing over each other.

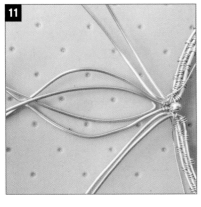

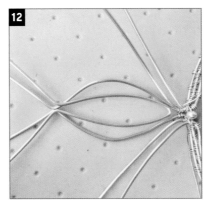

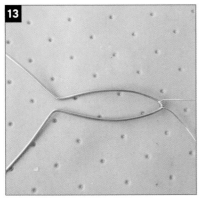

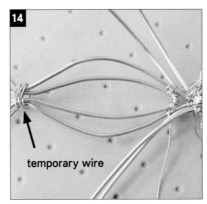

temporary wire

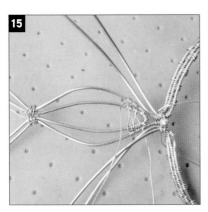

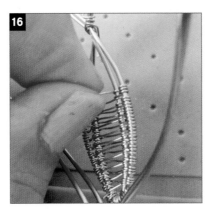

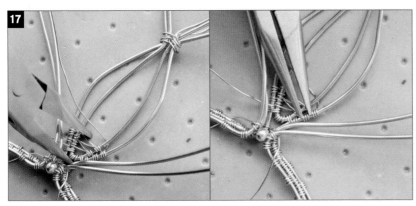

11 Take the cabochon setting and shape the end wires that are projecting from the outer frame shape at the back of the cabochon setting into a slightly larger leaf shape with the wire ends bent away at the end of the leaf shape. In this image I have also placed the smaller leaf shape (from Step 10) inside the larger leaf shapes you have just formed from the bale wires of the main cabochon setting.

12 Bend the wires at the end of the smaller leaf shape at the same level as the bends made in the larger cabochon leaf bale shape. The smaller leaf shape wires should run inside the wires splaying from the larger cabochon leaf shape.

NOTE: I also splayed the wires from the middle and inner cabochon leaf frames to either side as shown.

13 Take the inner leaf shape made in Step 10 and wrap five or six times around the tip of the shape using 120in (3m) of 26AWG (0.4mm) wire. One end of the 26AWG (0.4mm) wire should be about 12in (30cm) long; the rest of the wire will be used to weave the bale.

14 Place the inner leaf shape inside the larger leaf bale shape. Attach the shapes together with two wraps around the larger leaf frame bale wire and the inner leaf frame wire just above the wraps at the tip of the inner leaf frame, on both sides, followed by two wraps around the middle cabochon wire. I also wrapped a temporary fixing at the other end of the bale using scrap wire to help keep the bale wires stable while they are being woven (see arrow).

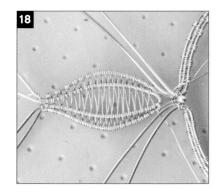

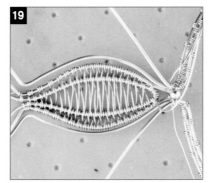

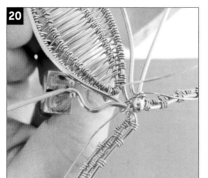

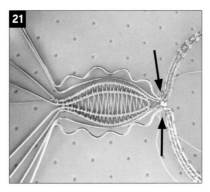

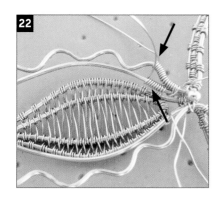

15 Start a basket weave up the leaf-shaped part of the bale using the longer end of the 26AWG (0.4mm) wire used to attach the leaf shapes together. This is an adaptation of the simple basket weave described on page 24, as you are weaving across four frame wires and not just two. (This technique is also used for the Seahorse Pendant; see pages 171–172.)

16 In the middle section of the weave, make sure the weave wires are kink free by pulling and stroking your fingers along the wire.

17 Neaten up the weave as you go with side to side gentle plier squeezes of the wraps along the side bale wires (see image on right) and of the whole midline weave (see image on left). A tight bind around the frame can also help, as the wire will grip into the frame better.

18 As you near the end of the leaf bale weave, about three-quarters of the way along the bale, remove the scrap wire. There is then more space to weave the wires, as you can move them up and along from the end of the bale. Stop weaving once you reach the end of the leaf shape bale. Do not trim the end weave wires; you will need them later to weave along the bale end wires.

19 Shape the middle frame bale wires around the middle woven leaf shape, following the lines of the leaf shape on either side.

20 Start to shape the outermost bale wires (the ones that originate from the front cabochon frame wire) into gentle wavy curves using round-nosed pliers to hold the wire while bending the wire around the pliers with your fingers, alternating the directions of the bends from side to side.

21 Make sure the little curves are the right size to place a 3mm bead in the widest space in the curve when placed adjacent to the next curved bale wire. I made four curves on each side for this size bale. Make sure the curves are even and symmetrical on either side. Take 80in (2m) of 26AWG (0.4mm) wire. Attach with the midsection of the 26AWG (0.4mm) wire at the base of the two outer bale wires on one side of the bale (see arrows in image).

22 Wrap one end of the 26AWG (0.4mm) wire along the inner of the two bale wires on one side of the bale up to a point opposite the midpoint of one of the wavy shapes. Wrap the other end of the 26AWG (0.4mm) wire along the outer bale wire until you reach the outer/top/ midpoint of one of the wavy shapes, at the same level to where you wrapped on the inner bale wire (see arrows in image).

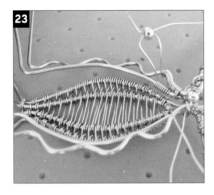

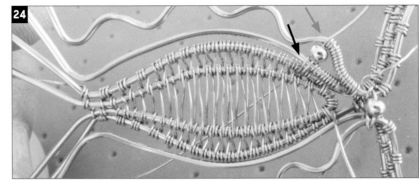

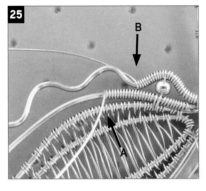

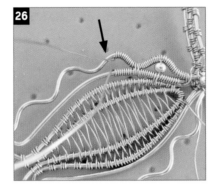

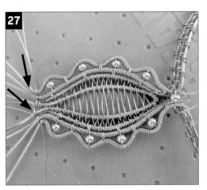

23 Thread a 3mm bead onto one 26AWG (0.4mm) wire end; thread the other 26AWG (0.4mm) wire end through the opposite side.

24 Pull both 26AWG (0.4mm) wires firmly until the 3mm bead pulls into place in the middle of the curved shape. Wrap the wire you have wrapped toward the inner of the two bale wires around both this wire and the outer wire of the leaf shape a couple of times to bind them both together. The black arrow in the image indicates this binding point. Wrap that 26AWG (0.4mm) wire around the inner of the two outer bale wires, not around the leaf shape. The other 26AWG (0.4mm) wire end is on the outer wavy bale wire (blue arrow).

25 Wrap the 26AWG (0.4mm) wire along the inner of the two bale wires you are working on until the midsection of the next bulgy wave (arrow **A** in image). Wrap the other 26AWG (0.4mm) wire along to the point at which the two bale wires lie closest together (arrow **B**). Bind the 26AWG (0.4mm) wire at point **B** around both bale wires twice. Then wrap along to the same level as point **A** on the other bale wire.

26 The black arrow here shows the level to wrap to. Repeat actions from Steps 21–25 along this side of the bale, adding in 3mm beads to the wavy sections and binding to the inner leaf-shaped woven section of the bale until you reach the end of the woven bale section.

27 Repeat along the other side of the bale. Bind the bale wires together with one of the 26AWG (0.4mm) wires you used to weave the bale with, using a few basket-weave-type wraps along all the bale wires (see arrows in image).

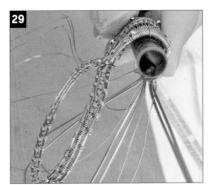

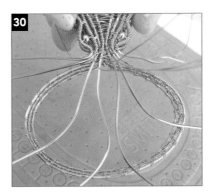

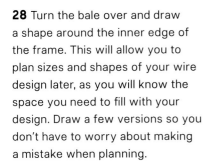

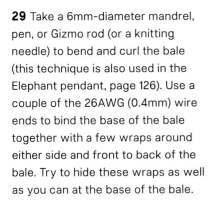

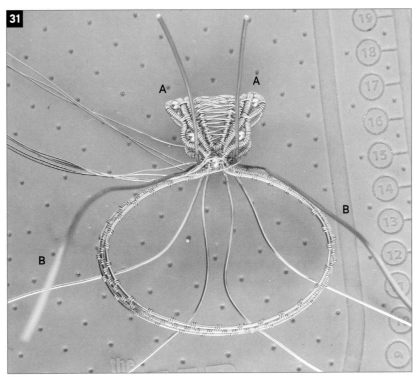

28 Turn the bale over and draw a shape around the inner edge of the frame. This will allow you to plan sizes and shapes of your wire design later, as you will know the space you need to fill with your design. Draw a few versions so you don't have to worry about making a mistake when planning.

29 Take a 6mm-diameter mandrel, pen, or Gizmo rod (or a knitting needle) to bend and curl the bale (this technique is also used in the Elephant pendant, page 126). Use a couple of the 26AWG (0.4mm) wire ends to bind the base of the bale together with a few wraps around either side and front to back of the bale. Try to hide these wraps as well as you can at the base of the bale.

30 The central four bale wires will form the backing frame for the cabochon. Bend these four 18AWG (1mm) wires from the middle section of the bale along the back of the pendant and shape them symmetrically using fingers and chain and round-nosed pliers. The image shows the back of the setting. Start to bend the outer four wires over the shoulders of the setting.

Tip

In some designs these wire ends may form part of the decoration over the front of the cabochon. In this case, the four wires will form decoration around the bale.

31 The outermost bale wires will end up as the top two bale wires pointing uppermost to the front of bale **A** in the image. The next bale wires inward from them will form the next lower bale wires, pointing downward over bale **B**.

I trimmed bale wires a so they project 2¼in (5.5cm) from the front of the setting. I have not trimmed bale wires b yet as they won't be completed until later. This image also shows the backing frame wires in early formation with the wire ends trimmed so that they project 1⁹⁄₁₆in (4cm) beyond the edge of the cabochon frame setting.

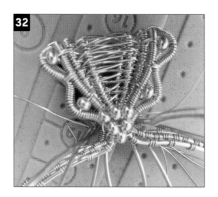

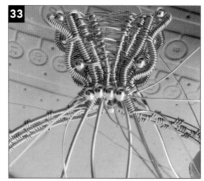

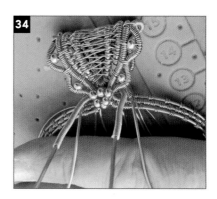

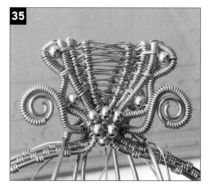

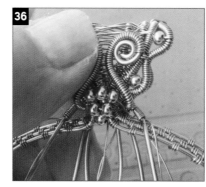

32 Feed one of the 26AWG (0.4mm) wire ends left from wrapping the bale back through the base of the bale. Add on more beads above the first one added in Step 8. This can be fiddly; you just have to find a little space with the wire. Pull the wires tight to cinch the beads into place with the two beads fitting nicely above the single bead. You can add as many or as few beads into this space as you like, both for detail and to ensure the frames fit securely and tightly over the top of the stone. I added another row of three above the two already added in. You can add a cluster of beads here if you find it easier to fill the space and bind the top of the cabochon frame together.

33 Use one of the 26AWG (0.4mm) wires from weaving the bale to bind two to four 3mm beads at the back of the bale to hide any potentially unattractive wirework.

34 If the 26AWG (0.4mm) wire ends left over from wire wrapping the bale are long enough, wrap one up along the top bale wires on either side. Wrap for 1⁹/₁₆in (4cm), leaving ⁵/₈in (15mm) of bare wire at the end. Trim the 26AWG (0.4mm) wire using flush cutters. Tuck in the end neatly around the bale wire using chain-nosed pliers.

35 The two upper bale wires from Step 32 that you have wrapped along are ready for shaping. Curl and shape the bale wire ends using round-nosed pliers to start the curl and fingers and pliers to finish the curl (see page 27). When the wrapped section is outermost on the coil, stop using pliers or you will crush the wrapped sections; coil the coils with your fingers instead. Do not coil along the whole bale wire end; leave some uncoiled ready for shaping and folding the coil over the bale.

36 Press the bale's curled ends into place with your fingers and adjust them so they are balanced and symmetrical.

37 You will need to pull the curls inward toward the midline. Put this section aside.

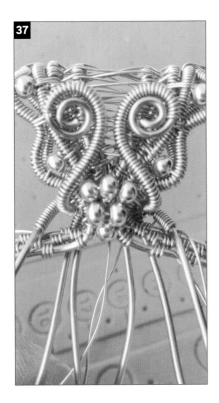

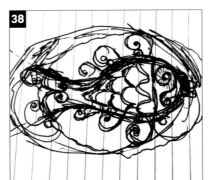

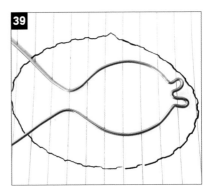

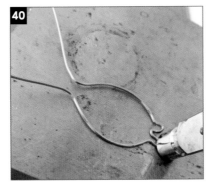

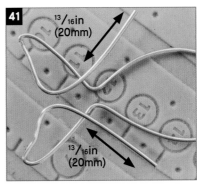

38 Take the cabochon setting you made in Steps 1–38 and press the front of the setting onto a piece of paper using the techniques from the Indian Elephant Necklace (Step 50, page 116) or Butterfly Cabochon Pendant (Steps 32–33, pages 242–243) to make an impression of the frontal space of the setting. Trace over the impression to get an internal frame size. Then plan your design to fit the space. This is a drawing I made; it is very rough and the finished article was slightly different, but it is good to start to work to plan the design to a certain size at this stage.

39 Take 12in (30cm) of 18AWG (1mm) wire and form an M-shaped curved lip/mouth section at the midsection of the wire using round-nosed pliers. This should be $^1/_4$in (6mm) long and $^3/_8$in (10mm)

wide, with each arch of the "M" $^1/_4$in (6mm) wide. Bend the wires at the side of the "M" away to the side using chain-nosed pliers at a 90–120-degree angle to start to form the body. Curve the body with your fingers upward and around for the back and downward and around for the tummy. Make a sharp bend with your pliers about 2in (5cm) along the back of the fish and $1^9/_{16}$in (4cm) along the tummy, splaying the wires to either side that will eventually form the tail.

40 Hammer the fish shape with a hammer on a steel block. Do not hammer the tail section as you have not formed it yet. You can flatten the wire as this will form an attractive flat reflective surface.

41 Start to form the tail section for the little fish. Bend the tail wires about $^{13}/_{16}$in (20mm) along on either side from the bend at the end of the body section. Bend the top wire sharply downward and toward the midline and the bottom wire sharply upward and toward the midline. This makes the tips of the tail section. Both wires after this bend need to be slightly angled toward the body. Shape the tail fin by making a small kink in the wire about $^1/_4$in (6mm) from the tip of the tail. Using your fingers, curve the wires back outward again about $^5/_8$in (15mm) from the tip of the tail so the ends pass over a point about $^1/_8$in (3mm) from the base of the tail. Take time to make the tail fins symmetrical. Trim the ends of the wire about $^{13}/_{16}$in (20mm) along from where they cross the base of the tail on both upper and lower tail fins.

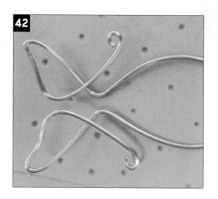

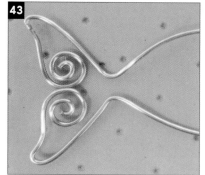

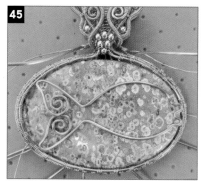

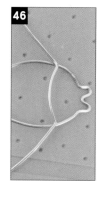

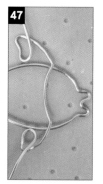

42 Loosely spiral curl the tail wires (see page 27). The bottom tail wire needs to curl downward and backward. The upper tail wire needs to curl upward and backward.

43 Make sure these spirals are as symmetrical as possible.

44 Hammer the tail shape. Here, I hammered the back of the fish so the front is against the block. This side ends up smoother and is less likely to be marked by the edge of the hammer.

45 Check this fish shape fits into the cabochon frame shape against the stone; make adjustments if required.

46 Take 6in (15cm) of 18AWG (1mm) wire and curve it gently in the center using your fingers. Lay this wire over the fish body frame. Make sure you place it one-third the way along the body from the tip of the lips. This makes a division between the fish's face and its body. Bend the 18AWG (1mm) wire where it crosses over the fish body frame.

47 Make upper and lower tail fins in the same way as the tail fins (but smaller versions). Make sure the tip of each fin touches against the side of the cabochon frame.

48 Make sure the top fin back edge touches against the top of the fish and the bottom fin back edge touches the tummy of the fish.

49 Do not cut the wire ends yet. Insert round-nosed pliers into the fin frame at the back edges of both fins and make loose spiral curls using the outer to inner spiral technique (see page 28). Cut the wire where the wire beyond the spiral crosses over the back edge of the fin (see arrow in image). Do this for both upper and lower fins.

MASTERING WIREWORK JEWELRY

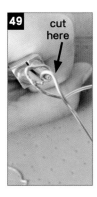

49 cut here

50

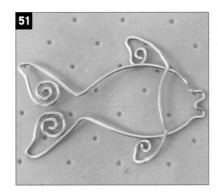

51

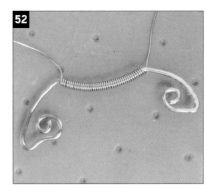

52

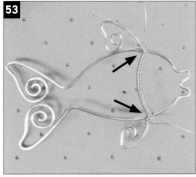

53

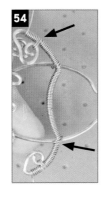

54

55

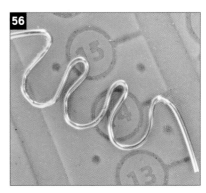

56

50 Hammer the back of the shape against a steel block so the front edge faces the block and ends up with a smooth surface.

51 Check this shape against the fish body. Make adjustments as required, as the hammering process tends to enlarge and distort shapes slightly.

52 Take 40in (1m) of 26AWG (0.4mm) wire and start wrapping from the center of the 26AWG (0.4mm) wire along the curve of the fin component wire from Step 46 until you reach the point where the wire would cross over the fish's body.

53 Take the fin component and attach it to the fish body frame with three binding wraps of the 26AWG (0.4mm) wire around both fin component and body frame (see arrows in image).

54 Secure this wrap firmly by continuing to wrap the 26AWG (0.4mm) wire along the top and bottom fins for ⅛in (3mm). Do not cut the 26AWG (0.4mm) wire yet. Carry on winding the 26AWG (0.4mm) wire along the upper and lower fins, also binding around the curl detail in the fin where it touches the leading edge of the upper and lower fins (see arrows in image). Carry on winding the 26AWG (0.4mm) wire to the upper and lower fin tips. Stop winding and don't cut the 26AWG (0.4mm) wire.

55 Take a 4¾in (12cm) length of 18AWG (1mm) wire and make a scale section by looping the wire around the base of round-nosed pliers.

56 Make three loops with short ½in (12mm) tails on either side.

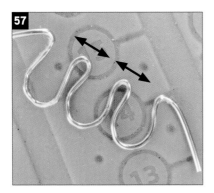

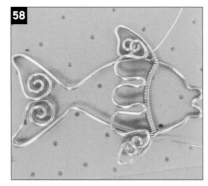

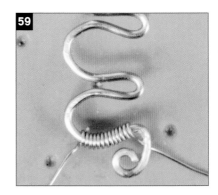

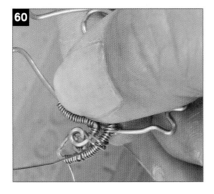

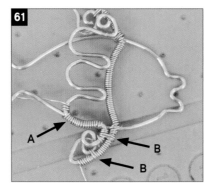

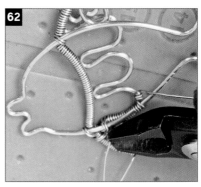

57 Squash the bases of the loops with side-to-side squeezes with your pliers at the arrow points in the image. This scale section needs to fit inside the body of the fish, with the wire tails projecting over the fin component.

58 The scales I made here are ¹⁄₄in (6mm) wide and ³⁄₈in (10mm) long. Curl the ends of the scale component. Hammer only the curls with the front of the shape against the block.

59 Take 40in (1m) of 26AWG (0.4mm) wire and wrap 8in (20cm) from one end at the base of the lowest scale, as shown.

60 The longest end of the wire needs to be directed toward the scales and the shorter end toward the lower fin. Place the scale section over the fish frame just below the edge of the face/gill curve dividing the head from body. Hold these frames in position over each other as you wrap along the fin. The wrapping process is decribed in the next step.

61 Bind the scale component to the fish body at two points with two or three wraps at the top of the bottom fin where it touches against the base (see arrow **A** in image). Bind at two points across to the front of the lower fin (see arrows labelled **B**). Bind only on the lower scale curl just below attachments **B**.

62 Then cut with pliers at the *back* of the fish so there are no sharp edges at the front of the fish.

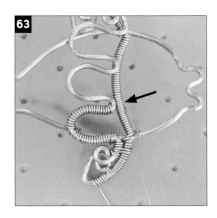

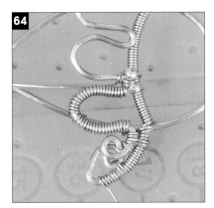

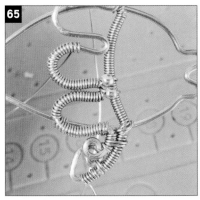

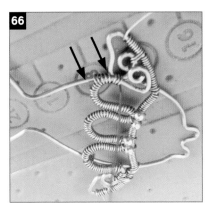

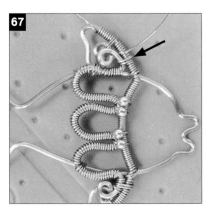

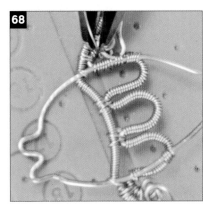

63 Continue to wrap up the lower scale until you reach a point where the upper end of the scale starts to touch against the face boundary part of the design (see arrow in image).

64 Bind across twice from the base of the scale to the facial boundary wire. Add on a 2mm copper bead and bind this to the front of the base of the scale with each wrap.

65 Continue wrapping the 26AWG (0.4mm) wire along the middle scale.

66 Wrap along to the next scale, adding in two more 2mm balls at the next base of the scale. Wrap up to the top edge of the top scale and bind to the upper frame at two points marked by arrows in the image.

67 Wrap along the back and up the curl at the top of the fin frame. Bind twice around the fin frame and the front edge of the top fin (see arrow in image).

68 Turn the fish over and cut the 26AWG (0.4mm) wire for the scale attachment and tuck in at the *back* of the fish.

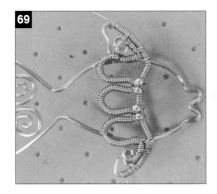

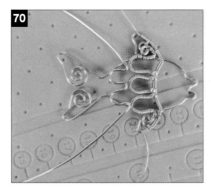

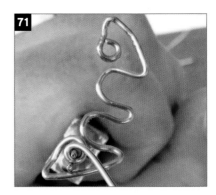

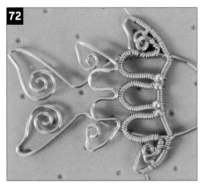

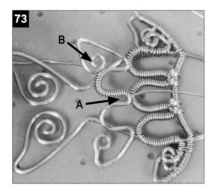

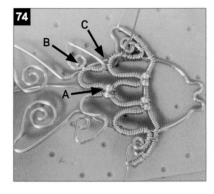

69 The fish should now look like this image.

70 Take 8in (20cm) of 18AWG (1mm) wire and make two scale shapes the same size as those in Step 55 with 2¹⁄₂in (6cm) tails of wire to either side. Make sure the double scale component fits into place along your fish shape; make adjustments to scale size as required. The scales I made here are ¹⁄₄in (6mm) width and ⁵⁄₁₆in (8mm) long, slightly smaller than the scales in the row of three.

71 Make upper and lower fin shapes for the double scale component in the same way that you did for the face shape component in Steps 46–50 and the scale component in Steps 55–58, shaping the back edge of the fins on upper and lower aspects. Then make spiral curls to fill the fin spaces.

72 Check the double scale component against the body of the fish for size. Hammer on the back of the components to flatten them. Check again for fit to the main body; adjust angles as necessary.

73 Take 40in (1m) of 26AWG (0.4mm) wire. Wrap around the upper of the two scales using the midsection of the 26AWG (0.4mm) wire down to the bottom of the top scale, ready to bind to the tip of the

middle scale in the row above (see arrow **A** in image). Wrap up to just beyond the tip of the upper scale ready to bind to the back of the fish (arrow **B**).

74 Bind the double fin component on to point a in the image across to the base of the middle fin. Use two binding wraps around both components, adding in a 2mm bead to the front with each wrap. Continue wrapping only around the double fin component as you work down along the lower scale. Bind across the back of the fish and the little loop in the top fin of the double scale component at point **B** in the image with two wraps of the 26AWG (0.4mm) wire. Continue wrapping along the scale until you reach the base of the scale (see arrow **C**).

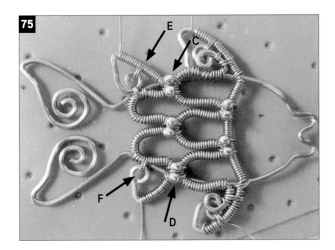

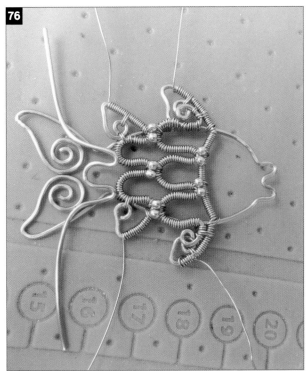

75 Wrap on from the base of the top scale, binding across to the tip of the upper scale in the row above and adding in two 2mm beads at this point (see arrow **C** in image). Then wrap on up the front edge of the fin with the 26AWG (0.4mm) wire, binding across to the curl detail of the wire inside the fin space (arrow **E**) for two wraps, then on up to the tip of the top fin, and stop. Do not cut the 26AWG (0.4mm) wire. Work along down the double fin component, wrapping the 26AWG (0.4mm) wire around the scale until it meets the tummy edge of the fish where you can bind across to the curled loop in the lower fin for two binding wraps (arrow **F**). Wrap along the lower scale until you reach the tip of the lowest scale in the row above. Bind across to this tip with two wraps (arrow **D**), adding in a 2mm bead to the front with each bind. Wrap on to the front edge of the lower fin. Wrap along this until you reach the tip of the bottom fin, and then stop wrapping. Do not cut the 26AWG (0.4mm) wire.

76 Make a third scale component to fit at the base of the body centrally between the two scales in the row above. Use 4³/₄in (12cm) of 18AWG (1mm) wire with 1⁹/₁₆in (4cm) wire ends curving away from the single scale on either side.

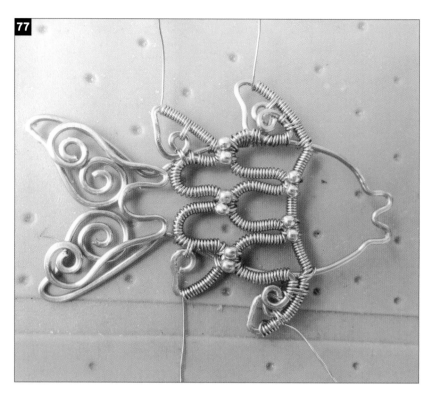

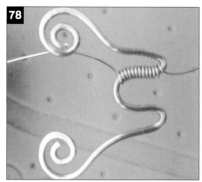

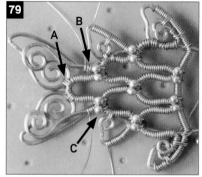

77 Make loose spiral curl details on the single scale component to form tail details sitting above and further along from the midline tail spirals formed in Steps 41–43. Hammer the back of the single scale shape to flatten it. Place over the fish again and make adjustments to the component so it fits into place.

78 Take the single scale component you made in Step 76, and wrap 20in (50cm) of 26AWG (0.4mm) wire from its midsection halfway along the top of the scale.

79 Place this section over the fish. You are ready to attach at two points to the rest of the fish. Bind at point a in the image with three wraps across to the main frame upper tail spiral. Make three wraps around the tip of the single scale only, then three wraps around both the single scale and the main frame lower tail spiral. Then wrap along the lower edge of the single scale. Bind in two more places to the main frame with wraps to the tips of the scales in the double scale component above at points **B** and **C** in the image.

NOTE: At points **B** and **C**, two wraps across, adding a 2mm bead on the front of the frame with each wrap, are required.

80 Working along from points **B** and **C**, in Step 79, wrap along the single scale component (at the side and base of the tail), binding it to the base of the tail on either side for three more wraps to the main body. In this image I have already wound along the bottom edge of the tail, wrapping along the tail frame only except for two points marked with arrows. Here I have bound across to the main frame tail curl with three binding wraps where it touches the tail frame (arrow **A**) and then also to the side of the single scale component tail curl, also with three wraps where it touches the lower edge of the main tail frame (arrow **B**). Continue wrapping along to the point of the tail. Stop here and don't cut the 26AWG (0.4mm) wire.

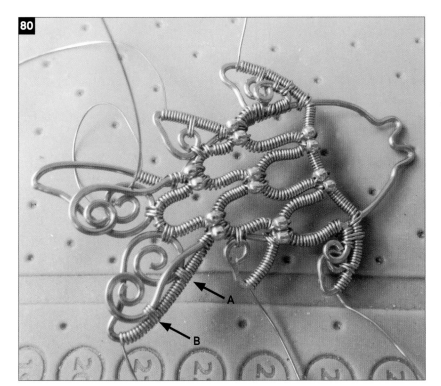

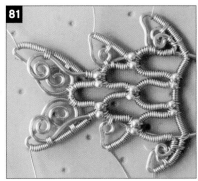

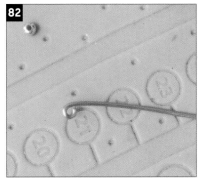

Tip

On the top edge of the tail frame, I have started to do the same wrapping as has been done for the bottom edge. I have bent the single scale tail curl away from the tail frame so that I can access the edge of the upper tail frame and wrap around it and reach the binding point more easily to wrap to the tail curl of the main frame. If I had not bent the scale frame away it would have been more difficult to achieve this. After doing these wraps, you can bend the scale frame tail curl back into place, ready to wrap and bind across to it as you work along the top edge of the tail.

81 Once you have completed Step 80, the fish frame should resemble the image. There are six 26AWG (0.4mm) unused tail wires for attachment to the cabochon frame. You may not need them all, but don't cut them yet until you know which ones you are going to use.

82 Start to make the eye. Take 6in (15cm) of 18AWG (1mm) wire and make a little spiral at one end using the tip of round-nosed pliers.

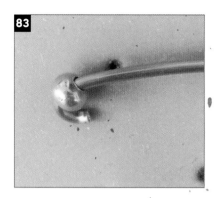

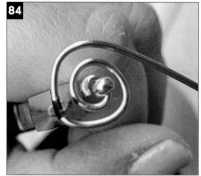

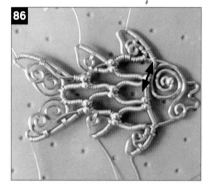

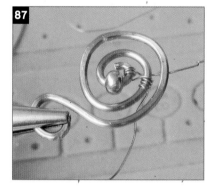

83 Open up the little spiral slightly and thread on a 3mm copper bead along the straight part of the wire until it sits inside the spiral curl.

84 Make a loose spiral curl in the 18AWG (1mm) wire. Use chain-nosed pliers to slightly flatten the side of the curl where it would touch the face edge wire. In the image I am flattening the wire with chain-nosed pliers.

85 Make a smaller spiral at the bottom of the first spiral using round-nosed pliers.

86 Check this shape against the face of the fish. The flattened surface made in Step 84 ensures the curve of the face edge frame fits the curve of the eye shape. See the black arrow in the image. Hammer this eye shape, avoiding the bead. Make sure this shape fits onto the lower jaw of the fish.

87 You can use 30AWG (0.25mm), 28AWG (0.3mm), or 26AWG (0.4mm) wire for this step. I chose 30AWG (0.25mm). Use a 27in (68cm) length and wrap the 30AWG (0.25mm) wire three times near one end of the 30AWG (0.25mm) wire around the 18AWG (1mm) wire spiral near its center and the little 2mm copper bead. Wrap the 30AWG (0.25mm) wire across to the adjacent part of the spiral clockwise in a figure-of-eight-style weave. Wrap around this

section five to six times. Don't cut the short end of 30AWG (0.25mm) wire nearest the 3mm bead until the weave is stable, then cut at the back of the eye to hide the end.

88 Wrap back to the central spiral for two wraps, then back to the adjacent outer spiral for five to six wraps, then back inward again. Work your way along the spiral in this way, clockwise in the direction of the spiral. Make more wraps on the outer spiral wire, as there is a longer distance to wrap along there compared to the more central spiral. You might have to miss out a traverse to an inward spiral frame wire where the 3mm bead is, as it gets in the way of the weave. Stop when you approach a level where you can start to bind to the facial wires for the fish.

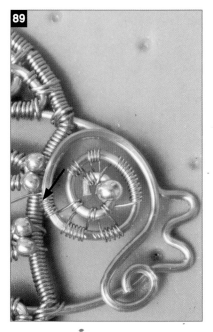

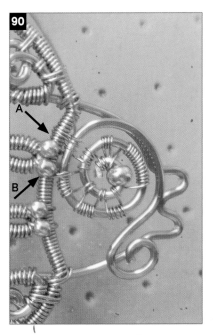

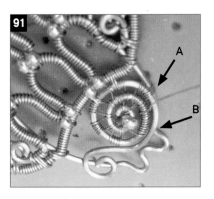

NOTE: Make sure the eye section lies to the side or in front of the facial wire, but not behind it.

91 Continue the spiral figure-of-eight weave around the top of the eye. By this stage you are starting to weave to inner spirals that have already been woven toward from the weave across central spirals. Find a space to weave toward and this will start to fill up the spaces in the wraps. As you weave to the outer and top edge of the eye, also bind around the top of the head (see arrow **A** in image). Continue this binding to the top of the head and the spiral weave to inner coils until you reach the level of the top edge of the lip (arrow **B**). Do not cut the 30AWG (0.25mm) wire. Carry on winding from the spiral with the 30AWG (0.25mm) wire over on to the top lip. Stop here and don't cut the wire.

92 I originally had seven wire ends from the tips of the tail fins to the tips of all the fins and the top lip. I decided not to use the wire ends from the smaller fin tips and cut these off (see arrows in image). I have tucked the ends in at the back of the fish.

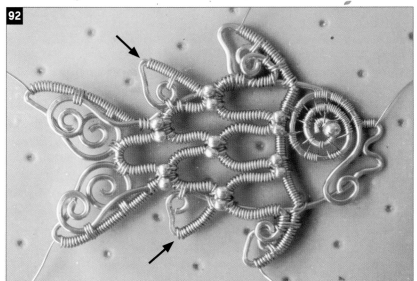

89 Continue weaving in the spiral figure-of-eight style, with more wraps around the outer coils compared to the inner coils, until you reach the edge of the coil where it has been flattened slightly ready to bind to the facial wire just below the 2mm beads attached to the scales (see arrow in image).

90 Bind the eye section to the facial wire by wrapping below the 2mm scale detail bead (see arrow **A** in image). Wrap back across to the inner spiral, then back across to wrap around both the outer spiral and the facial wire just above the upper 2mm scale detail bead (arrow **B**).

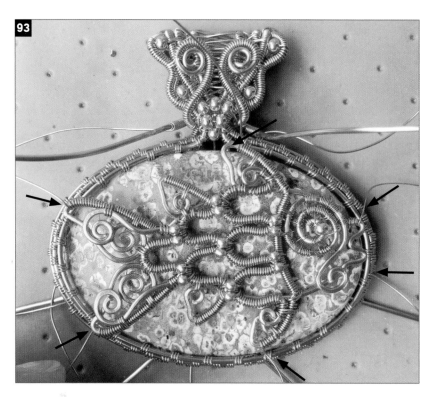

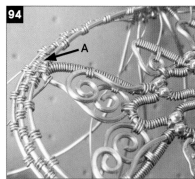

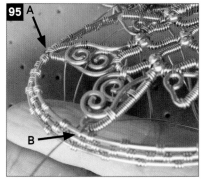

93 Check the fit of the fish frame in the cabochon setting with the stone in place and decide how you want your fish to appear. You can change the angle for the fish—whether you want it to swimming upward, downward, or straight across for example. Choose the points to which you are going to bind from the fish to the edge of the cabochon setting. There need to be spaces in the cabochon frame to bind to at all the six points marked by arrows on the image.

94 I made the first attachment of the fish to the cabochon frame by binding the 26AWG (0.4mm) wire at the tip of the top tail fin across to the space in between the inner/front frame wire and the middle frame wire for three binding wraps (see arrow **A** in image).

95 Fix this binding wrap in place and then continue to wrap on up the lower edge of the upper tail fin. Continue to wrap the wire along the bottom edge of the top fin. Stop when you reach the outer edge of the tail curl from the scale section (see arrow **A** in image). Cut the 26AWG (0.4mm) wire and tuck in the end at the back of the fish. Attach the lower fin (arrow **B**). Wrap the 26AWG (0.4mm) wire up the upper/inner edge of the tail fin. Stop wrapping at the edge of the tail curl (at the same level as on the opposite tail fin).

96 Cut the 26AWG (0.4mm) wire and tuck in the end at the back. Attach the lower and upper fins to the cabochon frame (see arrows **A** and **B** in image). Wrap from these attachments along the back edge of the upper and lower fins for a few wraps. Cut the 26AWG (0.4mm) wire and tuck in the end toward the back of the fish. Attach the top lip of the fish to the cabochon frame (arrow **C**).

97 Start to wrap along the top lip. Then wrap along the lower lip of the fish, attaching the fish to the cabochon frame at the sixth point of attachment at the level of the arrow in the image. Wrap along the lower lip of the fish, stopping at the edge of the lower facial curl detail. Cut the 26AWG (0.4mm) wire and tuck the end in at the back. Your fish is now attached in place over the setting.

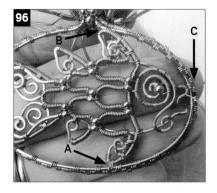

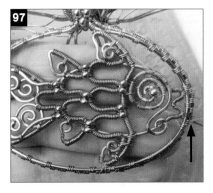

98 Replace the stone into the setting and check the fit again. Here you can see the frame has distorted a little with all the work that has been done to it. Press around the frame with your fingers to mold it to the stone evenly.

99 Take the stone out of the setting again. You are ready to shape the lower bale wires. You may have enough 26AWG (0.4mm) wire ends left from the bale wraps to wind along these bale wires. If you don't, add some on. Wrap up along the bale wires for 1³/₁₆in (3cm), leaving ⁵/₈in (15mm) of bare wire at the ends.

100 Now curl the lower bale wires. In some designs and shapes of cabochons you can curl these bale wires down to touch and bind to the design on the front of the gemstone, but in this case I felt the design did not need this. Curl and shape the wrapped bale wires as in Step 35. Press the curled wires down on the front and top of the setting at the base of the bale.

101 Turn the setting over and put the stone into it. Shape the four backing wires; they shape much more easily with the stone in place. Try to make the shapes as mirror-image symmetrical as possible. Cut the four backing wires so they project about 2¹/₂in (6cm) from the edge of the setting.

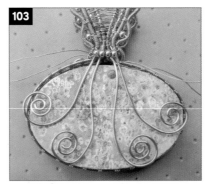

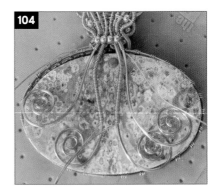

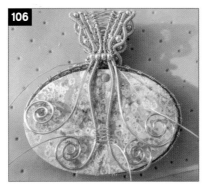

102 Make loose spiral curls at the end of the backing wires using round-nosed and chain-nosed pliers so that the edges of the curls touch against the edge of the cabochon frame. Try to make the two left and two right backing wires as symmetrical as possible in mirror image to each other. Lift up the backing curls gently so you don't bend the wires too much. Hammer the curls for each backing wire in turn to work-harden them, flatten them, and add detail.

103 The backing wires should resemble the image.

104 If you have some long lengths of 26AWG (0.4mm) wire left from weaving the bale then use them for this stage. You need 31in (78cm) for each side of the inner two bale wires. If they are too short, trim them, tuck in the ends, and add in new 26AWG (0.4mm) (26AWG) wire at the base of the wires. Wrap up each one until you get about two-thirds of the way along where the central backing wires are closest to each other.

105 For the next step you will need to hold the two middle backing wires apart and weave with one hand as shown or you will bind them too closely together. After you do a few weave traverses, the wires will hold themselves apart more easily and you will be able to weave without holding the backing wires to keep them apart.

106 Weave across to the opposite middle bale wire with one 26AWG (0.4mm) wire and wrap once around it. Take the other 26AWG (0.4mm) wire and weave across to the opposite wire as well. This forms a corset-style weave as you weave with two separate wires across the same space. If you find this too difficult, wrap down one bale wire then weave across and back, to and fro, only with the other wire. The "corset" weave should resemble this image.

107 Continue wrapping along the middle backing wires until they touch the cabochon setting sides. At this stage, bind the backing wires to the cabochon frame outer/back wire by wrapping around both three times using spaces between the weave in the back and middle frame wires. Wrap along the backing wires on each side with

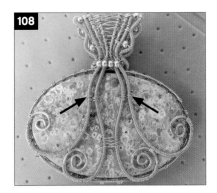

occasional weaves across to the cabochon frame, especially where the frames lie closest to each other (see arrows in image). As the backing wires travel away from the cabochon frame, bind around the backing wire only for a few more wraps. Then cut the 26AWG (0.4mm) wire and tuck in the end around the frame wire.

Tip

If the wire is difficult to thread through spaces, use your pliers to help grab the ends of the wire; your pliers will reach into spaces that your hands cannot. Trim the tip of the 26AWG (0.4mm) wire if it looks ragged and this will make it thread through gaps more easily.

108 If you have some long lengths of 26AWG (0.4mm) wire left from weaving the bale then use them for this stage. You need 31in (78cm) for each side of the outer two bale wires. If they are too short, trim them, tuck in the ends, and add in new 26AWG (0.4mm) wire at the base of the wires. Wrap up each one until you get about a quarter of the way along where the wires are closest to each other. At the level of the arrows in the image, make a few weaves across to the middle bale wires, keeping a small distance between them on both sides to strengthen the backing frame at this point.

109 Continue wrapping along the outer backing wires until they touch the cabochon setting sides. Bind the backing wires to the cabochon frame outer/back wire by wrapping around both three

times using spaces between the weave in the back and middle frame wires. Continue to wrap along the backing wires on each side with occasional weaves across to the cabochon frame, especially where the frames lie closest to each other (see arrows in image). As the backing wires travel away from the cabochon frame, bind around the backing wire only for a few more wraps. Then cut the 26AWG (0.4mm) wire and tuck in the end around the frame wire.

110 Your beautiful pendant is now finished. You can thread the pendant on a pearl necklace, a kumihimo braid in silver metallic thread, or mesh. You could also use a multiple-chain necklace or Gizmo coils.

Lion's mane pendant

The lion is a powerful symbolic design that works for both women and men. This project is for a copper wire and gemstone bead lion face pendant that can be easily adapted to attach to the front of cabochons of a variety of shapes and sizes.

Templates
See page 294 for the templates for this design.

Materials
18AWG (1mm-diameter) round wire
26AWG (0.4mm-diameter) round wire
30AWG (0.25mm-diameter) round wire
4mm round beads for nose and bale
4mm round beads for the eyes
2mm round beads for eyes and head details
4–5mm round or coin bead for ear details (you can use smaller or larger beads depending on the size of your pendant)
Ball-end headpins for dangles if you are making the pendant without the cabochon

Tools
General tools (see page 10)

Dimensions of finished piece
With dangles: 3³/₈ x 2in (8.5 x 5cm)
Without dangles: 2³/₄ x 2in (7 x 5cm)

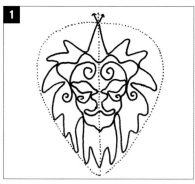

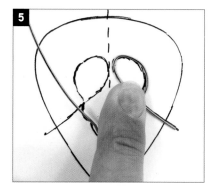

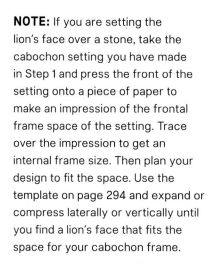

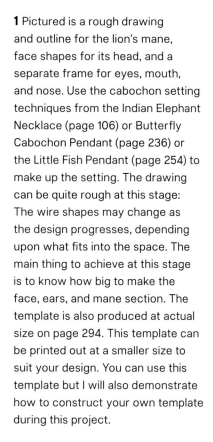

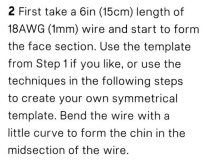

1 Pictured is a rough drawing and outline for the lion's mane, face shapes for its head, and a separate frame for eyes, mouth, and nose. Use the cabochon setting techniques from the Indian Elephant Necklace (page 106) or Butterfly Cabochon Pendant (page 236) or the Little Fish Pendant (page 254) to make up the setting. The drawing can be quite rough at this stage: The wire shapes may change as the design progresses, depending upon what fits into the space. The main thing to achieve at this stage is to know how big to make the face, ears, and mane section. The template is also produced at actual size on page 294. This template can be printed out at a smaller size to suit your design. You can use this template but I will also demonstrate how to construct your own template during this project.

NOTE: If you are setting the lion's face over a stone, take the cabochon setting you have made in Step 1 and press the front of the setting onto a piece of paper to make an impression of the frontal frame space of the setting. Trace over the impression to get an internal frame size. Then plan your design to fit the space. Use the template on page 294 and expand or compress laterally or vertically until you find a lion's face that fits the space for your cabochon frame.

2 First take a 6in (15cm) length of 18AWG (1mm) wire and start to form the face section. Use the template from Step 1 if you like, or use the techniques in the following steps to create your own symmetrical template. Bend the wire with a little curve to form the chin in the midsection of the wire.

3 Form the face on one side only first.

4 Place the half-formed face section over a blank piece of paper (over a soft bead mat, so it is easier to press an impression onto the paper surface with your wire).

5 Make sure the paper has a dotted line drawn down the midline and press over one side to make an impression. Turn the wire shape over and press onto the other half of the paper to make a mirror image of the face.

6 Draw over the impression you have made to complete the face frame with $^{13}/_{16}$in (20mm) lengths of wire projecting from the side of the face. This impression technique will help you keep the face balanced and symmetrical if you are not using the template.

MASTERING WIREWORK JEWELRY

7 Make the other side of the face and trim the wire ends so they project $^{13}/_{16}$in (20mm) from the edge of the face on either side.

8 Curl the wire ends for the face shape (see page 27).

9 Hammer the face shape on a steel block. You may need to reshape after hammering, as it tends to splay the shape outward.

10 Now take 4in (10cm) of 18AWG (1mm) wire and make an ear section. Use the impression technique to help you make this section mirror-image symmetrical if you are using your own diagram; otherwise, here is a template for you to use. Or see the templates on page 294.

11 The wire ends need to project about $1^{13}/_{16}$in (4.5cm) from either side beyond the ear. The image shows this wire shape fitted around the face section.

12 Curl the wire ends for the ear shape.

13 Hammer the ear shape on a steel block.

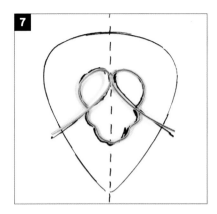

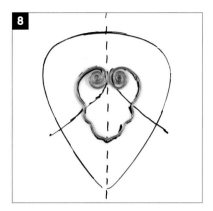

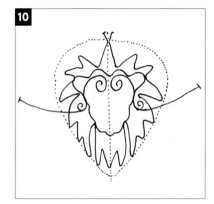

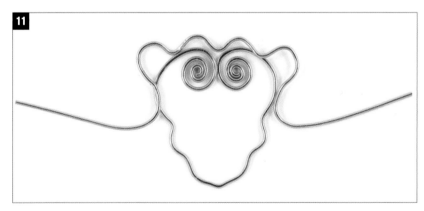

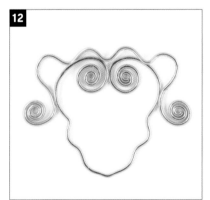

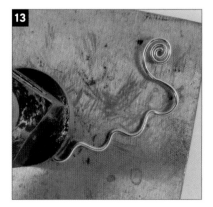

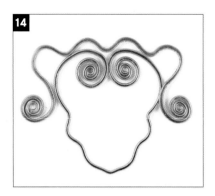

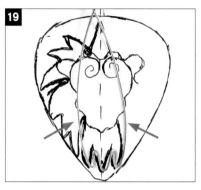

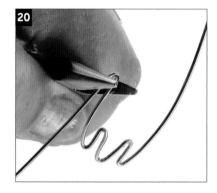

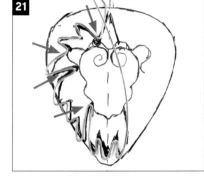

14 You may need to reshape after hammering as it tends to splay the shape outward. Check the fit of the ear shape around the face shape.

15 Take a new 40in (1m) length of 18AWG (1mm) wire and start to make the lion's mane, using the template from Step 1. This length of wire will leave a bit of excess if working on a large cabochon (the mane takes up more wire than you think so it is best to err on the side of caution). Start in the midsection of the wire and make the central pointed shape at the bottom of the lion's chin. Use the plier techniques (see page 24) to make the angle in the wire at the tip of the point as sharp as possible, clamping either side of the point repeatedly.

16 Make the next bends in the mane either side of the first V-shape you made. Keep placing the wire over the template to check the size. The first bends are made with pliers to shape them. The resulting shape looks like an "M."

17 The angle at the top points of the "M" needs to be tighter; clamp side to side near the top of the point with your pliers.

18 The shape you want to achieve should resemble the image pictured.

19 Make bends back upward on either side of the M-shape to make the lion's beard for his mane. Check against the template for fit.

20 Bend the wire at the top of the beard where it would touch against the lion's chin, using side to side squeezes with pliers. The red

arrows in image 19 show where you will need to shape the wire, Do this to both sides.

21 Make the mane shape on one side of the face using the template from Step 1. If your stone shape is different you will need to alter the lengths of each mane section to fit your cabochon setting. Keep placing the wire mane shape you are making onto the template, next to the face shape you have made, to make sure the mane fits around the face well. This will take time to achieve but it is worthwhile to make sure the fit against the face is good; this makes attachment easier later. Using chain-nosed pliers (near the tips) to make small movements in the wire, work along the shape from base to tip, then back to the next base point to shape each mane point. Make sure some of the mane point bases lie where

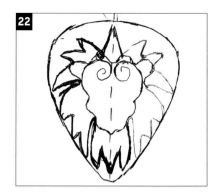

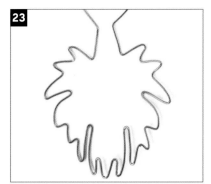

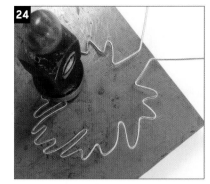

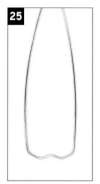

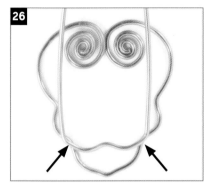

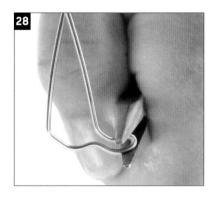

they could be bound at the side of the face, base, side of ear, and head (see arrows in image). These will be useful binding points later when you attach the pieces together.

NOTE: Leave 2–6in (5–15cm) of wire unshaped at the end of the top mane point on either side, depending upon whether you want to make a coil for the cabochon setting (shorter length) or a bale for a pendant—about 6in (15cm), depending upon the size of bale you want to make.

22 If you are making your own mane and not using the template, use the impression technique from Step 4 to make a mirror-image tracing of the mane shape to help achieve a symmetrical form.

23 Make the other side of the mane using the template on page 294, or your own drawing. Remember, if you are making the pendant without a cabochon setting, the wires at the top of the mane will make a bale. Make sure you leave long enough wire ends for the bale that you want to make for your pendant. The wire ends may need to be as long as 6in (15cm). You will only need 2in (5cm)-long wire tails for setting the lion's face onto a cabochon. The wire tails in this image are not long enough to make a large bale.

24 Hammer the back of the mane on a steel block, keeping hammer marks to a minimum on the front. Reshape the mane on your template as the hammering will splay the mane slightly.

25 Make the facial features, mouth, and eyes, referring to the template on page 294, or your own drawing. Take 12in (30cm) of 18AWG (1mm) wire and make a wavy shape for the bottom lip. Bend the wire ends upward at the end of the bottom lip. If you are working on a small cabochon, 20AWG (0.8mm) wire can be used as it is easier to shape to fit into a smaller space.

26 This lip should fit across the face at the points shown by the arrows in the image.

27 Make a bend at the edge of the lip to form the side of the mouth on one side. Make sure the returning lip wire follows the same curve as the bottom lip.

28 Bend the top lip wire upward where it reaches the midline of the mouth.

29 Squeeze the side of the mouth with chain-nosed pliers side to side to bring the lip wires close together.

30 Repeat in mirror image for the other side.

31 Check the fit of the mouth against your template and wire shapes.

32 About ¼in (6mm) up from the top lip, form a nose space using the same techniques used to make the bale detail shape on either side using the wires projecting up from the top lip. The lower edge of the nose needs to slope outward and upward before you make a bend about ¼in (6mm) along to bring the wire horizontally back toward the midline.

33 Bend the wire upward and outward ready to form the eye section. Do this for both sides in mirror image.

34 With one of the wires from the top of the nose, kink the wire slightly more upward about ⅛in (3mm) along and form the curve for the upper line of the eye.

35 Bend the wire back toward the midline and slightly downward to form the little curve for the lower edge of the eye.

36 Use the tips of chain-nosed pliers to squeeze the side of the eye, side to side, to form a point to the side of the eye.

37 Check against the head shape every so often.

38 Bend the wire sharply away again at the base of the eye.

39 Cut the end wire ¹³/₁₆in (20mm) from the base of the eye.

40 Form the other eye. If you find it easier, make an impression of the first eye using the technique from Step 4.

41 Curl the wires at the base of each eye.

42 Hammer the eye and mouth shape.

43 Reshape and balance the shape symmetrically.

44 Check all the components fit together over the cabochon and make any last adjustments to the shape. Plan where you will attach the pieces together. Find gemstones to fit the eyes and nose: 4–5mm gemstones work well in these spaces; try 3mm ones if using smaller face shapes. Take 80in (2m) of 30AWG (0.25mm) wire and wrap three times around the top of the forehead, joining the 18AWG (1mm) wires together using the midsection of the 30AWG (0.25mm) wire at the top of the forehead on the face shape. Add in a 3mm copper bead to these wraps for detail here. I passed the 30AWG (0.25mm) twice through the 3mm bead to wrap it on to add strength. I also bound around the frame wrapped above and below the bead to help keep it in place.

45 Wrap one of the 30AWG (0.25mm) wires a few times around the base of the bead to further stabilize it and form a bezel wire setting. Wrap around the bead below the girdle (widest girth of the bead) to prevent the wire wraps from slipping upward over the bead. Bring both 30AWG (0.25mm) wires up to the top of the head to bind to other components.

46 Holding the ear section with one hand, bind the ear section onto the head section using four or five wraps of the 30AWG (0.25mm) wire around both components near the midline (see arrows in image). Make sure the ear section lies slightly to the front of the head section.

47 Thread a 2mm bead onto each 30AWG (0.25mm) wire at the top of the head. Bind it across to the top of the brow of the ear section, leaving the 30AWG (0.25mm) wires directed upward ready to bind on the mane section.

48 Attach the mane to the head section. At this stage, if you are fitting your lion shape to a cabochon, make any final adjustments to the top mane tip size so that it fits to the top of the cabochon setting well. In my case I had to make the tip a little smaller. Bind the top of the mane wires together firmly with a little scrap wire so the mane section keeps its shape better during attachment.

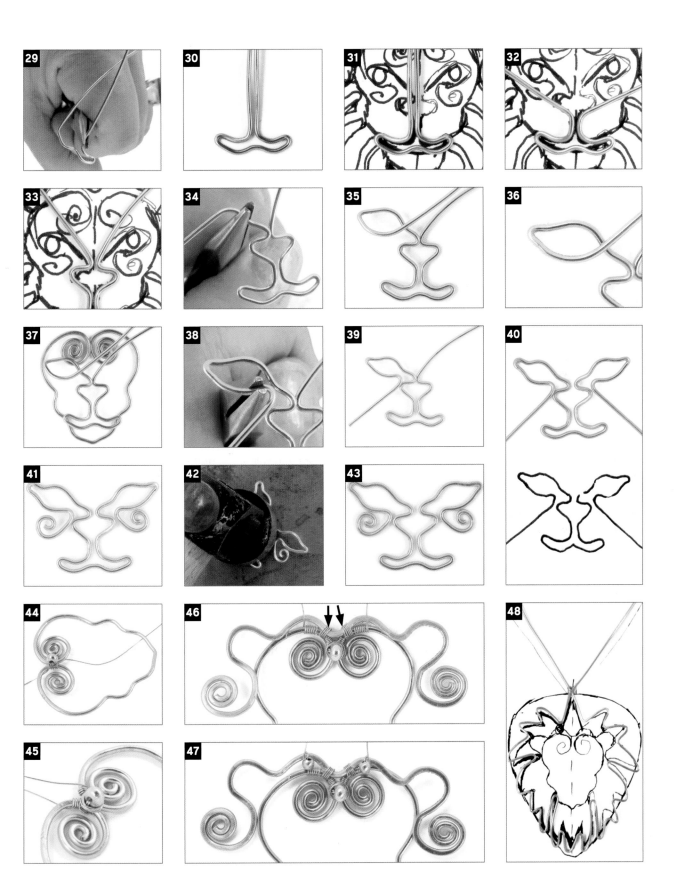

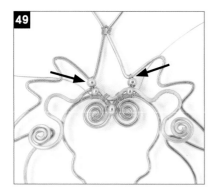
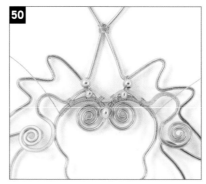
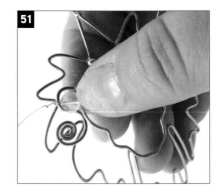
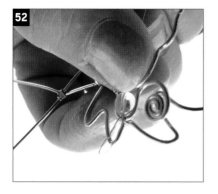
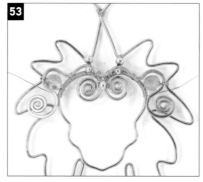
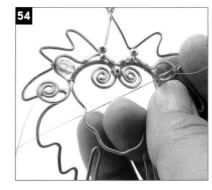

49 Thread on a 3mm bead to each end of the 30AWG (0.25mm) wires projecting from where you reached in Step 47. Bind it with a few wraps to the base of the top mane projection on either side (see arrows). 30AWG (0.25mm) wire is very delicate; to add strength, wrap back to the eyebrow section and back again to the base of the mane projection another time, before passing the 30AWG (0.25mm) wire back to the top of the head and starting to wrap along the top of the head only. If you can, thread the 30AWG (0.25mm) wire through the beads as you do this to hide the wires; otherwise, try to hide thewire behind the beads that you have attached.

50 Wrap the 30AWG (0.25mm) wire along each side of the top of the head, binding to the top of the ear with a few wraps. Continue wrapping along the head until you reach halfway along the ear section on each side.

Tip
Try to work along each side at the same level: This helps you to maintain symmetry and keep an idea of the balance of the face and head components.

51 Thread a 5mm coin or round (or a bead that will fill the ear space) onto the 30AWG (0.25mm) wire on one side. Wrap the 30AWG (0.25mm) wire around both the tip of the ear and the third notch down on the mane shape a couple of times. Keep the mane shape sitting behind the ear if possible.

52 Pass the 30AWG (0.25mm) wire back through the bead if you can to add strength to the attachment; if not, pass the wire behind the bead you have attached back down to the head frame wire.

53 Do this for both sides. Wrap along the head on both sides until just above the ear curl.

54 Cut the end of the 30AWG (0.25mm) wire a little to help you thread through more easily. To prevent the wire kinking as you pull it back through the bead a second time, catch the loop of wire in your fingers or round-nosed pliers, then remove your finger just before the last pull through.

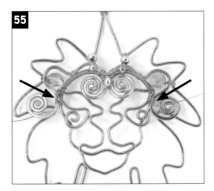

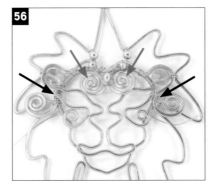

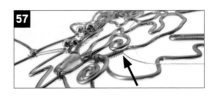

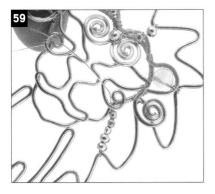

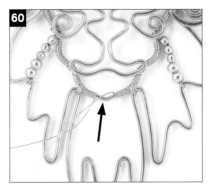

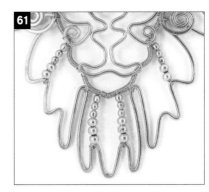

55 Place the face shape over the top of the head frame. Bind the 30AWG (0.25mm) wire around the base of the ear and the head from a few times on each side (see arrows in image).

56 Wrap a couple of times around the head frame on each side. Then bind the base of the ear curl and the fourth notch down on the mane a few times on both sides with the 30AWG (0.25mm) wire (see black arrows in image). Wrap along the face frame on each side until you reach the eye curl. Make sure the face frame is on top of the head frame except for the top head curls, which need to sit over the top of the eye frame shown by the red arrows.

57 Wrap along the side of the head on both sides, under the eye curl, for several wraps (see arrow in image).

58 Bind around the base of the eye curl for four to five wraps (see arrows in image).

59 From the level of the ear curl attachment in Step 57, thread on three 2mm beads then a couple of 3mm beads (thread on more or fewer to fit across the space if required). Bind to the fifth notch down the mane on that side with a few wraps. Pass the 30AWG (0.25mm) wire back through the beads (to add strength) and wrap around the ear curl.

NOTE: It may take some wiggling of the 30AWG (0.25mm) wire to fit the wire back through the beads, but it is possible if the bead holes are big enough.

60 Wrap along the side of the face frame until you reach the sides of the mouth. Do this on both sides of the face. Bind the side of the mouth to the head frame with four or five wraps. Then wrap along the head frame until you reach halfway along the chin to the midline (see arrow in image). Do this for both sides of the face.

61 Add on 2mm and 3mm beads to the 30AWG (0.25mm). Bind across to the lowest mane notches and back again as in Step 59. Wrap the 30AWG (0.25mm) wire ends toward the midline until they meet, then cut and tuck in the 30AWG (0.25mm) wire ends neatly around the head/chin frame wire. Make sure there is minimal gap here so it looks neat.

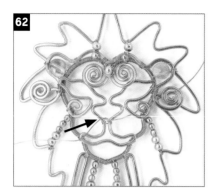

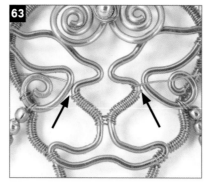

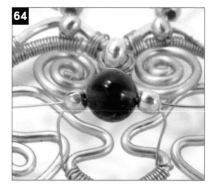

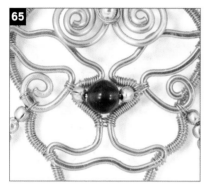

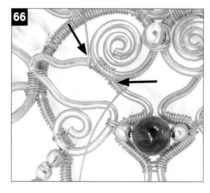

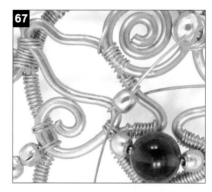

62 Take 16in (40cm) of 30AWG (0.25mm) wire and bind across the face wires at the base of the nose at the midsection of the 30AWG (0.25mm) wire (see arrow in image).

63 Wrap up the side of the nose on either side with the end of the 30AWG (0.25mm) wire on that side, until you reach the side point of the nose (see arrows in image).

64 Bind once around the innermost point of the eye curl (where it touches the side of the nose) on either side. Add a 2mm copper bead, then a 4–5mm bead, and another 2mm copper bead, onto one 30AWG (0.25mm) wire end. Thread the other wire end through the opposite end of the beads in a criss-cross bead wrap.

NOTE: Depending on the size of the nose space in your pendant, smaller, larger, or a different numbers of beads may be required.

65 Pull the wires tight to bring the beads down into the nose space. Bind a few more times around the eye curl and the nose to attach them together. Wrap a few times at the top of the nose on each side. Cut and tuck in the 30AWG (0.25mm) wire ends at the back so they don't catch, especially if you are making this as a face only pendant and not attaching it to a cabochon.

66 Take a new 12–16in (30–40cm) length of 30AWG (0.25mm) wire. Wrap using the midsection of the 30AWG (0.25mm) wire along the top of the eye binding to the forehead curl and also along the top of the

eye socket. Stop wrapping at the widest point of the eye socket and $1/16$in (2mm) along the eye toward the midline from the curl wrapping (see arrows in image).

67 Add a 2mm bead to the wire on the left and wrap up along the base of the eye socket with the 30AWG (0.25mm) wire. Two binding wraps through the 2mm bead will strengthen this attachment.

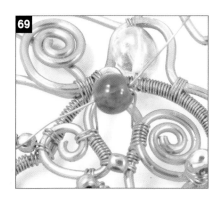

DESIGN ALTERNATIVE

To make this pendant without a stone, remove the scrap wire you attached to the mane in Step 48. Shape a bale following instructions in the Spring Daisy Necklace (see page 36). Attach 40in (1m) of 26AWG (0.4mm) or 30AWG (0.25mm) wire to the top of the mane and weave a bale as in the Daisy project. Attach a 3mm bead to the base of the bale. Make a curl in the bare wires at the end of the bale on either side. Bend the bale into shape and attach it front to back. Cut and tuck in any loose ends of wire neatly. Attach three dangles to the bottom chin mane to add movement to the piece, using beads threaded onto headpins. Attach these to the mane with neatly tucked in wrapped loops. Thread a chain through the bale and attach a clasp.

68 Wrap along the base of the eye socket with the 30AWG (0.25mm) wire. Stop at the same level at the widest diameter of the eye (see arrows in image).

69 Wrap the bottom 30AWG (0.25mm) wire around the top of the eye curl and add in a 4mm bead using a criss-cross binding wrap.

70 Continue wrapping the 30AWG (0.25mm) wire along the eye socket until you are two-thirds along the eye. Cut and tuck in the 30AWG (0.25mm) wires at the back. Do the same for the other eye, in mirror image. Your lion's face compnent is now finished and ready to attach to a cabochon setting or make up as a pendant without cabochon attachment.

71 If you want to make this up as a lion's face pendant without a cabochon, please see the Design Alternative box on the left. To attach the lion's face to a cabochon setting, adapt the techniques from the Indian Elephant Necklace (page 106) or the Butterfly Cabochon Pendant (page 236) or the Little Fish Pendant (page 254) to make up the setting and wire the lion's face onto the front of the setting. Curl the little frame wires at the top of the mane. Bind the top of the mane together, adding a 2–3mm copper bead as in Step 45–46. Then make up the cabochon setting, binding the lion's face in a curve over the stone you are using. You can thread the pendant on a pearl necklace, a kumihimo braid in silver metallic thread, or mesh. You could also use a multiple-chain necklace or Gizmo coils.

Templates

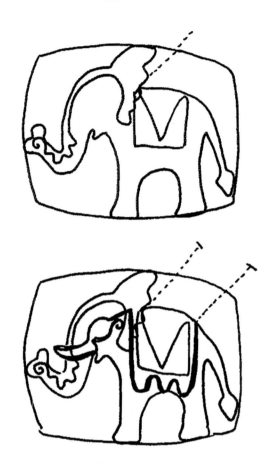

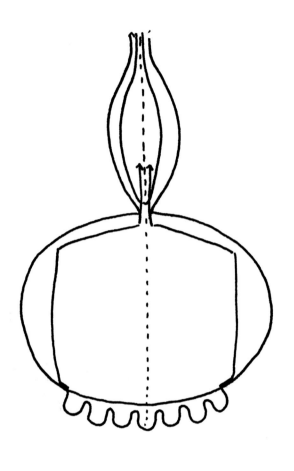

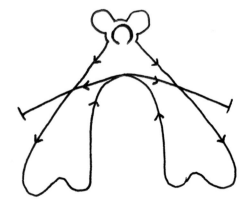

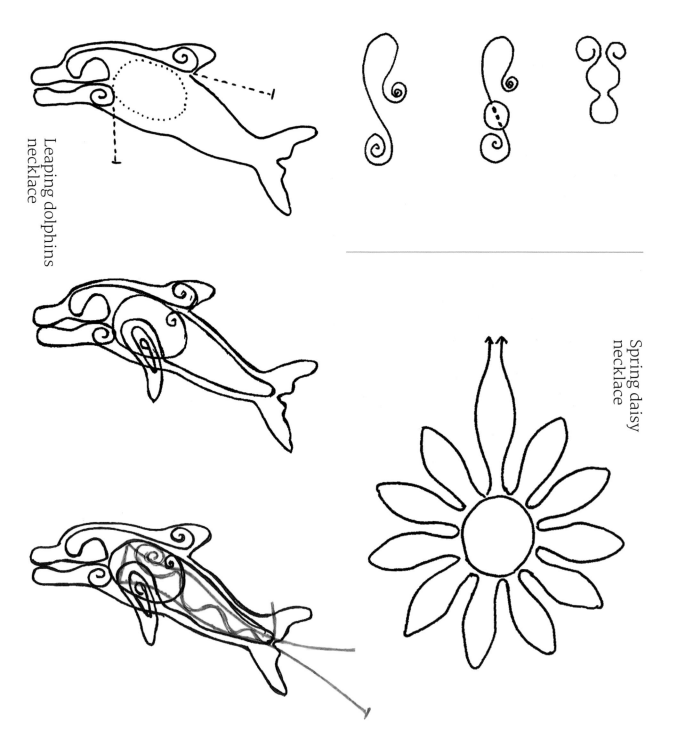

Leaping dolphins
necklace

Spring daisy
necklace

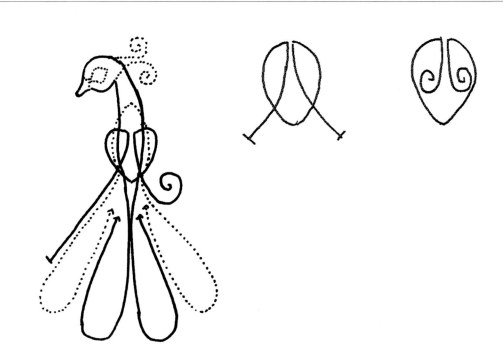

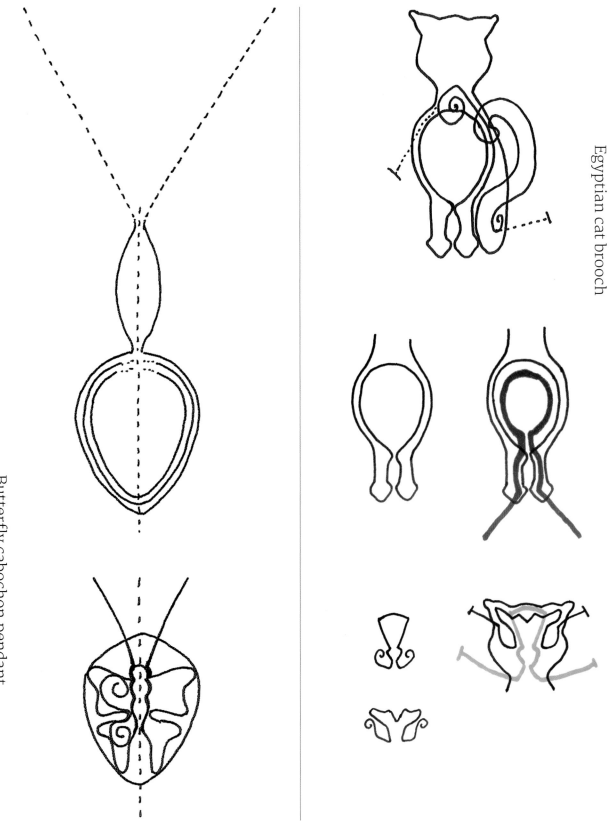

Egyptian cat brooch

Butterfly cabochon pendant

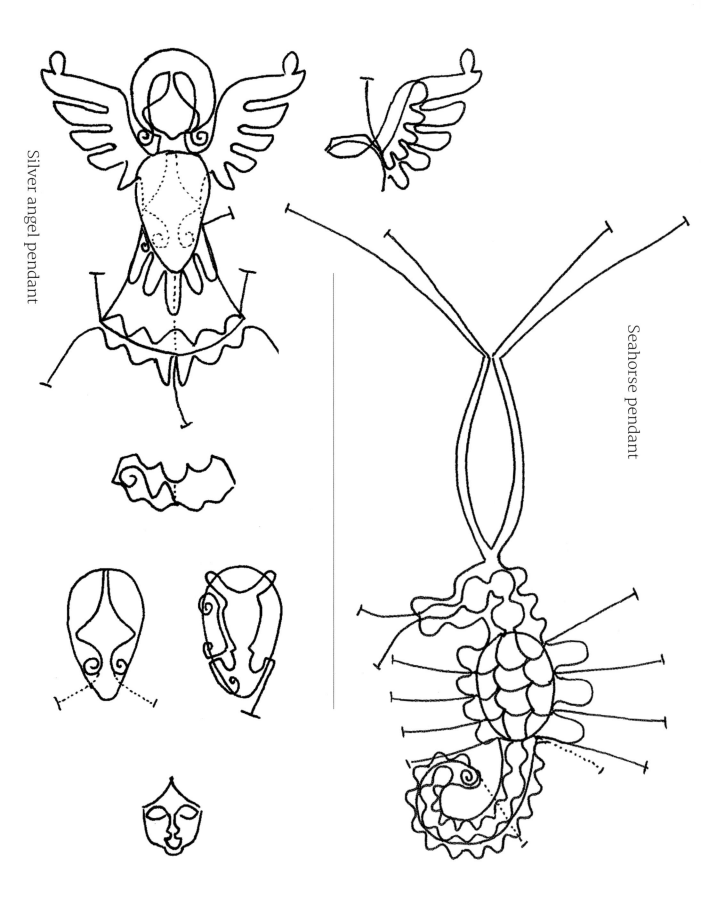

Silver angel pendant

Seahorse pendant

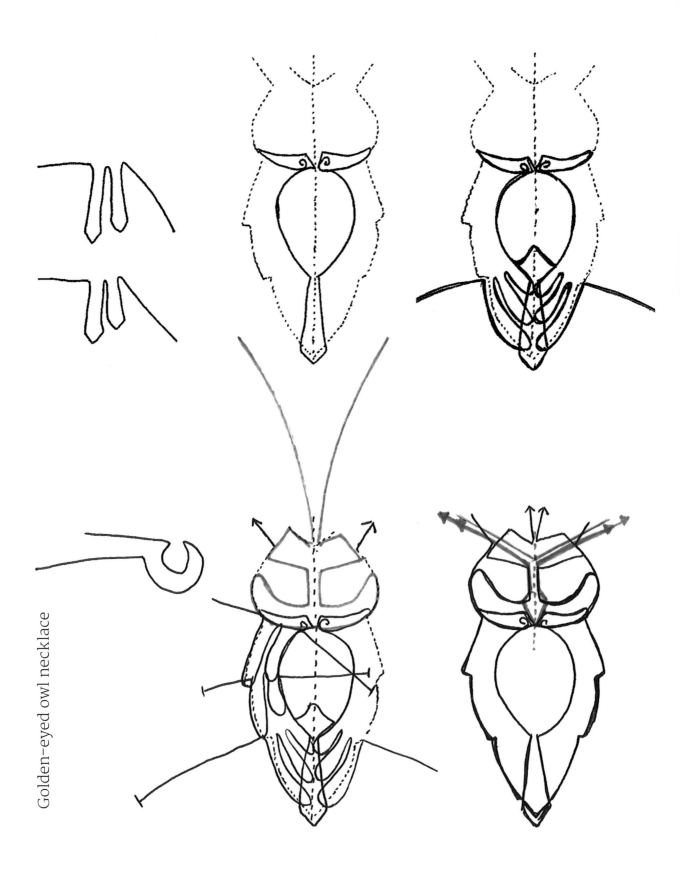

Golden-eyed owl necklace

Tumbling leaves
necklace

Gecko brooch

Bibliography

Books

Barth, Lisa, *Timeless Wire Weaving: The Complete Course*, Kalmbach Books, 2014

Bombardier, Jodi, *Weave Wrap Coil: Creating Artisan Wire Jewelry*, Interweave, 2010

Hook, Abby, *Wire Jewelry Masterclass*, GMC Publications, 2011

Jones, Linda, *How To Make Hammered Wire Jewellery*, Search Press, 2016

Jones, Linda, *The Complete Guide To Wire & Beaded Jewelry: Over 50 Beautiful Projects Using Wire and Beads*, Cico Books, 2009

Kaska, Firor, *Weaving Freeform Wire Jewelry*, Kalmbach Books, 2013

DVDs

Available via my Facebook Store: https://www.facebook.com/RachelNorrisJewelleryDesigner?ref=hl

Rachel Norris Wirework Masterclass, Edition 1, *The Beauty of Nature*

Rachel Norris Wirework Masterclass, Edition 2, *The Beauty of Nature: Air*

Rachel Norris Wirework Masterclass, Edition 3, *The Beauty of Nature: Water*

Gizmo DVDs by me available via the Jewellerymaker.com website:

Wire Gizmo Basics by Rachel Norris code FNMP63

Wire Gizmo Projects Edition 1 by Rachel Norris code OJMP68

Gizmo Wirework Projects Edition 2 by Rachel Norris code ZFMP03

Professional Gizmo Wirework by Rachel Norris code LKTY06

Suppliers

UK

Charming Beads
Singleton Court Business Park,
Wonastow Road,
Industrial Estate (West),
Monmouth NP25 5JA
Tel: +44 (0)843 2211 400
www. charming-beads.co.uk

Cooksongold
59-83, Vittoria Street,
Birmingham B1 3NZ
Tel: +44 (0)345 1000 1122 or
(0)121 200 2121
www. cooksongold.com

Hobbycraft
Hobbycraft DC,
E-Commerce Door A,
Parkway, Centrum 100 Business
Park, Unit 1,
Burton Upon Trent DE14 2WA
Tel: +44 (0)330 026 1400
www. hobbycraft.co.uk

Jewellery Maker
Ivy House,
Henley Road,
Outhill,
Studley B80 7DU
Tel: +44 (0)800 6444 655
www.jewellerymaker.com

Kernowcraft Rocks & Gems Ltd
Penwartha Road,
Bolingey
Perrnaporth
Cornwall TR6 0DH
Tel: +44 (0)1872 573888
www.kernowcraft.com

Palmermetals Ltd
401 Broad Lane,
Coventry CV5 7AY
Tel: +44 (0)845 6449343
www. palmermetals.co.uk

Spoilt Rotten Beads
7 The Green,
Haddenham,
Ely,
Cambridgeshire CB6 3TA
Tel: +44 (0)1353 749853
www.spoiltrottenbeads.co.uk

Wires.co.uk
Unit 3 Zone A,
Chelmsford Road Industrial Estate,
Great Dunmow,
Essex CM6 1HD
Tel: +44 (0)1371 238013
www.wires.co.uk

For palmstones specifically:

Crystal Age
Unit 29, Orbital 25 Business Park,
Dwight Road,
Watford,
Hertfordshire WD18 9DA
Tel: +44 (0)8454 300704
www.crystalage.com

Geofossils
Unit 16, Airlinks Industrial Estate,
Spitfire Way,
Heston,
Middlesex TW5 9NR
Tel: +44 (0)208 942 0488
www.geofossils.co.uk

USA

Beadaholique, Inc.
1506 Gardena Ave
Glendale,
CA 91204
Tel: 1-866-834-4618
www.beadaholique.com

Fire Mountain Gems
1 Fire Mountain Way,
Grants Pass,
OR 97526-2373
Tel: +1 800 423 2319
www.firemountaingems.com

ibead.com
www.ibead.com

The BeadSmith
37 Hayward Ave,
Carteret,
NJ 07008, US
Tel +1 732 969 5300
www.beadsmith.com

About the author

Rachel Norris is a specialist in vascular ultrasound. She lives in Cornwall, in the south-west of England, with her husband and three children. Rachel started making jewelry in 2010, shortly after her youngest son was born. She specializes in wirework jewelry, but also enjoys to work in polymer and silver clay, and loves incorporating these materials into her wirework designs.

Rachel has been on JewelleryMaker TV as a guest designer since September 2011, producing a collection of designs for one show each month, and demonstrating how to make these live on air. In 2012 she was voted Best Design and in 2016 she was awarded Design of the Year by the viewers.

In 2011, Rachel was Judges' Favourite on the BBC2 program *Paul Martin's Handmade Revolution*, with her design exhibited at the Victoria and Albert Museum in London. She was also voted Best Designer in *Beads & Beyond Magazine* in 2015.

Rachel regularly writes articles for jewelry-making magazines, including *Beads & Beyond Magazine*, *Bead Magazine*, *Making Jewellery Magazine*, and *Wirework US Magazine*.

In addition, Rachel has filmed six teaching DVDs with JewelleryMaker, and filmed and released a series of three Masterclass Wirework DVDs (*The Beauty of Nature* series) in 2013 and 2014. Rachel sells tutorials and DVDs via her Facebook store page, which can be found via this link: https://www.facebook.com/RachelNorrisJewelleryDesigner?ref=hl.

Index

To order a book, or to request a catalog, contact:

GMC Publications Ltd
Castle Place, 166 High Street,
Lewes, East Sussex, BN7 1XU,
United Kingdom
Tel: +44 (0)1273 488005
www.gmcbooks.com